Souls
united

About the Author

Born in 1940, Ann Merivale grew up in Oxford and Bristol. After graduating from the University of Bristol in French and Spanish, she made use of her linguistic expertise working for many years in support of the Third World. In 1969, her work brought her to Geneva, where she was employed by the American organization Catholic Relief Services and later with the World Council of Churches. In Geneva she also met her husband, David Pearson, who is now Emeritus Professor of Mathematics of the University of Hull. They returned to England in 1974 and, after bringing up three children (one adopted), she dedicated herself full time to research in spiritual matters, writing, and healing.

Merivale started practicing regression therapy in 1998 after earning a diploma from the London College of Past Life Regression Studies. Soon after that, she received further training under the Jungian psychoanalyst Dr. Roger Woolger (author of *Other Lives, Other Selves*), earning diplomas in Integral Regression Therapy in 2001, and then in Woolger's new technique of Deep Memory Process Therapy. Her first book, *Karmic Release: Journeying Back to the Self*, which was published in 2006, demonstrates graphically how Deep Memory Process Therapy works in practice and includes useful self-help exercises.

Ann and her husband now live in Shropshire, England, with Apu, their Cavalier King Charles spaniel. She practices her therapy in a clinic in North Yorkshire.

ANN MERIVALE

The Power of Divine Connection

Llewellyn Publications
Woodbury, Minnesota

First Edition
First Printing, 2009

Book design by Steffani Sawyer
Book edited by Ed Day
Cover art © 2009 by Stockbyte (hands),
        BrandXPictures (writing texture in background)
Cover design by Ellen Dahl
Interior art by Llewellyn art department

Llewellyn is a registered trademark of Llewellyn Worldwide, Ltd.

Library of Congress Cataloging-in-Publication Data for *Souls United: The Power of Divine Connection* is on file at the Library of Congress.

Llewellyn Publications
A Division of Llewellyn Worldwide, Ltd.
2143 Wooddale Drive, Dept. 978-07387-1528-5
Woodbury, Minnesota 55125-2989, U.S.A.
www.llewellyn.com

Printed in the United States of America

Dedication

To all those who are suffering the pain of separation from their twin, or the torment of agonizing relationships. That they may appreciate that it is only temporary, benefit from the learning that lies therein, and trust in the forthcoming joy of reunion.

Contents

Acknowledgments   xi

Introduction   xv

1   Identifying Twin Souls and Other Soul Mates   1

2   Incarnating Together for Important Work   27

3   Coming Together for Strength and Light   69

4   Teaching One Another Lessons   99

5   Things Don't Get Easier!   111

6   Same-Sex Relationships   123

7   Separation for Growth   129

8   Impossibility of Being Together   143

9   Guilt and Confusion   161

10   The Cords Can Never Be Broken   177

11   The Pain of Separation   197

12   Not Being Incarnate Together   211

13   Do Angels Also Have Twin Souls?   215

14   Twin Souls in History   227

15   Conclusion   285

Acknowledgments

The creation of this book has involved *so* many people, and I hope they all appreciate the extent to which I am indebted to them. I will list them, not in any order of priority, but simply as they come into my head, and with profound apologies for anyone that I might inadvertently omit.

Edwin Courtenay, Lilla Bek, and members of the Edgar Cayce Association—for introducing me to the concept of twin souls, and for teaching me about the different types of soul mate. And an extra thanks to Edwin for suggesting that I write a book on twin souls.

My son Christopher Pearson—for persuading me to take the book idea seriously, and for suggesting how I could improve on the first version.

My daughter Alice Pearson—for the illustrations, and for her general editorial skills, which have so helped me to improve my writing style.

My husband David Pearson—for his occasional editorial advice, his encouragement, and for his understanding when other things in the house got left undone.

My sister Philippa Merivale—for sharing a lot of the journey with me and for her ever-listening ear.

Eve Bruce and Patty Hall—for the translation into American and other editing. (I was used to a lift being an elevator, but had never realized the extent to which Churchill had hit the nail on the head when he spoke of "two nations divided by a common language"!)

Brian Davies—for giving me what I needed when I needed it!

Mark Young—for being such a wonderful therapist (and someone close to me in previous lifetimes), and for his unswerving belief in my writing as well as in my therapy.

Philip Cross—for his help in my spiritual development and for his dowsing skills.

Dr. Roger Woolger—for his excellent training in Bardo work, for sharing my passions for Bach and Elgar, for his endless supply of naughty jokes, and for introducing me to Lebanese wine.

William Grey Campbell—for being the only astrologer I have met to date who can identify twin souls from their charts.

Miriam and Leonard Darling, Elizabeth Barton, and Glenys Comerford—for input on Joan Grant.

François Reynolds—for his help on the Caddys.

All my friends and clients who have so diligently corrected my errors in recounting their stories.

Joan West, my agent—for all her hard work.

Carrie Obry at Llewellyn—for her editorial advice and for believing in the book from the word go, even though it was initially so much in need of professional input.

Anna Kummet at Llewellyn—for encouraging me to write an article related to the book for their online journal. And Ed Day at Llewellyn—for being such an astute editor and picking up on things that I should have noticed myself.

Introduction

You have risen above the world and can see what you could not see
when your feet walked upon the ground. Joy is the means through
which you ascend, and Clarity is the gift. Use this gift today . . .
Today is the day Perfect Clarity dawns.

—JESHUA BEN JOSEPH,
CHANNELED THROUGH JAMES TWYMAN[1]

E ven as a very young child, Judi knew that another half
of her being was out there somewhere, and at that early
age she began what she describes as a lifetime search for
him. When she was only about eight or nine, she thought
she saw him. Her parents were driving her to Petersburg,
Virginia, on Route 1, when a passenger bus passed their
car quite slowly. In the back of the bus was a boy about her

---

1.   James Twyman, *The Art of Spiritual Peacemaking—Secret Teachings from Jeshua
ben Joseph* (Forres, Scotland: Findhorn Press, 2006).

age and, during the brief moment in which the two vehicles were traveling at the same speed, their eyes met, and they "linked at some holy place." Judi, who now runs sound healing workshops and leads spiritual tours jointly with Tom (see www.tomkenyon.com), knew at that long-ago moment that the little boy she was looking at in the passenger bus had a beautiful singing voice and would one day play the guitar and write songs. Forty years later, Tom told her that, when he had been only eight or nine, he and his family had been traveling through Virginia on a passenger bus, and at one point the bus had locked speeds with a car in which a little girl was seated. He and the little girl had stared at each other until the vehicles parted, and he never forgot her.[2]

From almost any perspective, it is hard to believe that this story is pure coincidence. It is harder still from my point of view, since both my reading on soul-mate relationships and my work as a deep-memory-process (past-life regression) therapist have revealed many such cases of instant recognition. Some of the people that I have met either through this therapy or by chance have given me permission to share their stories with you. They are stories of love, of joy, of pain, of anguish, and of frustration, but because the purpose of our coming to Earth is learning, everything that happens is, I truly believe, for a reason. The names in these accounts have mostly been changed to protect the privacy of individ-

---

2. See Tom Kenyon and Judi Sion, *The Magdalen Manuscript—The Alchemies of Horus and the Sex Magic of Isis* (Orcas, WA: Orb Communications, 2002).

uals, and some small details have been altered for the same reason, but in each case the essence of the story remains.

"Twin souls" (also called "twin flames") do not meet with each other frequently on Earth, and when they do, it is invariably for a purpose—a purpose agreed by both parties prior to incarnating, and which I shall be exploring in each chapter. As we shall see, soul mates are by no means always "twin souls," and I shall be giving a full explanation of the three different types of soul mates in chapter one; but it is the occasions when twin flames do come together on Earth that inspire emotions profound enough to change a person's life forever.

For much of the information in this book I owe a debt to clairvoyants such as the famous Englishman Edwin Courtenay, as well as to one or two other books—particularly the beautiful one by Patricia Joudry and Maurie D. Pressman.[3] While drawing on their work, my aim has been a different one from any other book that I have come across in the field. For one thing, I have not attempted to write a guide for finding a soul mate (there are already enough good books on the market that do that!), and for another, I disagree with some of Joudry and Pressman's assertions on twinsoulship. While hoping that my examples provide some practical advice on relationships, my scope is in some ways broader than a typical

---

3. Patricia Joudry and Maurie D. Pressman, MD, *Twin Souls—A Guide to Finding Your True Spiritual Partner* (Dorset, UK: Element Books, 1995; Toronto: Somerville House Publishing, 1993).

self-help book. In other ways it is less broad, since I have
chosen to specialize in twinsoulship because in my experience, even among the spiritually aware, there are still many
people who have not yet studied the differences between
the varying types of soul-mate relationship.

If we accept that twin-soul connections are the strongest
that can exist between people and—theoretically at least—
the closest relationships possible on Earth, many people may
imagine that twin souls coming together will always make
for a bed of roses. This, however, is very far from being the
case, and the true stories in this book cover a wide range of
possibilities. I start with some examples of twin souls who
are very evolved spiritually and who have come together
in order to do important work for the uplifting of humanity, then tell the stories of some "ordinary" people who've
found their twin soul. Unlike the evolved twin souls whose
relationships work out beautifully, these ordinary partners
in these relationships grow over time and experience the
same feelings—all the joy, pain, fulfillment, frustration,
and disappointment—as anybody else. For, although clairvoyants are predicting that more and more twin souls will
be coming together to bring more light into the Earth for
the forthcoming Golden Age, such cases are at present still
fairly rare.

In chapter one, I make the important point that in
many of our lifetimes, we are happier with a soul mate who
is not our twin flame. We must also remember that we all
have lifetimes in which we have good reasons to be single.

Besides elaborating on the three different types of soul mate, I analyze the ways they can be identified. Distinguishing twin-soul relationships from less close ones is not always straightforward, and though I would hesitate to give myself the label of expert, I have nevertheless established certain criteria that can be looked for, and so I hope that listing these will be helpful for others.

When we move on to the stories, we will see that, while twin-soul relationships can be wonderfully romantic, they can just as likely be entirely platonic or even full of animosity. (One of my more evolved examples, whom I refer to as "Rose," is in her present life extremely happily married to her twin soul, but she has found a previous life in which they were brothers in an army and the younger one was jealous of the older because he was the one in command.) Twin souls can also choose to incarnate as the same sex in any given lifetime, which will not necessarily result in a homosexual relationship. Furthermore—as the story of the great American clairvoyant, Edgar Cayce, demonstrates—they can on occasion incarnate into the same family, which would obviously rule out a legal sexual relationship.

As I said above, our main purpose in coming to Earth each time is learning, and alas, human nature being what it is, often it is through pain that we learn the most. Since our twin is the soul who is the closest and the most important to us, he or she is often the one who is best equipped to teach us what we need to learn in a given lifetime. This explains why twin-soul encounters can on occasion be the cause of the greatest pain. This book gives examples of people who have learned from their pain and moved on to greater happiness for themselves and increased their capacity to contribute more for the benefit of society.

I end with some case histories of famous people and, though the majority of my examples in this chapter are of twin-soul relationships that benefited humanity, these also cover the full gamut from great pain to great joy. Strange as it may seem to put Elizabeth Taylor and Richard Burton in the same chapter as Saint Francis of Assisi and Saint Clare, I have good reason to believe they share the category of twin-soulship. In between these two extremes you will find, for instance, the uplifting stories of the Cayce family and that of the founders of Findhorn, the ecological village famous to so many spiritual seekers and to those interested in ecology.

This book explores the struggle, the pain, the passion, and the euphoria experienced both by ordinary and by famous people in the discovery of these extraordinary and divine connections. I am grateful to my clients and friends who have so kindly allowed me to share their stories with you, and wish you all both very happy reading and very happy, fulfilling relationships, whether or not they are soul-mate partnerships.

Identifying Twin Souls
and Other Soul Mates

All things in the universe
move from the subtle to the manifest and back again.
The character of your existence is determined by the energies
to which you connect yourself.
The way of the integral being is to join with higher things.
—LAO-TSU

My interest in the whole subject of reincarnation, karma, soul mates, and related topics dates from my attendance in 1991 at a lecture on Cayce given by John Walsh, who runs the British Edgar Cayce Centre in Durham. Until that time, despite having a growing interest in alternative medicine, I had been unable to believe in reincarnation because of my Catholicism, and so it was Cayce's Christianity that made me really sit up and listen. Walsh's lecture converted me almost instantly, and I promptly devoured a couple books on Cayce, joined the Edgar Cayce Association, and, the following

May, attended a conference with the late American psychotherapist and author, Harmon Bro. As a young man, Bro had
worked with the much-older Cayce, and later wrote a biography that I strongly recommend.[4]

When Cayce gave someone a life reading, he selected
from his or her etheric records the previous lives that had
the most bearing upon the present one, which people found
useful for correcting past mistakes or rediscovering latent
talents. His gift for reading the Akashic Records was unusual,
but fortunately not unique, and at this conference with Bro in
1992, I met people who had received Cayce-style life readings and found them most helpful. Since I fancied obtaining
a reading myself, Bro recommended Aron Abrahamsen (who
is discussed at length in chapter two), an American psychic
who followed directly in Cayce's footsteps.

When I received the reading from Abrahamsen, I was
fascinated by the five relevant past lives that he told me
about——not because he had seen me as anyone particularly
significant or famous, but partly because of the past links he
gave me with my husband and our three children (including the adopted one). Furthermore, I was amazed by the
assertion that I had come into my present life "partly as a
writer——to disseminate information on the spiritual life."
A couple years ago, my homeopath suggested that I write
a book, but I did not feel that I "had a book inside me."

---

4.   Harmon Hartzell Bro, Ph.D., *A Seer Out of Season* (New York: Penguin,
       1990).

However, soon after receiving Abrahamsen's reading in July 1992, my family and I went on holiday to Spain. On driving through a little place called Cariñena, we stopped for a picnic in the church square. This church had a high wall attached to it that was clearly guarding a convent or monastery, and this set me off reflecting upon the life as a Spanish nun that Abrahamsen had told me about. From this, I got the idea of writing an autobiographical book[5] that would show how my past lives were influencing my present one.

At the time that I was introduced to Edgar Cayce's work, one of my younger sisters was going through a difficult divorce. She had already met the man whom she eventually married, but there were many hurdles to overcome before they were both ready for the new relationship. One of the people who helped my sister at this time was a young English clairvoyant, Edwin Courtenay. He explained to her that the man with whom she had fallen in love was her twin soul. Since Courtenay's help proved so invaluable, and since I had already started writing my book and wanted further information about my distant past, my sister introduced me to Courtenay, who was at the time more accessible than Abrahamsen. (Courtenay has since become so well known that it is now much more difficult to obtain readings from him.)

---

5. Ann Merivale, *Karmic Release: Journeying Back to the Self* (Bangalore, India: Sai Towers Publishing, 2006). Available from www.puttaparthi.info/shopping/book

Not only did Courtenay answer all my questions, he also assured me that my book would be published and, as well as explaining in detail to both my sister and myself the concept of twin-soul relationships, he gave us further information about our past lives and our soul purpose. This proved to be a pivotal moment for us because it gave us deeper insight into our reasons for having chosen to incarnate into such a difficult family as ours. And also, since I had had grave misgivings about my sister's first marriage from the start, I was overjoyed to learn that a man who was so much more suitable for her was now on the horizon. Later, when I was on my first full workshop with Dr. Roger Woolger,[6] I found in the first regression that I did there, a life in which I had had the very same younger sister and where the dynamics of the relationship were similar to this time. But in that life she went off to the town to marry happily, leaving me to care for our aging parents. So this time around, things have been considerably better for me, and the two of us will not lose touch!

Courtenay's assurance that my book would be published increased my confidence, as well as my determination to complete it despite the pressures of caring for a growing family. Not long after meeting Courtenay, my sister

---

6.   Dr. Roger Woolger's excellent book *Other Lives, Other Selves* is published by Doubleday/Bantam USA (1988), and he also has a more recent book that includes a CD for practicing on one's own: *Healing Your Past Lives: Exploring the Many Lives of the Soul* (Boulder, CO: Sounds True, 2004).

introduced me to another person who was giving her a great deal of help through her difficulties. He is a renowned astrologer, and he predicted that my book would be published in another country first. (Little did I know that country would be India!)

When I first decided to write a book, it never entered my head that I would ever write more than one. However, once I thought that I had almost finished my first book, Courtenay suggested that since I had learned so much about the subject, I write a book on twin souls. He was even able to introduce me to one or two twin-soul couples and then, once the ball had been set rolling, I found myself bumping into them at regular intervals. And, after I had decided to train and practice as a regression therapist, the rate of "bumping into them" increased. Now I can see that, since I myself would probably never have thought of writing this book, my sister's first meeting her twin soul and then Edwin, and introducing me to Edwin too, was all part of a very much larger plan.

Not long after making friends with Courtenay, I got to know another very well-known clairvoyant, Lilla Bek, who gave me more information about my previous lives and also discussed twinsoulship with me. Had I still been needing proof of reincarnation, I would have believed I had been given it when Bek, quite independently of Courtenay (they were not personally acquainted), told me about the life he had already mentioned—when my adopted son and I had been priestesses together in Greece! She also foresaw my doing "a great deal more work in this field," yet it took the arrival in the mail of a leaflet about one of Woolger's introductory weekends to give me the idea of training in regression therapy.

Deep Memory Process Therapy

I had already been busy researching and writing about reincarnation and subjects related to it for a good five years before it occurred to me to train as a therapist. That first weekend in London reinforced my enthusiasm and, before I departed, I spoke to Roger Woolger about undertaking the training. He said that I should first do some body work since I was "too much in my head."[7] So I first went for some therapy with the man he had recommended for help with getting more in touch with my body, and then I obtained a diploma in past-life regression therapy from the London College of Past Life Regression Studies. This diploma course taught me a great deal of the theory and was a very useful introduction to the therapy. The more practical training that I subsequently did with Woolger gave me additional help in getting into my body, and Woolger awarded me his diploma in integral regression therapy in 2001. I then started practicing seriously what Woolger now calls deep-memory-process therapy and, after attending a refresher course with him in 2006, he gave me a replacement certificate with this new title on it.

---

7.   Merivale, *Karmic Release*.

Dr. Keith Hearne and Helen Wozniak, who ran the London course that I completed, are both hypnotherapists. (Dr. Hearne is also the author of numerous books.) However, hypnotherapy is not essential for accessing previous lives and, since it tends to dissociate a client from the past events that are retrieved, Woolger prefers to work mainly from the body. For, although we obviously take on a new physical body each time that we incarnate, the seeds of past traumatic events that have not yet been released (known as *samskaras*) are imprinted as scars on the soul and are then transferred to the new physical body. Strong evidence for this is to be found in the work of Dr. Ian Stevenson,[8] a Canadian psychiatrist who died in 2007.

A leading exponent of the hypnotherapeutic approach to regression therapy is Dr. Michael Newton, whose invaluable work[9] I treasure, even though I chose another path of study. Woolger's is simply a different method of working, and is the one that has helped me personally in my own process of healing more than anything else has. Woolger's one-week training workshops are all residential, and the fact of working, eating, drinking, laughing, and sleeping (please don't take that last one too literally!) together forges bonds between the participants and gives a strong feeling of security. This facilitates

---

8.   See Ian Stevenson, *Reincarnation and Biology, Volumes 1 and 2* (Connecticut and London: Praeger Publishers, 1997).

9.   Michael Newton, Ph.D., *Journey of Souls* and *Destiny of Souls* (St. Paul, MN: Llewellyn, 1995 and 2002).

the surfacing of trauma that has been buried very deeply, enabling profound, and often instantaneous, healing to take place. John Bradshaw, the American expert on "inner-child work,"[10] maintains that "the only way out is through," and so working through a past traumatic event with a trained therapist, and recognizing that it does not belong to the present, enables one to release it permanently.

In deep-memory-process sessions, much of the most important work is done after the client has been through the death in the previous life and gone into what is known as the *Bardo* (the term used in Tibetan Buddhism for the between-life period). In this state, the life review can be made with the aid of the client's spirit guides and other helpers on the other side. For, with their broader perspective, they are the best equipped to point out the lessons learned or still needing to be learned, and the therapist can join with them to encourage forgiveness—particularly self-forgiveness, which is often the hardest. In the Bardo state, too, people are often able to obtain information that is not so readily available in normal everyday life—this is how some of my clients have learned about someone being their twin soul. This has intrigued me particularly when the concept was a completely new one to the person concerned, and when the information has been relayed from the other side with little or no intervention on my part. So it can be seen how this therapy has afforded me

---

10.   John Bradshaw, *Homecoming: Reclaiming and Championing Your Inner Child* (New York: Bantam, 1990).

a great deal of interest and satisfaction, as well as providing me with further food for my writing.

Soul Mates

Although this topic tends to generate considerable interest, I have the impression that many people who are engaged in a hunt for their own soul mates are not always aware of the difference between the three different kinds: "twin souls," "companion soul mates," and "karmic soul mates." While no one can claim infallibility on the subject, my own view comes from years of reading on esoteric subjects, from talking to clairvoyants, and from finding an extraordinary amount of agreement in all the information gathered. So let me now draw on what I have learned by giving some definitions based upon this research.

Twin Souls

In the very beginning there was only God, but after God decided to divide into many parts for companionship, many different spirits were sent out. (Here I particularly recommend the books of Neale Donald Walsch.)[11] Once the worlds had been created and incarnation for growth had been decided upon, each of these spirits sent out not just one, but two souls, one embodying the masculine and the other the feminine energy. In their book *Twin Souls: A Guide*

---

11. Neale Donald Walsch, *Conversations with God, Volumes 1–3* (Charlottesville, VA: Hampton Roads Publ., 1998).

to *Finding Your True Spiritual Partner*,[12] Joudry and Pressman quote the Bulgarian Master, Omraam Mikhail Aivanhov, who in the 1960s wrote in *Love and Sexuality:* "Every human being has a twin soul. When man leapt like a spark from the bosom of his Creator he was two in one, and these two parts complemented each other perfectly, each was the other's twin. These two halves became separated, they took different directions, and they have evolved separately . . . "

To give the idea, let us think of the yin/yang symbol:

Think of this symbol as a spirit that has divided itself into two halves, representing the masculine and the feminine energies. Within the black masculine half lies the white seed of the feminine; in the white feminine side is embedded the eternal memory of her semi-masculine nature. And so the two can never be fully separated; the cords between them can never be broken. Hence all human beings' constant yearning to return to their other half, the feeling in each and every one of us that we are not completely whole.

The two now-separate souls left their joint spirit (otherwise known as the higher self) behind in the spiritual

---

12. Joudry and Pressman, *Twin Souls*.

realms, so that it could give them each the guidance they might need while playing their chosen roles on Earth. At the end of each lifetime, however, the soul returns to the higher self so the new learning can become incorporated into the whole rather than simply forgotten. Incarnation was never intended to be permanent, because God wants us all back eventually to enrich him/her (again see Neale Donald Walsh) and, since, to quote the poet John Donne, "no man is an island," the return cannot be made alone. There are many terms for what the Buddhists call Liberation, but whatever the term (God-realization, self-realization, etc.), the intention is clear: we need to escape from *samsara* (the Buddhist wheel of rebirth) by paying all the debts (*karma*) that we have accumulated and freeing ourselves from attachment to the Earth. Once both twins have done that, they can fuse once more and then, with the extra strength that this fusion brings, they can help those who are lagging behind along the path of return to God.

Plato, as early as about 385 BCE, showed an understanding of the twin-soul concept, as evidenced by his great *Symposium*. In this work, Aristophanes describes the rather curious eight-limbed hermaphrodites, who angered Zeus by attempting to become as powerful as the gods. As punishment, they were struck into two opposite halves and, because of their consequent feeling of being incomplete, each of these beings was then forced to wander the Earth in search of its other half.

In my opinion, the most comprehensive and beautiful
definition of twinsoulship is in a book by the French authors
Anne and Daniel Meurois-Givaudan, which is about their
previous life together as disciples of Jesus.[13] Anne and Daniel
are twin souls but, after writing and publishing a number of
books together, they separated and started writing independently. As far as I know, only their first book about Jesus[14] has
been translated into English, so for their definition of twin
souls you will have to bear with my own translation.

Anne and Daniel have the ability to travel out of their
bodies in order to read in great detail about their previous
lives from the Akashic Records. The word *akash* is the Sanskrit for "ether," and these records constitute the etheric
library in which is stored the information about everything
that has ever occurred since the beginning of time. When
Anne and Daniel knew Jesus, they were married, their
names were Simon and Myriam, and Simon had as a young
boy been trained for discipleship by the Essene monks of
the "Krmel." *Chemins de ce Temps-là* (Paths of that Time) is
the second of their two volumes about their life with Jesus,
and in it, when Simon begins to recover from the death of
his beloved Myriam, he recalls the teaching he had been
given by a monk named Moshab: "The story of love between

---

13.   Anne and Daniel Meurois-Givaudan, *Chemins de ce Temps-là* (France: Edi-
      tions Amrita, 1989).

14.   Anne and Daniel Meurois-Givaudan, *The Way of the Essenes: Christ's Hidden
      Life Remembered* (Rochester, VT: Destiny Books, 1993).

man and woman is the story of a long-lived nostalgia. In its utmost depths, in its very root, the human being clothed in flesh is both male and female. This root is the spirit, and the spirit, which animates each one of us, was created androgynous in the image of the Nameless One." While still thinking nostalgically about his beloved Myriam, Simon realized that the two of them had originally come from God and would eventually return to God together. He also realized that they had come from the same spirit, because Moshab had continued: "In the beginning, each spirit gave birth to two souls; two souls destined to sail across the worlds, over the lands, one clothed by the moon, the other by the sun. That is why each moon seeks its sun, and why each sun weeps for a moon, the ideal image of which it keeps locked in the depths of its heart . . . "

Returning to Plato for a moment, he was also a believer in reincarnation—a concept with which the twin-soul theme has always been inextricably linked. This is because concomitant with awareness of the original split goes the understanding that, before we can make the final return to God, we shall need to return together to the spirit part of our being—the part that remains in higher realms and does not incarnate—and fuse once more. And before that can take place, we need the experience of many, many lifetimes of learning, and we each need to have gained the confidence to stand on our own so that the coming together will be an enrichment for each soul rather than a codependent relationship. Moshab put it thus: "The man and woman who seek one another are like the right and left eyes of the same face. They need to learn to look in exactly the same direction, without either one of them taking precedence over the other. Ultimately, they are called to fuse into a single eye; then they will be the One Lamp shining on the brow of the enlightened being, of him who has remembered, has recognized . . . "

In view of the fact that, through our many incarnations, we often fall from grace and make mistakes that we later have to rectify, meeting our twin soul on Earth is not always blissful. For the relationship to be as it should, we need, as Moshab explains, to have learned to put God and other people first: "Twin souls only find one another again when their heart and their consciousness have achieved the great awakening. They are the same being twice over, and their union seals the end of the pact which they needed to make with the world of flesh. Such marriages are the ultimate transmutation from which the True Person can prepare to be born."

Rebirth has always constituted an integral part of both Hindu and Buddhist philosophy, and many people maintain too that the ancient Egyptians believed in it. The fact that the belief was also widespread in the early Christian Church is proven by the Council of Constantinople's decision in 553 AD to formally condemn and suppress it! Justinian, the Emperor of Constantinople at that time, was married to a powerful woman named Theodora, and she was averse to the idea of having to return to Earth as anything other than an empress. So she used her persuasive powers on her husband and, with the pope in prison during this Council meeting, the motion was passed by just a few votes. The Bible was subsequently purged of references to reincarnation, but one or two passages somehow escaped the censors. For instance, when Jesus asked his disciples, "Who do you say that I am?" he must have actually meant, "Who do you think I was before I came in this time as Jesus?" and he also stated quite clearly in chapter 17, verses 10–13, of Matthew's gospel that John the Baptist was Elijah.

It suited the clergy as well to have their people believe that they only had one life on Earth, since it gave the priests more power to control what everyone did with that life. ("Unless you do as I say, and give me such and such a percentage of your income, you will be condemned to eternal damnation!") As a result, for many centuries in the West, knowledge of reincarnation was restricted to sects such as the Gnostics or the Knights Templar, who resisted the domination of Rome, and so the concept of twinsoulship was also pushed under the carpet until the world was once again ready for this awe-inspiring knowledge.

Truth must always out in the end, and one of the most important people to raise the carpet and retrieve the buried treasure was the aforementioned great American seer, Edgar Cayce, who lived from 1878 to 1945 and performed trance readings for most of his life. These trance readings varied in nature from medical to prophetic to past life, and from the latter he worked out a whole philosophy of reincarnation that was entirely in accordance with his Christianity. Since I am writing at greater length about Cayce in my final chapter—Twin Souls in History—suffice it to say here that he was happily married to a companion soul mate while his twin soul was his devoted secretary. This book is based upon Cayce's definitions of the three different types of soul mate.

Companion Soul Mates

Through our many incarnations on this planet, we come back again and again in what are known as soul groups. We are drawn to others through overlapping patterns of karma that need to be worked out, or simply because of familiarity and affection. When two souls have been together many times as husband and wife, brother and sister, or parent and child, the affection will be deep and the familiarity strong. This makes a good basis for a marriage or a partnership. What Cayce termed "companion soul mate" relationships are therefore very often the most comfortable ones, and very often the envy of those who are in a difficult or painful relationship, or living alone. Moshab says, "Companion soul mates . . . [âmes-compagnes in French] must not be confused with twin souls," and Cayce stated that we can have about twenty companion soul mates, whereas we have only one twin soul.

Companion soul mates are perhaps the easiest to identify. Probably the majority of good, comfortable marriages and partnerships are between companion soul mates—people who have been together many times in varying relationships—and I personally feel sure that in Rita Rogers' book on soul mates,[15] many of the people she describes as "true soul mates" are in fact companion soul mates rather than twin souls. Companion soul mates can be sexual partners, or they can be siblings, parent and child, or close friends of either sex. My older son and my daughter are undoubtedly companion soul mates. Many of my friends' children displayed jealousy at the arrival of a younger sibling, however well they had been prepared for it, but when I brought Alice home from the hospital, twenty-month-old Paul welcomed her most eagerly. As they grew up, many of our acquaintances commented that they were like twins, and I did indeed find out about a previous life in which I had borne Paul and Alice as twins. Also, Edwin Courtenay told me that they had been married to each other, probably in several previous lives. Nowadays, at thirty-four and thirty-two, they remain as close as ever.

Basically, companion soul mates are really good friends. (Ideally twin souls are that too, of course, but—whether good or bad—are normally more intense.) Companion soul mates support each other, work well together and, when they fall in love, are not possessive but respect one another's independence. They have enough interests in common to make for a good partnership, but may also have markedly different personalities.

---

15.   Rita Rogers, *Soul Mates* (London: Pan Macmillan, 2000).

Karmic Soul Mates

As its name implies, "karmic soul mates" are couples who come together on account of an outstanding piece of karma that needs to be worked out between them. In his book on soul mates,[16] the American author, Jess Stearn, relates a dramatic example of this type of relationship taken from one of Cayce's readings. The subject of this reading had in one of his previous lives murdered a woman of his acquaintance. In order to pay the debt incurred by this murder, he met her again in his present life, fell in love with her, and married her. The marriage was apparently a successful one, but Cayce explained that their karma was now complete and that they would not need to come together again.

However, the karmic link does not have to be such an extreme occurrence. I am sure my younger son had a karmic debt to his ex-wife, which he had to pay before being able to break free from what unfortunately proved to be a very unsatisfactory relationship, but I can also give a much happier example. A friend (I'll call her Jill), who started exploring spiritual topics at about the same time as I did, was told by the well-known clairvoyant Edwin Courtenay that in a previous life her husband had disowned her for following Jesus. The two met again in this life, fell in love, and married. It seems to me that he (I'll call him Jack) fell in love with Jill this time around because he had a debt to her

---

16.   Jess Stearn, *Soul Mates: Perfect Partners, Present and Beyond* (New York: Bantam, 1984). Now out of print, but nevertheless available on Amazon.

from the life in which he had rejected her. Jill is a woman of great faith, and in her present life, though a Catholic in the beginning, she later became an ardent devotee of the Indian *avatar*, Sathya Sai Baba. The word *avatar* means "divine incarnation." Jack has not followed Jill's spiritual beliefs, but he is currently paying his debt from abandoning her by completely supporting her spiritual path. He is an excellent and devoted husband despite the fact that he has no wish to visit Sai Baba's ashram himself.

While these are the three different types of soul mate defined by Cayce, there are also many credible variations. Sue Minns, in her very good book on the subject,[17] gives yet another definition of the term. She describes a soul mate as anyone who comes into one's life for a specific purpose. This purpose may be one of loving support, or it may be a painful challenge, but whatever it is, we can view it as something from which to learn and grow. This book of mine, however, is concerned with relationships based on love and mutual attraction, and I have focused on twin-soul relationships because I believe this concept to be one that still requires greater understanding in many quarters.

    Having discussed the three different types of soul mates, I feel I should now point out that distinguishing between them is not always totally straightforward. I believe that even the best clairvoyants can occasionally make mistakes. One

17.   Sue Minns, *Soul Mates* (London: Bloomsbury, 2004).

criterion for deciding on the nature of a couple's relationship is the fact that, when twin souls are seated side by side, their auras can be seen to merge. People such as Edwin Courtenay often use this method. However, since I have also heard from Dr. Roger Woolger that clairvoyants can sometimes observe the same phenomenon occurring in sessions with a therapist and a client, I personally doubt its total reliability for identifying twin souls. When Courtenay gave my friend Jill her reading, he said that she and her husband were twin souls. Since she was extremely happily married, this idea pleased her, but over the years in which I have known this couple well, I gradually began to have my doubts. That is why I have given them as an example of karmic soul mates. I feel that studying the question of twinsoulship in depth enables one to develop a sort of sixth sense about couples one meets, and to me Jack and Jill feel far too different in character to be twin souls. Also, twin-soul couples tend to challenge each other a lot more than these two do. I am no doubt much less infallible than Courtenay, but when I consulted independently two well-known dowsers about it, both pendulums gave the same answer: that Jack and Jill were karmic soul mates and that neither of their twin souls was at present incarnate. Therefore, if I and the pendulums are not mistaken, Jack's karmic debt to Jill is now fulfilled and this couple will not need to reincarnate together again (though they will, of course, always be free to do so by choice).

Speaking of developing an intuitive sense about the nature of couples' relationships, I sometimes find myself nowadays even recognizing twinsoulship among fictional characters! Many people will unfortunately not have seen the wonderful German movie *Heimat*, but it was broadcast on English television a few years ago. The series consisted of eleven quite lengthy episodes, which started at the end of the First World War, and covered several generations of one family. I was intensely moved by the story of the two main characters, who were both gifted musicians. Hermann ultimately became a successful conductor, Clarissa was a cellist, and they met when they were students. Though clearly in love, they somehow failed in their youth to make a relationship. After leaving the university, they both had unsuccessful marriages with other people, and he had one daughter and she one son. When they met again years later, they became able to express their love, which was to my mind clearly twin-soul love, and spent their last years blissfully together, with Hermann touchingly supporting Clarissa through cancer.

For me, another good fictional example of a likely twin-soul couple is in Jane Austen's famous novel *Emma*. Mr. Knightley, who is considerably older than Emma, has known her from her childhood, and never hesitates to reprimand her for undesirable behavior. Only when she has matured and learned her lessons sufficiently well to satisfy him, does he finally tell her how much he loves her, and then how unbounded is her joy! Knightley would undoubtedly have had several other opportunities for matrimony but, having recognized his twin soul, he waits patiently until she is ready to make him an ideal wife.

Why do twin souls tend to challenge one another more than other couples? Because their growth depends upon it! The fusion (or re-fusion) that we are all aiming for cannot take place until both individuals are at exactly the same level, and so each half of the whole has to keep pace with the other in order to attain the ultimate goal of not needing to be reborn. We shall see in the forthcoming chapters that on occasion one partner seriously lags behind the other, but this is never permanent. One twin soul soaring ahead spiritually will inevitably affect her partner's development as well, even if he appears to fail to catch up in any particular lifetime.

Joudry and Pressman

Through my years of reading on esoteric subjects, one of the books that has impressed me the most is one I referred to earlier: Patricia Joudry and Dr. Maurie Pressman's *Twin Souls: A Guide to Finding Your True Spiritual Partner.*[18] Patricia Joudry (like Eileen Caddy, one of the founders of the well-known ecological village of Findhorn in northern Scotland, whom you will meet in the history chapter at the end of the book) was given the image of twinsoulship in a vision. Joudry explains that she then sat with the concept for thirty years before her meeting with Pressman (when she was sixty-eight) finally made it possible to give birth to the book. She is dead now, but her autobiography has been published on the Internet (www.lib.unb.ca/Texts/Theatre/joudry/autobio10

---

18.   Joudry and Pressman, *Twin Souls.*

.htm). This makes it clear, while the book does not, that she and Pressman are indeed twin souls. (It was an awkward situation because Pressman was—and still is—married to someone else, whom he loves dearly.)

Joudry and Pressman point out that, despite the collective amnesia that caused the twin-soul concept to be almost forgotten for centuries, the notion of the individual being divided at the start into masculine and feminine has been transmitted down through the ages by mystics. Besides the quotation from the Bulgarian master Omraam Mikhael Aivanhov that I gave earlier, they quote Plato, from whom came the name *Androgyn*. ("The original human nature was not like the present, but different. The sexes were not two as they are now, but originally three in number; there was man, woman, and the union of the two.") Joudry and Pressman also cite the sacred literature of Sufism, an ascetic and mystical Islamic movement that had its origins in Persia in the eighth century: "Out of the original unity of being there is a fragmentation and dispersal of beings, the last stage being the splitting of one soul into two. And consequently love is the search by each half for the other half on earth or in heaven, a search that can become desperate . . . " (This echoes both Plato and Moshab!) "As twin souls are so alike to start with, it seems necessary for them to go their different ways before they can complete each other. Identity and complementarity are the two driving forces and axes of love . . . For the complete blending there must be a blending of the two."

The Joudry-Pressman thesis is that for many centuries the world was not ready to take the twin-soul concept on board again, but that now, with the dawning of the Aquarian Age, the time is ripe for it to resurface fully. And clairvoyants of my acquaintance maintain that more and more twin souls will be coming together at this time since the world is in need of the greater light that their combined forces are able to generate. Patricia Joudry says toward the end of her introduction, "What we have written here is hardly the last word on twinsoulship; it is only a beginning. There is much more to be discovered about this beneficent law of love." Hence this book of mine!

Though I cannot recommend their book more highly, the Internet now reveals that Joudry and Pressman's case histories—unlike my own, which are all genuine—are actually fabrications based upon their personal experiences with each other. This (might I say somewhat limited research?) is presumably the reason for their making four assertions with which I take issue. First, they say that twin souls never incarnate in the same family. Well, we shall be looking later at the Cayce family and, since this story is so well known in esoteric circles, I am surprised Joudry and Pressman overlooked it. But we are all human, not omniscient. While I am impressed with Patricia Joudry's internal revelations, I myself have obtained all my information from others. Second, Joudry and Pressman maintain that when twin souls incarnate together, they are always opposite sexes. Third, they say that twin souls who are together will never separate. Fourth, they state that an upright man will never forsake his partner for his twin soul. Well, I believe that my research has disproved all of these assertions.

Authors such as Richard Webster and Dr. Michael Newton talk of twin-soul union as though it can only happen in our final incarnation. But neither Newton nor Webster give their reason for having this idea, and I am puzzled as to where they got it from. (I am sure it was not from Plato!) As the Cayce story shows, there is no doubt that, over the eons of earthly existence, twin flames do meet up from time to time—not only in between incarnations, but also on Earth. I cannot go along with the Bulgarian master, Omraam Mikhail Aivanhov, who apparently said that twin souls meet on Earth twelve times, because I do not personally believe that something like this is ever so firmly cut and dried, but my book now is endeavoring to show the various reasons for these meetings. Many of them are joyful, but also, since many of us still have a long way to go before reaching perfection, equally many of these stories are extraordinarily painful. Why? Because people who mean little to us have little or no power to cause us pain; it is the most intimate of relationships that affect us profoundly, and the twin-soul bond is of course the closest of all. And, as Joudry and Pressman pointed out, we evolve through pain until we finally learn to evolve through joy.

So now, without further ado, let us proceed to the stories!

Incarnating Together for Important Work

Wake up lovers, it is time to start the journey!
We have seen enough of this world, it is time to see another.
These gardens may be beautiful but
let us pass beyond them and go to the Gardener.
On this perilous journey only love can lead the way.
—Rumi

Edgar Cayce's death in 1945 at the age of only sixty-seven (caused basically by overwork due to his desire to help victims of the Second World War) was mourned not only by those close to him, but also by large numbers of people who were still awaiting one of his readings. Fortunately, people worldwide are still being cured of numerous ailments through the vast Cayce legacy of medical readings, and nowadays also there are other people who have his gift of reading the Akashic Records for an individual's benefit and spiritual progress.

While Cayce chose a companion soul mate as his life partner, some highly developed twin souls choose to live together in sexual as well as spiritual partnership, with the realization that the strength of their unique bond enables them to bring more light into the world. It is as though the fusion (or rather re-fusion) of the masculine and feminine energies of the one being has caused a huge explosion of light; and when such wonderful light comes into the world, it expands naturally to embrace others. Hence, you will never find evolved twin souls who are wrapped up only in each other. One such couple is Aron and Doris Abrahamsen, who are now aged eighty-seven and eighty-one, and whose wonderful spiritual work on Earth is no doubt not quite over.

Aron and Doris Abrahamsen

The Sanskrit word *akash* means "ether," and everything that has ever happened since the beginning of time has been recorded etherically and is available to be read. When I, or any other deep-memory-process/regression therapist, work with clients, we help them tap into their own Akashic Records stored in their own subconscious memory. This technique is very effective because the subconscious knows what the individual needs and is ready to deal with. Reliving trauma and working through it makes it easier to release it and thus free ourselves permanently from its effects. However, what both Edgar Cayce and Aron Abrahamsen did was to put themselves into a trance state and read the Akashic Records for their clients. The skill of Cayce, Abrahamsen, and other good clairvoyants lies in selecting for another individual the past lives that have the most bearing upon his or her present life. I hasten to add, however, that these are very often not quite what the person concerned was most wanting to hear! But Aron Abrahamsen has been a true master of the art of counseling people on how best to rectify their past mistakes and integrate their learning to better their spiritual development.

Aron is Norwegian by birth, but emigrated to the United States to earn his degree. Born a Jew, Aron converted to Christianity following his marriage to Doris. Aron describes in his autobiography[19] how his wife encouraged him in his search for all that God had for him, and joined with him in that journey. For twenty years, he had a distinguished career as an electrical engineer, and was at one time a member of the scientific study team that paved the way for the Apollo Space Program. His longtime desire to know God was achieved through Christ, studying the Scriptures and teaching them, and through prayer and meditation. Aron and Doris were both ordained as ministers under the American Ministerial Association and they both also hold honorary doctor of divinity degrees from Trinity Hall College and Seminary.

Meaningful spiritual experience came to Aron quite early on in his engineering career, and he started giving readings to people in a small way before eventually deciding to devote himself to that full time. He and Doris did not advertise, but they achieved an international reputation simply by

---

19.   Aron Abrahamsen, *On Wings of Spirit* (Virginia Beach, VA: ARE Press, 1993).

word of mouth, and during the twenty-five years in which Aron gave these readings, thousands of people were helped by them, even as far away as Japan.

Doris herself has more than thirty years experience in counseling and has been well known for her expertise on the subject of sound dynamics, healing of memories, and meditation, teaching classes and workshops on these subjects for many years. The two of them also conducted seminars, conferences, and workshops together in both the United States and Canada, covering topics such as spiritual growth, Earth changes, and dreams. For more than two years, they were on the speaking circuit for the Association for Research and Enlightenment (on the topic "Be your own psychic"), and Aron appeared on TV and radio while on a speaking tour across America.

Edgar Cayce described the Akashic Records thus: "Upon time and space is written the thoughts, the deeds, the activities of an entity—as in relationships to its environs, its hereditary influence . . . the record is God's book of remembrance, and each entity, each soul . . . either makes same good or bad or indifferent . . . "[20] And in Reading 294—19, Cayce described the (quite lengthy!) journey he would make when he left his body in order to read someone's history. It culminates, "Quite suddenly I come upon a hall of records. It is a hall without walls, without ceiling, but I am conscious

---

20.   Taken from Cayce's Reading 1650-1.

of seeing an old man who hands me a large book, a record of the individual for whom I seek information . . . "

Aron had already been doing readings for people for a while before he had his own dramatic introduction to the Akashic Records. On the occasion in question, he had been asked for help by a young man who was having difficulty in choosing between jobs, and he was sitting, as was his custom, in his favorite rocking chair, praying for the young man, when suddenly "something dramatically different happened." He then found himself out of his body—on the roof of his house. From there, he soared upward, traveling along a path (which felt comfortable despite the uniqueness and unfamiliarity of the experience), eventually coming to a Grecian "temple-like palace" that contained an enormous library. There his guides selected the volumes that were relevant to the young man, and Aron obtained the information he needed before saying goodbye "with an inner knowing that I would return." This turned out to be the prelude to well over seven thousand past-life readings made between 1970 and 1995, when he stopped because of health concerns. Now he and Doris are enjoying a well-earned retirement in Florida.

A great lover of music, which he often incorporated into his counseling (often advising people what to listen to), Aron likened his and Doris's role to that of the timpani in a symphony orchestra: "When it's important, it's time for them to be heard." Their good friend, the psychotherapist Harmon Bro, who died in 1997, worked with Edgar Cayce and wrote an excellent biography of this most famous of all clairvoyants.[21] In a recorded interview with Aron and Doris, Bro described the couple as being like two musical instruments playing together. He commented that, although Doris had fewer passages to play, they were tuned in to the same material. For—like Gladys Davis Turner, who took meticulous notes of all Edgar Cayce's readings—Doris was always present, asking pertinent questions on behalf of the subject of the reading. Aron said that, even though he was in trance, he always knew if Doris left the room and would be "helpless until she had returned." Her role was more than that of helper—she was a vital part of the whole enterprise.

Aron always stressed that he wanted people to use the readings as a jumping-off point—a motivator saying "look at this," to entice them to "look around the corner." Like all good therapists, the last thing he wanted was to be a crutch for anyone. In the interview with Bro, Aron said, "Usually a reading poses more questions than answers. People have to start working and stretching themselves." I can personally endorse that because, when he told me in 1992 that I had come "partly as a writer, to disseminate information on the spiritual life," Aron did not suggest that I write books, nor tell me if or when I would get published. Still less did he suggest that I train in regression therapy.

God, and a person's individual relationship with him, always forms the core of Aron's readings. He urges people to begin right where they are, because "that's where God

---

21.   Bro, *A Seer Out of Season*.

accepts you. God can guide you little by little to be the person you should be." Then he encourages them to grow in richness with their day-to-day process, learning to listen, to be aware, becoming a better person, living a more meaningful life. He says, "See how your relationship with your spouse can improve, and as you communicate with God, you can communicate better with spouse, children, and anyone else." Above all, Aron encouraged people to take responsibility for their life, explaining that it was not his task to know what God had in mind for them. We need to listen to that still small voice and then set out in faith, one small step at a time. "We grow, sometimes through pain, difficulties, and hardship. There is instant coffee and instant tea, but there is not instant illumination." When Aron and Doris pray for people, they pray that God may make that person a person after his heart.

Aron always began his readings with a prologue, and a fascinating thing about these prologues is that he had no conscious knowledge of the reasons for saying what he said. To Bro, he cited the instance of a prologue for one young man that was entirely about what happens to a soul that commits suicide. Seven months later, this young man's best friend committed suicide!

The next part of the reading would always be the "life seal"—a symbolic representation of the person concerned, "even if they don't recognize it." One might describe it as a pictorial guide to the character, and Aron said that each symbol he gave helped people to discover themselves. Never were two of Aron's life seals alike. Cayce apparently did not give these in as much depth, and when he was particularly busy he omitted them all together. Bro says that Aron's seals really gleam with meaning and excitement; and many people have had them painted and framed, or even made into something such as a stained-glass window.

After the life seal come influences: whether someone is people-oriented, goal-oriented, what their psychological influences are, what things tug at them. This is a broader picture than an astrological one, unpacking the life seal. Aron encourages people to move ahead without fear of being wrong, and also sometimes gives warnings about what to engage in and what to stay clear of. For instance, to someone who had been a gambler in previous lives, he would warn to avoid that now, lest it be their downfall again. According to Harmon Bro, Aron was "the most skilled psychic at discerning patterns and trends."

When it came to the past lives, Aron usually cited five. In the early days, when he gave information about ten lives, Aron found that many were simply repeats. He never found any Napoleons or Caesars, but plenty of gladiators, lawyers, attorneys, and so on. Just as I have found with regression therapy, sometimes people are not aware of their latent interests and talents, and getting in touch with their past can give them a chance to discover these and maybe make use of them again. Sometimes it takes as long as five years for people to resonate with the information they obtain from the reading, but eventually they normally find that it all makes a great deal of sense. Very importantly, Aron says, "Don't postpone what you can do now. The longer you procrastinate the harder it becomes to get started; negative patterns get reinforced." So, if you procrastinate now, you will almost certainly procrastinate in your next life. Perhaps the main purpose of the readings was to help people avoid making the same mistakes. Rather than simply being snapshots of previous lives, Aron would invite people to take responsibility for their past mistakes and rectify them.

In the same interview with Harmon Bro, Doris movingly described her sense of awe as a reading was taking place and the emotion she felt rising up within her concerning the person Aron was talking about. Sometimes, she explained, she would become aware of a question that needed to be asked about the person to further draw information that might be helpful. The process was a journey in spirit for the two of them together.

After finding the person's most relevant past lives, Aron would speak about their color vibrations, which he explained tell people their purpose. "Red can be dangerous for some. Too much purple can drive you insane, or be depressing." If someone doesn't like the colors they came in on, it means that they are not responding well to some aspect of themselves. Therefore, they need to draw these colors back into their lives—maybe a little at a time—in order to become more integrated with themselves. The color therapists I am acquainted with would certainly agree with that.

The final section of Aron's readings always concerned one's purpose in one's present life. This is particularly interesting because Aron said that very often what someone was doing professionally had nothing or little to do with his or her purpose. Aron had come to the conclusion that the separation of career and purpose was often by design. After all, people can lose their jobs. Apparently our purpose has often started eons ago!

Doris commented that the readings had taught what should be our order of priorities: God, family, work, and other people. These four, she said, never change, while other priorities can. And, concluding the interview, Bro said that Aron and Doris' purpose was to open the doorway for people. Such a reading is one of the greatest gifts that anyone could receive.

Ann and Ken Evans

How like a winter has your absence been
From me, how seeming endless are the years
Without your presence, till I only dream
Of days I spent with you without these tears,
It makes me sigh to see your paintings still
With humour, pathos, seeing nature's pain.
—ANN EVANS, NOVEMBER 2005

Ken was a struggling artist, Ann an ex-nun, still devoting her life to serving other people. They first met at a charity event that Ann was involved in to raise funds for African nuns. Ken was exhibiting there, and Ann's initial reaction was one of sympathy "for this poor man trying with some difficulty to put up his paintings." It is, however, usual for twin-soul recognition to be more or less instant, and their courtship was only three months. Ken, who was about sixteen years older than Ann, had already married, had a son, and later got divorced, before they first met. They then had two daughters, Jessie and Christine, seven years apart and both very gifted and creative. Jessie, now twenty-nine, studied fine art sculpture and while at college gradually steered toward film. She is running Plantagenet Film and has a partner and a baby son, while Christine, who has been designing and making jewelry, is at present doing an art foundation course in Somerset (in southwest England).

Twin souls very often incarnate into similar circumstances and, although Ann's family was well-to-do while Ken's was extremely poor, they both had eccentric mothers and difficult childhoods. Ann was born in 1940, her father was killed in action, and the family was caught up in problems caused by the Second World War. She and her brother were even sent to boarding school for a term when they were only two and three years old. Ann's mother had won a scholarship to the Royal Academy Schools and, while talented, interesting, and artistically inspiring for her children, she was also difficult to deal with. This, Ann says, gave her many challenges to overcome at an early age, and—like many people who have difficult childhoods—she ultimately became a healer. Ken's mother had a special talent for music, but was eccentric in similar ways to Ann's, and as a result did not understand her son very well. Additionally, the family's poverty led him to suffer from malnutrition, which Ann feels may have contributed to his death from a stroke at the age of only sixty-two.

Ann is clairaudient and clairvoyant, and as a child she had a secret garden where she would meet Jesus and talk to him. Her family, who were Catholics, could not understand her, and later on there was no one in her Catholic boarding school with whom she could talk about her dreams and her communications with spirit. So her childhood, like Ken's, was very lonely.

After a year spent on a farm looking after horses and teaching riding, Ann went to teacher training college with the aim of teaching the blind. However, rather than entering the teaching profession, she obeyed an order to become a nun which came, quite unexpectedly but very clearly, during one of her daily "listening to God" sessions. While the idea horrified her at first, she said her nine and a half years as an Assumption Sister were "an incredible teaching in contemplative prayer, awareness, and gentleness." Ann adds that in ordinary life it is difficult to be calm within, and harder still to achieve inner silence, but that in the religious life people can concentrate on awareness of the divine and tune in to God's love and wisdom. While she was a nun, Ann spent three years in Africa, and more recently she went out to Tanzania with her two daughters to teach people there to make solar ovens. Though happy in the religious life, Ann gradually felt that God was telling her to move on, and she subsequently became a Quaker.

When Jessie was three years old, Ken heard a radio program about Major Bruce MacManaway, who drew many people together for healing, including the general commanding the army in Scotland and Peter Caddy, one of the founders of Findhorn (the famous ecological village). This gave Ken the desire to do one of MacManaway's courses at the Westbank Healing Centre in Fife, Scotland, and, since the Evanses were short of money, the MacManaways kindly lent the family their caravan for the duration of the course. Ann has been using her healing abilities ever since and, at very early ages, before they had each started to do their own thing, Jessie and Christine regularly worked together with her in this field.

Ann says that during their married life she and Ken were literally never apart, so his sudden death was a terrible shock. However, while still looking at his body, she was immediately consoled by feeling his presence at her side and hearing him tell her not to worry, since what had happened was for the best. Also, in life he often used to stand just behind her and hold her on the upper arms in a comforting way, and one day shortly after he had died, she felt his hold again. This was naturally a great comfort to her. Later, when their older daughter Jessie was eleven, she had a near-death experience during which she met her father. He explained to her that he had promised before he came into that life to return as soon as he was needed again for his work on the other side.

Four months after he died, Ken started waking Ann up at around four o'clock in the morning and telling her about the meanings of all his paintings. These words have been written by Jessie, in beautiful calligraphy, into a book of reproductions of the paintings that Ann and Jessie have produced together.[22] I made friends with Ann only some time after her husband's death in 1987, but this book has helped me to feel that I know him too. Ken said of the painting entitled "Keyhole in the Hill" that when he started it, he saw a donkey blocking the path and realized that this was a warning of his hourglass running out. He struggled with the painting for months and sees it as a deep cleansing both for himself and for others. The angels in the painting are sounding the trumpet to say that it is time to come to the rising sun. Ken comments, "That is what death is: a coming to the sunrise, full of hope, light, love, and joy."

Ken explained to Ann that, when he had first passed over, his work in spirit consisted of helping people who had just died to make the transition to the other side. Whereas the Africans, for instance, know only too well that "getting to heaven" is not always straightforward, and that some people need help and guidance to find the route, we in the West have long since forgotten about this. Tibetan Buddhists continue reading the *Bardo Thodol* (known to us as *The*

---

22. Ann Evans and Jessie Plantaganet-Ford, *An Artist's Life after Death* (Somerset, UK: Wincanton, 1996). Both this book and cards of Ken's paintings can be ordered via www.kenevansprints.co.uk

Tibetan Book of the Dead) to people for some time after they have passed away, and in Africa it is also the custom at death to "escort the soul across to the other side." The great African shaman, Malidoma Patrice Somé,[23] (whose name means "one who makes friends with the stranger") now lives in the United States and runs workshops in the West.

With his great sensitivity to such things, Malidoma finds much of our atmosphere in the West to be polluted by souls who have been lost, often for a very long time. First of all, those who did not believe in God and an afterlife will tend to stay asleep when they die rather than coming to an instant realization that there is no such thing as death. Furthermore, when people die very suddenly, in, say, an accident, they often do not have time to realize that they are dead. The astral plane, which is immediately "above" the earthly one, looks exactly the same as this one, and so people sometimes need to be convinced of the fact that they have left their physical bodies. And finally, there are many other reasons for souls getting stuck in the astral plane, such as attachment (either to drink, food, etc., or to people) or a desire for vengeance. Those who believe in praying for the dead, and those who do shamanic work, can help such souls jointly with evolved souls such as Ken who are in spirit. Ken has also been able to use his art therapeutically with those who were

---

23.   Malidoma's three books are published by Penguin Compass, New York, and I particularly recommend his extraordinary autobiography, *Of Water and the Spirit*.

struggling to come to terms with their death; he told Ann that he painted with light and that the people he was helping could change the pictures if they wanted to.

Later on Ken informed Ann that he had moved on to work with souls who had got stuck at levels beyond the astral planes. We carry on evolving spiritually in between incarnations, moving ever-on through deeper planes but, just as people on Earth can often get caught in the thralls of materialism, so do souls who are not incarnate some-times lose interest in their own advancement, remaining absorbed in a particular pastime (of which there are at least as many available on the other side as there are here—see, for instance, the books of Dr. Michael Newton).[24] Ken, as a highly evolved soul, had the ability to inspire people with enthusiasm for the most worthwhile pursuits, but he apparently often found it difficult to stir souls out of their apathy!

One of my favorites of Ken's paintings is of two hands stretching up toward the sun. For me, this is a good symbol for twin souls reaching out together toward God, which is precisely what Ken and Ann did throughout the ten rich years of married life. Ken, who said, "I paint the beauty of nature so that people will stop destroying it before it is too late," always put God and the spiritual life at the very center of his work.

In recent years, Ann has not only become a sculptor but has also trained in reflexology and as a chiropractor. She has

---

24.   Michael Newton, M.D., *Journey of Souls* and *Destiny of Souls*

developed her own, more gentle form of the latter, which she calls "alignment therapy" (see www.alignment-therapy .co.uk). She would like one day to go back to Africa to teach her therapy and maybe to join a group of women in Uganda who are using reflexology to help with AIDS. Her mother was, at ninety-four, still living alone, gardening, and driving a car, and she had only just given up riding a bicycle because of a knee operation! She died recently at ninety-six while having tea with friends. So Ann, now only sixty-eight, feels that she still has a lot of work left to do on Earth before she can merge with Ken. To show how fit she must be, she thoroughly enjoyed her first skiing holiday a couple of winters ago!

Ann and Ken's great work together (and apart) demonstrates a high level of spiritual understanding. Our planet needs to have souls of different levels incarnate at the same time, just as we usually need to return here regularly in order to pay our debts and advance spiritually. As the well-known clairvoyant Lilla Bek once explained in "Agony Aunt's column" in the magazine *Caduceus,*[25] when people evolve they become "more collective;" that is, more interested in the welfare of everyone and less concerned about finding their own twin flame or soul mate. Ann says that she has always had an inner knowing that she and Ken were one being, but she also feels the two of them to be part of something much greater and even more wonderful. She feels that she is almost at the point where all the individual drops merge into

---

25.   *Caduceus* issue number 28.

the great ocean of love that is God, and it seems that Ken
has already done this.

Nirvana, yes, but does that mean obliteration of individuality? Personally I have always preferred to think not,
and in Graham Bernard's book *Eternal Ties: The Reality behind
Relationships*,[26] the author's deceased friend Richard explains,
"We are all one in God. Remember, each fellowship will
ultimately become a distinct organ in the augmented Body
of God, each member contributing an individual, unique,
and perfect element of that organ, without which it would
be incomplete. . . . The more truly we are one with God,
the more we become one with all. The more we become
one with all, the more we are individual." Well, what Ken
says coincides with this description. After a period of purifi-
cation during which it was very difficult for Ann to communicate with him, he moved on again. (Some clairvoyants and
spiritual books talk of higher planes, but Ann says that that
is not an adjective Ken ever uses.) Now it seems that he has
"arrived," or merged into the whole—an amazingly wonderful concept that is very difficult for us on Earth to grasp.
Ken explains that he is completely filled with light, unclut-
tered with anything that is not light and love. His star—his
uniqueness—is purified and wonderfully itself now; in fact,
he feels more fully himself than ever. So this is the state in
which Ann will join him when she has finished her work on

26.　Graham Bernard, *Eternal Ties: The Reality behind Relationships: A Conversation
　　　with Richard* (Rochester, VT: Destiny Books, 1990).

Earth, and it is also, I am very happy to say, the state that we all have to look forward to!

Graham and Elfie Courtenay

Being the older brother of Edwin Courtenay, who must be one of the best-known clairvoyants in England, was initially far from easy for Graham, but in recent years he has become well established in spiritual work in his own right, and living in Germany with his German wife now helps keep him from being overshadowed by his younger sibling.

Despite a happy childhood in a very loving family, Graham had a difficult start to his adult life. After leaving school at sixteen, he went to college to pursue a four-year degree in graphic design, but failed to obtain the qualification. He then spent a number of years searching—not only attempting other courses, but also seeking a satisfactory relationship. Graham is quite sure that he incarnated with a determination to find Elfie (her image deeply engraved in his soul!), because he says that all the girls with whom he did achieve brief relationships looked very similar to her. "They all," he said, "had dark hair and bobbed haircuts just like Elfie's, and some of them were also spiritual, if less so than her."

They met on a guided tour of the sacred sites of Cornwall, where Edwin had offered Graham a free place when he was feeling particularly depressed following the end of a relatively long relationship. This tour had been organized for a group of Germans, and Elfie was acting as interpreter for them. She had been told, not long beforehand, both by

Edwin and by other clairvoyants, that she would be meeting her twin soul within three months, so she was much better prepared for the meeting than Graham was. For her, the recognition was therefore more or less instant, while for him, feeling something of an outsider in a group of whose language he knew not a word, the week was a much less happy one—that is, until the fifth day.

On that completely unforgettable day in August 1995, Graham told Elfie that he had dreamt that she had asked him for the ring he was wearing. He then suggested that she try wearing it the next night and see what happened. Of course what happened was the realization that there was something between them, but they then only had a couple of days left to get to know each other. A very eventful couple of days because, in meditation, they both had visions of previous lifetimes they had shared.

Graham then returned home extraordinarily happy on one level, but at the same time very confused. First, he had been accepted for a degree course in sculpture, which was slated to start shortly in the following September; second, he had no money to pay for traveling to Germany to see Elfie; and third, at that point he had very little knowledge about twin souls or soul mates and his previous negative experiences in relationships made him somewhat scared about the whole thing. However, Edwin had arranged to do some workshops in Germany a few weeks later, and Graham was already making healing wands and sets of rune stones, which they both believed would sell well at the workshops.

Elfie was more than happy to lend him the money for his fare to Germany, but it would mean renouncing his degree course—a difficult decision.

Elfie's upbringing—unusually for twin souls—was rather different from Graham's. Eager to be free and independent of her parents and older brother, she left home at nineteen after studying pottery for three years. She then worked for a couple of years before deciding to go to England as an au pair in order to learn the language. On her return, she worked again in pottery workshops, and then she went back to college and studied to become a master of pottery. This qualification gave her the confidence to set up her own workshop. Two years later, she met her first husband, but they separated after nine years, when their daughter Verena was only two years old.

Elfie's difficult years of supporting and bringing up her daughter on her own were helped somewhat by the spiritual reading that she had already embarked upon. She had also, before her daughter was born, taken courses in esoteric psychology taught by Thorwald Dethlefsen in Munich. She says that all this had given her a great deal of help in understanding life from a different perspective, that she consequently knew that there were no accidents, and that she realized that she had to take responsibility for the circumstances of her own life.

For a few years, Elfie was naturally very tied to her home and her workshop, but at the end of 1988 she suddenly found herself able to attend a New Age conference where she met the famous American channel, Janet McClure. This proved to be the real beginning of her spiritual life, and in 1990 she started to organize programs with different spiritual teachers. Since most of these came from America, she decided to resume her studies of English, and after another couple of years her English had improved so much that she was able to translate readings for people and take on the task of translator for Edwin Courtenay's workshops.

All the channels whose visits she organized told Elfie that there would be a man in her future, but they all said that she had to be patient. She had by then developed a great deal of faith and trust, and in any case she was too busy to worry about finding a new partner. Despite being more prepared for their meeting than Graham, the fact that she is fourteen years his senior made her a little apprehensive. Another concern was that, if Graham were to renounce his place on the degree course, he would lose his unemployment benefits as well as his grant.

Whatever qualms Elfie had, however, were not as strong as the feelings of love and yearning that the Cornwall encounter had stirred deep inside her. She was nevertheless determined not to put any pressure on her twin flame, and to leave him to decide for himself where his path lay. The weeks of waiting and reflection proved a fascinating time for both of them. First, the information concerning the nature of their relationship came through two weeks after the end of the Cornwall workshop, in a channelling received by Edwin from the Archangel Michael. Second, the two of them seemed to be in constant contact not only by telephone and letter, but also telepathically. On one occasion, they each bought the other a postcard with a picture of seagulls on it; on another occasion, Graham's card to Elfie written in a spiral crossed with one from her in which the words were also written in a spiral! All this gradually gave Graham the confidence to believe that his destiny lay with Elfie and to trust that, if this really was the case, they would be taken care of financially. So—very apprehensive about flying for the first time—Graham renounced his place in the degree course, accepted Elfie's offer of a loan, and booked for himself to join Edwin on the forthcoming workshops in Germany.

During these workshops Graham's artifacts sold well and, though it was the least of her concerns, he was soon able to pay Elfie back the money for his fare. Spending more time together was wonderful, but they both needed to make many adjustments. Graham did not know a word of German, and Verena was not used to having a man in the house. But since Verena already had a father she saw regularly, Graham resolved to make himself her friend rather than a stepfather, and he began straight away to make a serious attempt at learning German. Elfie too, after so many years without a partner, preferred to take things slowly, and so Graham for the next few months came and went with his brother, who was at that time giving regular workshops in Germany.

Graham says that Elfie was "way ahead of me spiritually," but this was no doubt simply a result of her years of study and of contact with distinguished people in the field. Twin souls always catch one another up spiritually, and under Elfie's influence, Graham soon started to soar ahead. A great deal of his work nowadays has to do with symbols, which he channels, and it is interesting that his real introduction to this dates from the Cornwall trip when he and Elfie first met.

During that tour, Edwin led a meditation around a rock that was originally part of an ancient temple. This rock was engraved with two spirals, and it was obvious that a third spiral was missing. During the meditation, Graham found himself plunged into a post-Arthurian lifetime in which he had been a knight connected with that very temple. In that life, he evidently had an important role resisting a group of people who were trying to stamp out the local religion. To his amazement, in the meditation, Graham saw himself actually removing the piece of rock which held the third spiral! It was a terrifying experience because he was surrounded by armed men who were intent on killing him, but he knew that it was vital for him and the fellow lightworkers of his religion to preserve the spiral. By fleeing he was able to leave the temple and the other two spirals safe, because the enemies were then more intent on catching him than on wreaking further destruction at the site. He managed to escape and eventually, after walking probably for months, he met Elfie, who was a high priestess at Glastonbury Tor, which was at that time an island. (This is a very famous holy site in England, connected with King Arthur. The Tor, which is an ancient Celtic word meaning "conical hill," stands solitarily just outside Glastonbury in Somerset and is a land-mark for many miles around. It is topped by the roofless St. Michael's Tower.) Together with two other people, they broke the slab of rock into four and, while the other two each took a piece off elsewhere, Graham and Elfie walked all the way back to Cornwall with their pieces of the rock and threw them into Dewsmary Pool, which is also where Arthur's sword Excalibur is supposed to have been thrown. The day after this meditation, a local person told Edwin about a theory that someone had forced the third spiral off the rock face!

The following year, with their relationship now firmly established, Graham and Elfie went on another one of Edwin's guided tours, which this time included a visit to Avebury (an important archeological site in the south of England), and here the end of the story came clear to them. In Avebury, Graham found himself drawn to a really big stone somewhere at the end of the site, and he could not walk away from it. So he leaned against it, closed his eyes, and meditated. Once again he found himself plunged into that same post-Arthurian lifetime, and it seems that he sacrificed himself to save Elfie. They both believe that they were on their way to a sanctuary near Avebury, where the energies are particularly strong and protective, because they were still being chased by the ene-mies. Graham told Elfie to go on while he stayed by that big stone to fend them off, and there he was killed by a knight in black chain mail, who plunged his sword through Graham's armor and his solar plexus (an area in his present body that tended to be particularly sensitive).

Although Graham and Elfie have found various other shared past lifetimes, they regard this one as the most significant for their work in this life. Once Graham had moved to Germany permanently, they gradually started to work as a couple independently of Edwin (though Elfie still does some translation for his workshops). By 1999, they had established themselves sufficiently in their spiritual work for her to be able to give up her pottery and move to a home near Munich that was more suitable for them as a couple. They married in November 2001, and nowadays they do certain things individually and other things together. As well as working in Germany, they lead spiritual walking trips to power places in the south of England and in Ireland.

Elfie comments that one of the keys to their strength as a couple is the understanding, acceptance, and support of each other's individuality and path as well as of each other's talents and needs. She realizes that soul partners may have to follow individual pathways in order to express certain gifts of the soul, and that they sometimes come together in order to complete certain experiences—some of which, just as Aron Abrahamsen says too, may have started literally eons ago.

Graham and Elfie have both qualified as healers with the Healing Society of Germany, and Elfie has also qualified both as a nature and landscape guide and as a herbal teacher. She works as a guide in German and English at the nearby *Glentleiten*, which is an open air museum. Graham has recently been concentrating more and more on developing his abilities as a channel, connecting to the Akashic Records and receiving symbols from there, and also working (like Edwin) with crystal skulls. A friend of theirs is publishing a card deck of her own photographs, which she has combined with symbols that Graham has channelled and which represent the energy of the picture. These cards are useful for meditation and connecting with certain energies and powers.

Today they are a very busy, as well as a very happy, pair! As for Verena, she is living with her partner and working for a security company. Up to now, she has not begun to explore her spiritual pathway, but Elfie is quite confident that this will happen when the time is right.

The "Pink Twins"

Whereas tradition in the West for the past two thousand years has been that there could only be one divine incarnation ever (Jesus Christ), in India it has always been believed that the divine incarnates on Earth during times of great need. Such incarnations are know as *avatars*, which bring varying amounts of power with them, the most powerful being known as *poorna* (full) avatars, who exhibit sixteen different attributes of the Godhead. Krishna (who pre-dated Jesus by approximately three thousand years!) is said to have been a poorna avatar, and Rama, whose name is also well known even in the West (and who pre-dated Krishna by another very long time) was very powerful too.

There is no question that our present era is a time of great need. (As I write, the television screens and newspapers are full of terrible pictures of the appalling devastation wrought by the May 2008 cyclone in Burma.) Consequently—and in accordance with prophecies made thousands of years ago—the Earth is at present being blessed by a triple incarnation of major avatars (as well as some minor ones such as Mother Meera, who resides most of the time in Germany, and Amma, "the hugging one," who travels very widely as well as having an ashram in Kerala). The first of these was Sai Baba of Shirdi, who is venerated as a great saint throughout India and whose shrine in Shirdi, in the state of Maharashtra, still receives a constant stream of pilgrims. He died in 1918, and just before leaving his body, he stated that he would return in eight years.

Sathya Sai Baba was born into a poor family on November 23, 1926, in the tiny village of Puttaparthi in the state of Andhra Pradesh. His mother, Easwaramma, said that when he was conceived she saw a blue light coming toward her and felt it entering her womb, and instruments in the house played on their own at the moment of his birth. From a very early age he did things that displeased his family, such as taking food from the house to give to people who were poorer still, as well as exhibiting amazing powers of healing and manifestation. He would, for instance, run his friends up the hill to a tamarind tree and pick from it whatever fruit each one of them asked for. At the age of fourteen, He threw down his school books, declared Himself as Sai Baba, and stated that it was now time to begin His mission. Sai Baba, incidentally, means "Divine Mother and Father," and Sathya means "truth." Many people who were devotees of Sai Baba of Shirdi during His lifetime came to recognize Sathya as his reincarnation (He teased one of them that he still owed him three rupees!), and he says that eight years after leaving his present body in 2022, he will return as Prema Sai (*Prema* means "love") and incarnate near Mysore in the state of Karnataka. Sai Baba of Shirdi embodied the masculine energy of God, known as Shiva; Prema Sai will embody the feminine, known as Shakthi; but Sathya Sai, the most powerful poorna avatar of all, embodies both Shiva and Shakthi.

Very many fascinating books have been written about Sathya Sai Baba in many different languages, but I will just recommend those of the American authors John Hislop, Dr. Samuel Sandweiss and Diana Baskin; that of the Italian Catholic priest, Mario Mazzoleni; the book by the English couple Peggy Mason and Ron Laing (Peggy produced a wonderful Sai Baba quarterly magazine until a couple of weeks before she died at the age of eighty-eight!); and the book by Phyllis Krystal[27] (who is probably best known for *Cutting the Ties that Bind* and is still, at ninety-four, running workshops!). Baba's message is a simple one: "Love all, serve all, help ever, hurt

---

27.   Phyllis Krystal, *Sai Baba: The Ultimate Experience* (Los Angeles: Aura Books, 1994).

never; there is only one religion—the religion of Love . . .
There is only one caste—the caste of humanity." And people
of all creeds and none, and of countless nationalities, throng
to his ashram in their thousands—or rather millions. Puttaparthi has grown from an insignificant rural village to a
vibrant hubbub of people ever clamoring for even the tiniest
glimpse of the five-foot, two-inch form in the orange robe
with his shock of hair (an afro that is now rather thinning in
his eighty-second year); and he also has a smaller ashram in
Whitefield on the outskirts of Bangalore.

Even more important than his healing of individuals
("Cancer canceled" is one of his oft-repeated phrases) and
the manifestation for them of such things as diamond rings,
gold chains, and watches, are Baba's education, health, and
social welfare programs. The latter extend far afield: thanks
to Baba, the entire vast area of Chennai (formerly Madras)
is now enjoying clean water. Sathya Sai schools abound
in India; there are also a few in other countries, and Puttaparthi and Whitefield each has a university and a large,
super speciality hospital that provides free treatment from
some of the best-qualified medical staff. Puttaparthi also
now boasts a music college and a wonderful sports complex, which was inaugurated not so long ago by a game with
the Harlem Globetrotters. The Sri Sathya Sai Education in
Human Values (SSSEHV) program—based on the five prin-
ciples of *sathya, dharma, prema, shanthi,* and *ahimsa* (truth,
right conduct, love, peace, and nonviolence)—is spreading
throughout the world and is already being used in between

three and four hundred schools in Britain. There is also now a Radio Sai station, and the monthly magazine, *Sanathana Sarathi* (*The Eternal Charioteer*), produced in several languages by the Sri Sathya Sai Books and Publications Trust, relays his discourses and reports on the activities of Baba groups all over the world.

In 1996, I helped to found a Sai Baba group in my neighborhood, and in 1998, the leader of the group and I paid our first visit to Puttaparthi. Since then I have made eight more pilgrimages there, and each time something occurred that made a major improvement in my life. (On none of these occasions was it something I was expecting or even asking for.) And that is how I came to know of the "Pink Twins," who had started to go to Puttaparthi from Australia years before I had.

When people are looking for a soul mate or their twin soul, they will normally, unless they are gay, be thinking in terms of someone of the opposite sex. However, since most of us change sex regularly between our numerous incarnations, the chances of one's twin flame actually being of the opposite sex in any particular lifetime are presumably not more than 50 percent. This is another of the instances on which I disagree with Joudry and Pressman, who maintained that twin souls always incarnated as opposite sexes. Of course, when twin souls do plan an incarnation of working together, it seems very likely that they will also decide to live in a sexual relationship, but even this is by no means always the case (like Edgar Cayce and Gladys Davis Turner).

I find it interesting that in French twin souls are called, not twins, but *âmes-sœurs*—"sister souls"! Well, my final couple in this chapter are not only quite literally sister souls, but also twins in both senses (which clairvoyants tell me is fairly unusual for twin flames). Among the millions of people who visit Sai Baba's ashram, there can be no better known or more greatly loved figures than Dorothy and Moyia O'Brien, whose nickname was given to them affectionately by Baba because they like to wear pink, and because pink is the color of love and therefore totally appropriate for two people whose lives have been filled with nothing but love since the very beginning.

Dorothy and Moyia were born in Toowoomba, in Queensland, Australia, in 1923 (the same year as Sathya Sai), and Dorothy died—I will not say "sadly" because the whole thing was organized absolutely perfectly and beautifully by Baba—on January 18, 2004. Their sister Nell is just one year older than they are, and their father, who was badly wounded in the First World War, died when they were only three years old. The twins still have a few happy memories of him and can remember feeling sad at his death, but the pain of loss was greatly alleviated because they could take comfort in always having each other. The loss was much harder for their mother, but she was a very courageous, as well as a

very loving, woman, and the twins' beautiful autobiographical book[28] speaks only of happy childhood memories.

The O'Brien family was Catholic, and Dorothy and Moyia
were educated by nuns. From their earliest years they always
talked of God, and were unpopular at school because they
were seen as goody-goodies. They never showed the least sign
of selfishness, and even their mother—wonderful Christian
though she was—sometimes had problems with her twins'
habit of giving things away to poorer children.

I was also brought up Catholic and can well remember
my reluctance, from the age of not more than about seven,
to believe in eternal damnation. This idea always seemed to
be totally at odds with the concept of a loving God, and so
I was fascinated to read about the twins' refusal to believe
in hell at an equally early age. However, unlike myself, who
felt a great deal of pride in my religion after having been
taught that only Catholics were right and everyone else was
wrong, Dorothy and Moyia also questioned that teaching.
The youngsters even dared to ask the nuns why God should
favor Christians more than, say, Buddhists or Muslims!

Such spiritually advanced, inquiring minds prepared the
way very well for their first coming to Sai Baba in 1981. Mrs.
O'Brien, the twins' mother, was born in 1900, lived to be
ninety-four, and was also a great spiritual seeker all her life.
Although they had already read widely on spiritual matters

---

28.   Dorothy and Moiya O'Brien, *The Touch of the Lord—On the Life of the
       O'Brien Twins* (Queensland, AU: Divine Print Publishers, 2000).

and come to believe in reincarnation, Dorothy and Moyia's attachment to the Catholic Church was at the time still so strong that, when a healer friend first spoke to them about Sai Baba, they were not interested. Very shortly after that, however, their mother read one of Howard Murphet's books on the avatar and urged them excitedly to read it. They then decided to take her to India to meet him, and ever since then there has been no turning back.

When, in 1981, Mr. Shastri, the Nadi Gruha in Bangalore, told Dorothy and Moyia that they were twin souls, it made perfect sense to them. *Nadis* (or *naadis*) are the keepers in India of prophecies that were made thousands of years ago, inscribed on palm leaves and handed down carefully from generation to generation, normally, I believe, in the same family. Several of my acquaintances have been to see the Nadi in Bangalore, since it is not too far from Puttaparthi, and have been amazed by the accuracy of what they were told. I myself have paid two visits to Mr. Murthy (Shastri's successor), and he was able to find the bunch of palm leaves in which I was recorded from my birth details and some minimal facts about my family. In 2002, after relaying much of my life history without a single error, Mr. Murthy told me, among other things, roughly when (though not where!) my first book[29] would be published, and that my husband would retire the following year rather than in 2004 as we had long assumed. (Three months later, David's

---

29.   Merivale, *Karmic Release.*

university suddenly announced a major financial crisis, which made him volunteer to leave a year early.) In January 2008, I was told that my writing would be complete when I was seventy-three—five years to go and I am sure that I still have enough to keep me busy at it throughout that time! An interesting book has just been published, whose subtitle is *The Mystery of India's Naadi Palm Leaf Readers.*[30]

To return to the Pink Twins and their reason for not doubting the Nadi's assertion that they were twin souls: before they were born, Mrs. O'Brien had no idea that she was expecting twins, nor had there been any previously in the family, and it is Dorothy and Moyia's belief that they almost always choose to incarnate together. Immediately after the birth, they were placed at either side of their mother's bed, and the attending nurses were astonished to hear them saying "ah, ah" to one another as if they were already missing each other! Mr. Shastri further told them that they had shared many incarnations and that service was all that they ever thought about. This ties in with something they were told by a clairvoyant woman who has been with Sai Baba all her life. She said that the two of them had been with Sai Baba of Shirdi when he died, and that Moyia used to stroke his arms. She still does this to people, and once in Moyia's present life Baba did it to her!

---

30.   Andrew and Angela Donovan, *The Hidden Oracle Of India—The Mystery of India's Naadi Palm Leaf Readers*, (Winchester, UK: O Books, 2008).

The twins always did equally well at school and, since they were both very artistic, they thought initially of careers in the field of art. The war, however, changed things for them, and they left school a year early in order to do twelve months' voluntary service. Once the war was over, their sister Nell, who was by then working as a nurse and had observed how much joy and happiness occupational therapists were able to bring to sick people, suggested that they train in that. This idea had an instant appeal for them and, although people around them said that it would be difficult for such "country girls" to move to Sydney, Australia, for their training, they did not hesitate. They say that they have always had undaunted spirits when they believe that they have made the right decision. Although they did not in the end choose art as their profession, the twins' artistic abilities have been put to great use in the creation of a number of beautiful picture books about Sai Baba.

Living in Sydney inevitably brought opportunities for them both to meet charming young men, but they always felt that their commitment to each other should rule out matrimony for either of them. After graduating, Dorothy and Moyia got jobs in Brisbane. Although these posts were not in the same institutions, they were both working with disabled people—something they found immensely rewarding and continued almost up to normal retirement age. But retirement was not for them because, in 1977, SWARA was born from their mutual desire to help brain-damaged people no one else was helping.

SWARA stands for Sunshine Welfare and Remedial Association. Dorothy and Moyia chose the name because for them the word "sunshine" represented the energy and love that they bring to people, but they later were pleased to discover that the acronym also had appropriate meanings in two different Indian languages. In Sanskrit, *swara* means a sound or a note, and the other meaning of the word is "a force like the breath that maintains and sustains." The latter sums up their work perfectly, and they say that they also like to think that they "started a sound or a note on how disabled people should be treated, by introducing a novel concept where we let them run the place themselves with minimal supervision." There seems little point in my repeating here the history of SWARA when that, and an excellent description of its wonderful work, can all be found in Dorothy and Moyia's own book.

Dorothy and Moyia always lived together and, until Moyia started sometimes to go to India on her own while Dorothy stayed behind to look after SWARA, they were scarcely ever apart. Their book recounts many, many wonderful miracles that Sai Baba has performed either for them or for others in their presence. Twin souls tend to suffer from the same illnesses or physical problems. Well, Dorothy and Moyia have both been very troubled by arthritic knees. In 1990, instead of obeying the doctors who said that Dorothy needed an operation, they chose to go to India for treatment by the "divine doctor." Dorothy had at that point been in a wheelchair for some time, and Moyia was walking with crutches after breaking a femur. Baba healed them both and they went home walking quite normally!

But great spiritual advancement does not signify the end of physical suffering. Personally I see this partly as karma, partly as something that can help our compassion. How could we understand other people's pain without personal experience? Memories are not always long, and, in her joy after a birth, a woman will even forget the most intense pain of labor. Moyia still has trouble with arthritic knees, and Dorothy had a stroke some months prior to her last visit to India.

Some good friends took them both to India for Christmas after Dorothy's stroke. They all had an interview, which proved to be Dorothy's last one, and shortly afterward she was taken into the general hospital just outside the ashram. Baba came to visit her there on the very day that she passed over. It was incredibly beautiful: besides Moyia, three friends were around the bed; Baba spoke to them all, made *vibhuti*[31] and put some of it into Dorothy's mouth. Later he sent word that he would take care of everything, and Dorothy passed late in the evening of January 18. She had an Indian cremation at half past ten the next morning. Baba sent a white[32] sari for her to be dressed in, and *vibhuti* to put on her. There

---

31. Vibhuti is the healing ash that Sai Baba materializes all the time, and which also forms on his pictures in the homes of very spiritual people who follow him.

32. White is the color of mourning in India.

was a lovely service held in a more private part of the hospital grounds. They sang five or six English *bhajans* (devotional songs), and also a Sanskrit one written specially by an Indian gentleman. Three people spoke about Dorothy and she was covered in flowers. Then she went to be cremated. A friend performed the ritual with the help of a doctor who lives in the ashram.

Twin souls who are acquainted on Earth tend to die within a short span of time one from the other, but we have already seen an exception to this with Ann and Ken Evans. When Moyia and Dorothy had the reading from the Nadi Gruha, he said that Moyia would be the one to die first and that Dorothy would pass over six months later. However, nothing is ever set in stone and, when an avatar as powerful as Sai Baba comes into the equation, anything can happen! Moyia, who, at the time of my writing (May 2008), is still going strong and has just returned from yet another visit to India, is not at all concerned about the "mistake" in the reading; she just feels that Baba must have decided to change it. She is totally accepting of what happened and very happy indeed that Baba took care of everything for her.

There can be no doubt that Moyia has moments of missing Dorothy, but Baba has not really given her very much time to be lonely! The morning after Dorothy's funeral, he took Moyia and a good friend of hers into the interview room and was very sweet to her. He said that it had been Dorothy's last life and that she was now with him. Baba then told Moyia to go back to work at SWARA and to keep busy.

He said that he would take care of her and that he would give her strength and good health as well as his love and help. The friend who was supporting her in the ashram comments that she was extraordinarily brave throughout the whole thing. Since her sister's passing, Moyia has had other interviews and Baba has given her permission to travel and talk about him and about Love. She has been to Russia and other countries in Europe, and also to Tasmania twice, and has given a great number of lovely talks to many people. When she is not traveling, Moyia still works at SWARA three days a week. When she is at the ashram, she uses a wheelchair to get to *darshan* and back (in the Indian heat, it can seem a long way for anyone!), but apart from that she is remarkably fit. *Darshan*, by the way, is a Sanskrit word which means "seeing and beholding the Lord and receiving His blessing"; Sai Baba normally comes out among the devotees once or twice a day.

With the ever-increasing crowds at Sai Baba's ashram, it is getting harder and harder for people to be granted an interview. So nowadays those who receive this great privilege are mainly in three categories: those who work closely around him (teachers, doctors, etc.), those in greatest need, and those who are the most deserving from their previous lives. Dorothy and Moyia undoubtedly come into the third category. (I myself come into none of them! However, much though I would love the experience of an interview, I know that he is watching over and guiding me all the time, and that the most important is what Baba calls "inner view," i.e., getting in touch with the God inside oneself.)

And finally I would like to end this chapter with a quotation from Dorothy and Moyia's own book: "Not long ago we were in an interview with Baba and we said to him, 'Baba, we cannot get down to touch your feet. Can we touch your hand?' Now he puts out his hand every time we go for an interview and we both touch it, sometimes one hand each. So you see how twin souls live—we even get to touch the hand of the Lord together!"

3

Coming Together for Strength and Light

Love alone can unite living beings so as to complete and fulfil them
. . . for it alone joins them by what is deepest in themselves.
All we need is to imagine our ability to love developing
until it embraces the totality of men and of the earth.
—TEILHARD DE CHARDIN

In Indian tradition, the history of the world is divided into *Yugas* (ages), each of which lasts many thousands of years. Even within India there is no consensus as to exactly where the divisions are made—or even as to which era we are in at present—but there is much agreement that the age from which we are almost due to emerge is the Kali Yuga. It need hardly be said that it is an age of darkness (Kali is the goddess of death), when evil is coming to the surface, but the good news is that we are in a time of real purging and that our beloved Earth is preparing herself for a Golden Age. (Edgar

Cayce predicted that, once the cleansing was complete, the souls who have been causing so much havoc at present would not be allowed to reincarnate for a thousand years, thus permitting a thousand years of peace and harmony.)

According to the renowned Mayan Calendar, this present age of darkness is due to end on December 21, 2012. Whether we follow that closely, whether we have been brought up in the Hindu tradition, whether we are New Agers excited about the dawn of the Aquarian Age, or whether we are Christians eagerly awaiting the Second Coming of Christ, we can all agree that the world is in a sorry state at the moment and that things might get worse before they begin to get better. But I hope, too, that everyone agrees that there are glimmers of light to be found all over the place. Mature twin souls who are together can be extra strong glimmers because, as we have just seen, working together increases their strength. I have four examples from among people I know, but first of all I should like to quote from a channelling brought through by Celia Fenn from the Archangel Michael, for the spring equinox 2006. This coincides with what I have for long been told by clairvoyants such as Edwin Courtenay, who claim that more and more twin souls will be coming together in order to amplify the light being brought in for the New Age. Fenn is a channel, spiritual facilitator, writer, and speaker/performer, who lives in South Africa but travels the world working with groups of people. Previously a university academic in English literature, she now works with the energies of Archangel Michael, the Cetaceans, and Mary Magdalene to bring information about the transformation and ascension of the planet, the significance of the Grail Codes and the Sacred Heart, and the work of the indigo and crystal beings at this time. Here is the extract from Fenn's circulated e-mail:

" . . . with the opening of the new light meridians in the Galactic Lightbody, you are . . . returning into alignment with the Cosmic pulsations of the Great Heart at the Center of All. . . .

. . . you may also feel very emotional and vulnerable at this time, and you may be experiencing clearing away of old energies around relationships and love.

For the implications of this moment are deep and far-reaching for all of you. As you bring your masculine and feminine energies into balance, you open the way for perfect balance in all relationships. This includes also the moment when you will begin to feel the connections with your Galactic family in a very real way as you begin to align on the same energy frequency of Galactic Harmony and Love. And also, this is the time when it becomes possible for Soulmates and Twin Flames to enter into relationships of perfect Balance and Harmony."

So now let us look at some more examples of twin flames coming together as extra strong forces of light during these times of great need.

Christine and Bruce

"I'm going to marry that man!" said Christine to the friend who had persuaded her to accompany her on a hypnotherapy weekend at a college in London. At the time, Christine was going through a particularly low phase over her divorce and was glad to have the distraction. Her friend, knowing Bruce to be married already, was surprised and a trifle shocked by Christine's words but, being very familiar too with her predictive powers, she replied that she would introduce them, and she further told Christine that Bruce was a scientist.

Christine, who was born toward the end of the Second World War, has always been psychic, but it took a few years for her to decide to make it her career. Since her father was in the RAF (Royal Air Force) and her mother worked in a factory during the war, Christine spent a lot of her childhood with her grandmother and a couple aunts, who were all quite intuitive. While these understanding relatives did not think it strange when she saw such things as cats who had died two years earlier, their empathy also contributed to a difficulty common to many psychics—not realizing that only a select few had this ability. When she was about six, however, Christine started noticing that people looked at her strangely after she had stated that something was going to happen, and so then she decided to keep quiet about the things she saw except with her understanding relatives. She has always known that she has lived before, and at an early age she started to have flashbacks to a brief lifetime that had ended earlier during the Second World War. (Occasionally we do come back extremely quickly. I myself was gassed by the Nazis before returning early in 1940.)

Interestingly, Bruce has had flashbacks to the same life-time. They know that they met in London and that they were both killed before they were able to get married. He was a bomber pilot, she a nurse; he was shot down in a daylight raid over France, and she died, probably (as often happens with twin souls) shortly afterward, in one of the London Air Raids. They feel that they came back this time not only as helpers, but also to complete what they were unable to do together in their last life. But in this life, they both had some very difficult times to get through before attaining the joy of meeting up again.

Christine (who always wanted children, while Bruce never did) knew from a very early age that she would marry and have two children in quick succession, and after leaving school at fourteen she went to work in a factory. At age twenty-one, she married a man who was several years older, got pregnant very quickly, and had two sons born eighteen months apart. This twenty-year marriage was hard, not only because her husband never shared her spiritual interests, but also because his health was very poor. Since he was constantly in and out of hospital, she had to be the breadwinner, and so for some years she worked nights as an auxiliary helper in a clinic that performed cosmetic surgery.

I have learned from clairvoyants that, though our spirit guides change throughout our lives according to the work we are doing, we all tend to have one main guide who remains with us from birth. Christine started hearing the voice of her main guide when she was very young, and later, when she sat in a psychic development circle, she started to see him as well. He is a Native American she calls White Cloud and, at a time she still needed to support her family, he told her that she should give up her job and go into psychic work full time. Initially this seemed too scary a challenge, but she finally got the message after the clinic she worked in closed down, and the two subsequent jobs that she took had folded!

Christine had no idea how to begin, or even how to advertise herself, but a friend who was a medium kindly offered to send some of her clients, and then the work just grew from there. She says that no one who works in this field could ever get rich because one has limited energy for a task that is so tiring and taxing, but that she herself has always managed to earn a living. Nowadays people get in touch with her for a wide variety of reasons, ranging from a desire to contact someone who has passed over, or for guidance in important personal or business decisions, to a need to locate a lost pet or object. Christine is also very gifted in psychometry[33] and has discussed this on television and radio.

Since Christine's ex-husband never had any interest in her psychic work, they drifted apart after their sons had grown up. She has never been in the habit of making friends with her clients, but once, seven years before she met Bruce,

---

33.   Psychometry involves holding an object and obtaining by psychic means information from it concerning its owner, past history, etc.

she felt an impulse to telephone an astrologer who had come to her that day for a reading and suggest that they meet for lunch. This woman, who rapidly became a firm friend and gave Christine a great deal of support when her marriage was breaking up, turned out to be the hynotherapist who invited Christine to the weekend where she first met Bruce.

Bruce was brought up strictly Catholic, but was interested in the paranormal from an early age. He did a degree, followed by a doctorate, in applied chemistry, but rigorous scientific training did nothing to divert his interest away from the spiritual. He drifted away from Catholicism when, as a student, he was seeking answers that the Church failed to supply, and ever since then he has been making his own way philosophically rather than turning to any other religion.

After working for some years with a major multinational chemical company, Bruce gradually became increasingly dissatisfied with his work and keen to do something more worthwhile. He then trained as a hypnotherapist and was working at it part time when he attended the conference in London. When they first met, Bruce was still married to his first wife, but that relationship, which had been deteriorating for quite some time, was in its final, agonizing death throes.

Bruce was already sitting in the refectory when Christine and her astrologer friend arrived at the college for the hypnotherapy weekend. Christine commented that she noticed his "very long legs" the moment that they walked in. After making the introduction, Christine's friend took her off to another table to meet some other people, but later Bruce came over to say "Hullo," and said he was really interested in what she did (surprising words from a scientist, she thought). During a fairly brief conversation, Christine found that they got along extraordinarily well but, while she felt the attraction immediately, Bruce was far too troubled about his marriage to let the thought of another relationship enter his head. Since he was still married and her divorce was only just going through, Christine kept well away from Bruce for the rest of the weekend, but she knew that he traveled all over the country and so, just as she was leaving, she gave him her card and said, "If you're ever in the area and need a psychic reading, just come down."

During the next few weeks, far from feeling impatient to meet Bruce again, Christine knew that, when something was meant to be, it would happen when the time was right. The hypnotherapy weekend had taken place in January, and the following April, when Bruce's business had taken him to Christine's area, he decided to get in touch with her simply because he had found her an interesting person. On arrival at her house, the first thing he said was, "I'd better tell you straight away that my marriage has just broken up." He says that no one could have been more astonished when she replied by exclaiming, "Oh good!" In fact, he claims to have been "absolutely flabbergasted" when she continued, "Because I really like you and I think that we ought to be together." Christine explains that, since he traveled so much with his work, she did not know when they would meet again, and that in any case her conviction that they were destined to be together was very strong.

The next step for Bruce was to decide whether to run away as fast as he could or whether to let Christine go ahead and do the reading for him. The final years of the relationship with his first wife had been so traumatic that the thought of embarking on another one made him panic, yet he bravely opted for the latter course. They met again the very next day, and within six weeks they had found a house to rent and moved in together!

It is rare for twin souls not to see eye to eye on all the most important things, and Christine and Bruce have the same tastes in such things as art, music, and décor, and they prefer to live in exactly the same sort of place. In addition, they share a love of animals (at one time they kept goats as well as having a dog and several cats), and of walking in the countryside. There are also differences between them, of course—the sort of differences one would expect between a scientist and someone who is more artistically inclined—but, like the other couples in this chapter, that makes for useful complementarity; and where they differ greatly, they work hard at meeting in the middle.

It is easy for those of us who did not have Christine's exceptional abilities at an early age to imagine that these are gifts that one is either born with or not, whereas in actual fact we all have the potential to be psychic. Twin souls who are together tend to find not only that their own talents are enhanced, but also that each gains something from the other.

Bruce soon found that living with Christine enabled him to develop his own psychic powers, and some years ago they started to run workshops together on developing psychic ability. Not too long after they were married, Bruce felt sufficiently confident in his other work to be able to give up his industrial career completely. He particularly enjoys working with the tarot and finds it a very useful tool in helping people. They are also as a couple interested in helping people who are having difficulty in relationships; they feel their own past negative experiences to have been useful training in that field.

As for Christine, who felt sure from a very young age that she was going to have to wait quite a long time for her life to really begin, she says that after so many years of struggling on her own, she at last feels complete—"as though I've got the other half of me." And, although her psychic work always involved therapy to some extent, they both feel that this has been enhanced by Bruce having been able to pass on to her the fruits of his therapy training.

Nowadays they are an extraordinarily busy couple, and courses that they have put on in a further education college have always been oversubscribed. In addition, Bruce, who never liked the idea of fatherhood, has found himself suddenly plunged into grandfatherhood! But that, he says, since it is not full time, is both enjoyable and interesting.

Rose and Danesh

Rose and Danesh were by chance in the same London pub one evening, each in the company of a friend of the same sex. Rose describes her friend as "absolutely gorgeous," so when this gorgeous-looking girl repeatedly walked to the telephone to call her boyfriend, each time brushing past Danesh and his friend in the cramped pub, the men couldn't help but comment. The comments turned into a conversation between all four of them, with Danesh and Rose subsequently arranging to meet again a few days later. After this second meeting they met every day. Rose describes the experience as extraordinarily intense, since they both felt that they had always known each other from the start. In fact, she says that she felt so happy and complete that she would not even have minded dying the very day that they met! But she also says that going into a relationship at such lightning speed took a good deal of courage.

In contrast to Christine and Bruce, Rose and Danesh met when they were quite young and have been very happily married for many years. However, their coming together was not completely straightforward either, since they had both had previous relationships, which made for the usual difficulties. Furthermore, they are an interesting match because their cultural heritage is very different, he being Indian and she Eastern European. In fact, the cultural factor is precisely what gave Danesh some hard times prior to finding the joy of meeting his twin soul.

Nevertheless, there are also striking similarities in their family backgrounds, which can in both cases be described as distinguished. Although one tends to think of India as a poor country, it contains wealthy sections, and Danesh is of royal blood. His father, who is a *rajput*, is one of a lineage of kings of a tiny kingdom—a kingdom that even has the tradition of a two-gun salute! The society in which Rose was brought up was, on the other hand, a socialist one, where no one had very much in terms of material wealth, but her father comes from a very old family, well known in the area. Her great-grandfather was given as much land as his eye could see in return for his contributions to the kingdom, and her father's family was mentioned in poems. Twin souls commonly incarnate into similar circumstances, and in this case, Rose explains, despite the cultural differences, both their fathers come from prestigious backgrounds and both their mothers come from relatively wealthy families.

Danesh was sent to a boarding school in England when he was thirteen, but the tradition in India is for parents to arrange the marriages of their children. After obtaining his degree, Danesh complied with his mother's wishes by returning to India to marry. Astrological compatibility may be used in the selection process, and Indian marriages are often very successful indeed, but there are also exceptions (we shall meet another one in chapter eight). In Danesh's case his mother pushed him into the relationship before he even felt ready to marry at all. The poor girl that his parents chose had been seriously messed up by a deranged mother, and living with her actually made Danesh become ill with dangerously high blood pressure. The girl was a part of the richest families in India, and in their strata of society there had only ever previously been two divorces. Therefore the "unimaginable scandal" was very hard for his parents, not to mention how difficult it must have been for Danesh to make and then announce his decision to divorce. However, he literally felt that his life was at stake, and I have no doubt that he was helped and supported through it by the subconscious knowledge that marriage to his twin soul was part of his Life Plan.

A broad plan for each of our lives is made before we come into it, and the extent to which we ourselves participate in its formation depends very much upon the level of our development. There is always room to maneuver after we have incarnated, but the main characters in the forthcoming script tend to be decided beforehand in accordance with the lessons that we choose (or agree) to learn, the karmic debts that we decide to pay off, and so on. We vary in the ease with which we discover our Life Plan, but there is always a good reason for everything that happens to us— good or bad.

Rose had also, before they met, had an offer of marriage, but she has a good understanding about the Life Plan and knows that that relationship would not have worked out. She and Danesh complement each other like Christine and Bruce do, since Rose is less academic but more intuitive than Danesh.

Danesh's family was very keen for him to have a good education, and so he was sent to boarding school in England when he was only eleven, and he subsequently obtained several degrees before embarking on a business profession. Rose was also sent to the best schools available, but shortage of money prevented her completing her degree. In any case, her talents lie more on the artistic and creative side. She loves acting, and during the time she was at university she found many other worthwhile things besides art to distract her from her studies.

Soon after leaving university and finding a job, Rose decided to come to England to study. She began with a language-proficiency course, but then her plans for further academic study were thwarted by the two great loves of her life: yoga and her twin soul! She started attending a yoga class in London in her spare time and quickly decided to train as a teacher of it. She soon followed that with trainings in alternative therapies and, after she had met Danesh, Rose found that simulaneously continuing all these studies left her with insufficient time to spend with him. So she abandoned academia and is now an accomplished therapist and yoga teacher who has helped many people with a combination of skill and delightful character. Since Danesh's career is in business, one can say that their professional interests are complementary.

Neither Danesh nor Rose has ever been very religious, but they have both always been spiritual. He was brought up Hindu, and she feels an affinity with Hinduism but inclines more toward Tibetan Buddhism. So for both of them the idea of having lived before, as well as having known each other "for ever," seemed natural. She has in any case had various past-life regressions, and in her very first one of these she went straight into a masculine life in which she and Danesh were twin brothers (once more—sorry, Joudry and Pressman!) and leaders of an army that looked to be Greek or Roman. A sad thing about that life was that there was jealousy because she (then he of course), as the older of the twins, was given the main command, but after her (I mean his!) death, she could see a river of people in shaded light walking toward the source of bright light. The two brothers were gliding above the other people, of the same color as the source and connected to each other with a cord. Her image of their two souls was a wonderful one of two triangles connected with a strong cord and merging into a larger triangle, which in turn was merging into the Source, in a blindingly bright golden light. This is what first made Rose appreciate fully that she and Danesh were twin souls. At the end of that life, after the soldier that was Danesh had died, Rose channeled him and was able to lift off some dark attachment that he had had. She says that that is something that only twin souls can do for one another—something that transcends the ordinary soul mate level—and that "clearing out one another's stuff" is still a thing that they do now for one another. She believes that at some point when they were in the light together, they took an oath always to be there for one another in that way.

Like many twin souls, Rose and Danesh are telepathic with each other, and, she says, they are one another's strength and can do things for one another that no one else can do. They had their birth charts analyzed at an early point in their relationship and found that there were certain things about her that were evident in his chart, and vice versa. The two charts "match" exactly because where there are gaps in certain of his houses, her chart fills them in, while the houses in his chart fill the gaps in hers.

In another regression that Rose did, she found herself as a king in, maybe, Kashmir, and Danesh was her—or rather his—queen. There was a terrible famine in their land and the king prayed to God for the salvation of his starving people. The answer to his prayer was a very painful one: salvation for the people in exchange for giving up his queen. He made this difficult sacrifice for the sake of the people, but then not a day passed without him thinking of his beloved queen and, after she had died, God rewarded his devotion by bringing her back to life in his arms. They then spent the rest of that life together.

Rose says that one thing that she can never bear is to see Danesh suffer. She tends to be very protective of him, which she sees as stemming not from the fact that he is eighteen months her junior, but rather from a previous life as his mother in which they both died during labor. Nowadays, whenever he is suffering or has any big problem to deal with, she says that she is always able to lift it from him by praying sincerely from her heart to God. Such wonderful faith is surely a mark of a totally successful twin-soul relationship! But Rose further says that, although they are one, learning is something that he has to do for himself.

When twin souls are less evolved than this couple, living together often entails huge challenges. This is because, as Rose says, they can do for one another things that no one else can. Though these challenges are sometimes unbearable and may even cause a temporary split between a pair, they are normally beneficial. Why? Because if a twin-soul partner is quite literally one's other half, it makes sense to really push him or her to do what is needed for their mutual spiritual development. But in Rose and Danesh's case, challenge is not necessary because they are so much in sync and so firmly on the spiritual path that there is virtually no conflict between them.

Although they function in a similar way, Rose and Danesh are very different, and they complement each other in everything. Perhaps unusually in such a close relationship, they do not even like the same sorts of movies and, while she loves the outdoors and nature, he prefers creature comforts. (Rose says that, if they went on a skiing holiday, she would be joyfully hurtling down the slopes, while he would prefer to be discussing some topic with an interested listener, sitting next to a warmly inviting fire.) Such differences can be extremely useful. For instance, Rose says that anything to do with finance or money is a total blur to her, but Danesh, being business-oriented, can help her in that area. He grounds her in a way that no one else could; and where she is weak he will advise and be her strength, while she can protect and be there for him whenever he needs it.

Finally, neither Rose nor Danesh sees their cultural difference as a problem. She says that there could be difficulties because his culture is so strong and structured whereas hers is all about individual freedom and respect, but they get around it simply by always making the other partner a priority. Rose feels that the differences really only come alive when they go to India, or Danesh's parents visit them, but she feels herself to be fortunate because they are lovely people and very laid back by Indian standards. In any case, from my personal knowledge of Rose, I am sure that her in-laws must feel most fortunate too in having her as a daughter-in-law.

Ekavir and Faatina

Ekavir was forty-seven and had been married for eighteen years when he met Faatina at his local Sai Baba center. Whereas he had been going there regularly ever since his days as a student twenty-seven years ago, it was her first visit despite the fact that she was thirty-one and her family were Baba devotees. It was November 23, 2007, and they were both involved in organizing a celebration for Baba's eighty-second birthday. Ekavir was busy cleaning up the place, sweeping, clearing garbage, and walking here and there collecting cups and plates. He passed Faatina now and again as he went back and forth placing garbage bags outside the center, and had to say "excuse me" a couple of times. As it is the custom at Sai Baba's ashram for the men to dress all in white, Evakir had already dressed smartly for the occasion in an Indian white suit. Faatina noticed him, thought to herself how handsome he was, and wondered why an educated-looking man should be there cleaning up garbage. He noticed her too and, taking her for younger than she really was, immediately thought to himself, "Hey, she must be a new youth that I can recruit for my Human Values Classes for Teenagers." So he stopped to say "hello" and asked whether she was local, to which she replied that she was at present working away but that her family lived nearby. So he gave her his card, and suggested she call him when she could.

Although I believed Joudry and Pressman's assertion that an upright man would never leave his partner for his twin soul to be unsubstantiated, I did not find an example of this until after I thought that I had completed this book and met Ekavir and Faatina. They are friends of an acquaintance of mine, who, during my most recent visit to Sai Baba's ashram, in January 2008, picked up my first book and then sent them to me for therapy. I cannot quite call them a couple, since Ekavir is still married to someone else, but he now knows that it his destiny to be with his twin soul for the rest of his present lifetime and is greatly looking forward to getting together with her fully.

Ekavir and his wife recently lost their young daughter through illness, and I have heard that only about 30 percent of marriages survive the loss of a child. Even before this tragedy, however, the two of them had been growing apart. (Sai

Baba likens partnerships that end when their time is up to logs drifting down a river. They come together for a while and then drift apart again when the current takes them in different directions.)

Ekavir says that he forgot about Faatina after that first meeting on Baba's birthday, and nothing transpired between them for a month until he received a text message saying "hello." He replied by calling to find out who she was, and then, a couple of weeks later, she suddenly phoned him, sobbing that her boyfriend had left her. Later, when they had got to know each other, Faatina explained that she had made the call after pulling her car onto the curb because she was so desperate to talk to someone, and that his was the first number that had appeared in her "received calls" diary! She also told him that she had come across his card when clearing out her handbag after resigning from her job, and, feeling a sudden, unexplained urge to contact him, had sent the text message because she did not have the courage to call. They arranged to meet when Faatina was due to return to her family after leaving her job in the city. Although Faatina had been with her boyfriend for nine years and the parting was difficult, she quickly became aware of imperfections in that relationship and things between her and Ekavir developed rapidly into love.

When I met them for the regression, it was shortly before Ekavir had to fly home, but Faatina came later for a session on her own. Ekavir explained that the attraction had been so sudden and so powerful that he was anxious to find out the reason. In the regression that day, he went straight into an Egyptian life as a tall, dark, lean man, working at a construction site. There he found himself chiseling stones in a desert area, and could see something that was obviously a pyramid. In the next scene, a "water girl" walked by and, when she offered him a drink, he immediately noticed her very beautiful smile. (This was the first thing that had attracted him to Faatina. And she does indeed have a beautiful smile!) In the regression, he described the girl as being the most wonderful bronze color. It was love at first sight, and it appears that he did not wait long to ask for her hand in marriage. Next he saw himself in a tent with lots of people, merrymaking and drinking, and it was clear that the occasion was his marriage to the girl with the beautiful smile.

Later we moved on to a much sadder scene, where his beloved wife was on her deathbed. By this time, he was old and had a white beard. Their son was beside him, tall and lean. His wife died smiling at him, but he could not bear the grief. So he walked out of the hut into the desert, and died near an oasis "all shriveled up with the grief of my wife's death."

After Ekavir as the Egyptian had died, he floated up toward the light, where he first saw yellow/green colors. Then he saw his mother and Gayathiri, his daughter from his present life, who was walking toward Sai Baba. He called his daughter's name, and then she turned back, smiled to him, and said "Swami [Baba] is calling." Then she walked toward Baba and merged with him, which enabled Ekavir to understand that Gayathiri had completed all that she needed to do on Earth.

I then encouraged him to ask Baba the questions to which he wanted answers.

First of all, he asked Swami why he had had to lose Gayathiri. He replied, smiling, that she had come to teach him both love and grief. Seeing Baba in the Bardo, with what he described as "lovely, pinkish, lotus-like hands and a beautiful smile," he called out, "I love you, Swami, I love you Swami, I want to join you, Swami." Then he saw Barry (the person who had introduced us) coming, holding the hand of a girl with a beautiful smile. Ekavir recognized the smile, but could not immediately place the girl. Barry's face was floating in and out, and Ekavir asked him who he was. Barry replied that he was Ekavir's guardian angel and, when Ekavir asked him who the girl was, he said, "She is your twin soul." Many tears flowed when Ekavir saw his beloved mother and daughter, and then he asked Barry and Baba what his future was. Barry replied that there was nothing to worry about, as "Swami says he will take care of it."

Ekavir's grief then turned to joy when he focused on the girl with the beautiful smile. She seemed to be so full of joy herself, and he started asking, "Is it you, Faatina? Is it you?" Then, before she had replied, he came quickly back down to Earth and into an Indian life. In this past life he was wearing sandals and white cloth, and was walking in a marketplace toward a hut. Inside the hut he saw a woman, who turned around and gave him a beautiful smile. She was wearing a green sari, had a dot on her forehead, and was sitting by the fire. He now recognized her as Faatina, and then he saw their child running toward him.

This regression moved Ekavir deeply. He had not heard of twin souls, so I had to explain to them both what it meant. When Faatina came to see me on her own a few days later, she wanted to work through some lingering issues from her previous relationship. However, it was also clear that, much though she loved him too, she had concerns about the idea of Ekavir leaving his wife for her—especially when she was also suffering so greatly from the loss of their daughter. A tough one, but it seemed clear from the two regressions that, since they were both such ardent devotees of his, Sai Baba had brought them together to work for him. Thanks to e-mail, it has been easy for us to keep in touch, and Ekavir (whom I am sure Joudry and Pressman would describe as an upright man!) explains that, since he is very concerned about the welfare of his wife and their son, he and his twin soul have agreed to give themselves three years in which to make all the moves necessary for getting together fully. He further says, "My regression has opened up a whole new experience for me, Ann. I am reading books that I never dreamed of reading, have taken up clinical hypnosis classes (London Class of Clinical Hypnosis) and am also now taking up music lessons. My outlook on life has changed completely, and I am taking some wonderful new steps, hoping that all this will lead to a more fulfilling life. Thanks, Ann and Barry, for giving me the opportunity to experience a new life." So this is what meeting one's twin soul can do when one is sufficiently well prepared for it spiritually! And here is confirmation of the fact that an upright person will on occasion leave his or her partner for a twin soul.

When I asked Ekavir by e-mail to give me some more information about the things that he and Faatina had in common besides being Baba devotees, he sent me the following list:

- both of us love to read books, and we share interesting passages
- both have the same interest in hypnosis
- both have a passion for teaching children
- both love traveling, especially to Baba's ashram
- both love to look good
- both have the same passion in love
- both love to sing and to learn to play musical instruments
- both love swimming

He further commented that he fits her ideas of what her husband should look and be like, and that she fulfills his dreams of the ideal wife in a way that his first wife never has. Also, when they met, Faatina was keen to leave her "fast and furious life in the city" for a "more passive and spiritual life" and that she has found that possibility with him. He is aware of the pain that their getting together will bring (to Faatina's family, who disapprove of her marrying a divorced man, as well as to his own), but sincerely believes it to be for a good reason. A couple years ago, Sandy Stevenson gave a workshop in England, in which she said, "If your partner leaves you, it is for your own good because it is helping you to learn to stand on your own." And it is my personal belief that whether a meeting between twin souls leads to a Platonic relationship or a divorce depends entirely upon the lessons that the individuals concerned had chosen to learn before coming in.

May and David

May was running a florist's shop, and she always made a habit of warning her assistants when she was in a bad mood, giving the reason for it. One day, however, she felt restless from the moment she woke up, became increasingly anxious as the morning wore on, but said nothing because she could not understand what the matter was. Eventually one of the girls asked what was worrying her. She replied that she did not know, and then decided to telephone David's superior to find out whether he was all right. David, her husband, was working in the Navy (where he spent seventeen years). The superior promised to phone her back in a couple hours, and when he did, he told her what David had asked him to tell her: that he had been feeling poorly for a few days with a little bit of ulcer trouble. However, as we have already seen, twin souls are commonly telepathic with each other, and May realized straight away that he was not telling her the whole truth. So the superior then admitted that David had had an operation and was very seriously ill, with not more than a 50 percent chance of surviving.

The superior was very concerned indeed, and so, being aware that May was the only person who could give David the will to live, he urged her to send him a telegram. A couple days later, to his colleagues' complete astonishment, David made an amazing recovery and went straight back to work as usual. Throughout his years in the Navy, they wrote each other long letters more or less daily, and once when May had gone to a shop for something she needed, she found herself also picking up a packet of turquoise pen refills. This puzzled her as it was a not a color of ink that she ever used, but on returning home she found that there was a letter from David awaiting her, in which he asked her to send him some turquoise pen refills!

May and David are sadly both dead now, but when I made their acquaintance they were doing an excellent job of running a highly successful alternative health clinic. David, however, was a bit of a workaholic all his life, and it was probably overwork and exhaustion that caused him to have a fatal car accident while driving to a meeting shortly before his fifty-seventh birthday. May, who was five years his senior, gallantly carried on the work single-handedly for a while, until she fell seriously ill and passed over to join him on the other side, where I feel sure that they now have a great deal of important work to do together.

It is not unusual for more advanced, mature souls to have flashbacks to previous lifetimes. This makes sense because obviously they have more lives to remember. Once, when David and May were out walking together in a part of the country they had never visited before, he said to her, "I'm sure there's a church around here." They hunted and hunted until they saw a sign that said "To the church," and when they had found it, David recognized it as very familiar.

May and David also knew that they had both worked as healers for a very long time indeed. In ancient Greece, during a time of great civil unrest, he was a healer-priest in a small temple dedicated to Asclepios, the Greek god of medicine. In that lifetime, he was a lot older than her, and they met after she and her mother had been stricken by plague and journeyed a long way to the temple for healing. David failed to save her mother, but May eventually recovered after he had nursed her for a while. Then, having no family to return to, she stayed in the temple while he taught her all his healing arts. She became his assistant, lover, and, in due course, also a priestess, and they practiced their skills together to heal those wounded in battle.

During the Middle Ages they were again involved together in helping people through a time of war. In that incarnation, May was married initially to another man, who was a comrade of David's. David brought her husband back to her when he got wounded, and he told May on his deathbed that he was entrusting her to David's care. In due course the couple fell in love and married, and they then ruled jointly and benevolently over their combined lands, making use of spiritual philosophy, herbal remedies, and other healing arts in which May was an expert.

In their current lifetime, May and David were born first cousins. This is probably no more common for twin souls than incarnating as twins, but another such example can be found in a previous life of the writer and regression therapist Joan Grant. Though published as novels, all the deceased in Joan Grant's beautiful books are actually her own pastlife stories (taken from what she calls "far memory"—the title of one of her books).[34] In *Scarlet Feather,* she recounts the moving story of the twin souls Raki and Piyanah, who were suckled together by Piyanah's mother following the death of her sister, Raki's mother. Like Raki and Piyanah, May says that in this lifetime, she and her twin flame were really never not in love, though it took some time, and other failed relationships, for them to decide to marry. They had a large family, and after David had finished a career in the Navy, they took over a hotel. When they felt that the time had come to move on and the health center post came up, some of their children were able to succeed them in running the hotel.

David felt that he was nearing the end of his earthly incarnations all his life, but he also believed that this time round he had had a very strong determination to be born as a helper. His parents' marriage, which had been one of convenience, was never happy, and his conception was the

---

34. All Joan Grant's books are published by Ariel Press, Columbus, OH, and *Scarlet Feather* was republished in 2007 by Overlook/Duckworth, USA and London.

result of an extramarital affair. Hoping to keep this secret, his mother decided to have an abortion, but she did not know that she was bearing twins, and only David's twin was aborted. He did not find out about this until long after he had grown up, but he was conscious throughout his childhood of feeling different, of missing someone, and of being incomplete. Of course, once he had married May, she filled the gap and made him feel complete and better able to fulfill his life's purpose. Nonetheless, after finding out the truth about his conception, he remembered his older brother asking him, "Why is it that *you* are always the subject of our parents' rows?" Then his difficulties in childhood suddenly made sense. His mother had really loved his natural father, and David and May were pleased to get to know him toward the end of his life.

May and David's background was conducive to their healing work as well as to their innate spiritual nature. The grandfather whom they shared was a healer and herbalist, and both their grandmother and David's mother were clairvoyant. Both their mothers were Christian Scientists, but they did not force their beliefs onto their families, which left the pair free to search for their own spiritual path, and they eventually ended up as Quakers. They both always had auric sight (the ability to see people's auras), and they also often used to see spirits. Though they both had psychic gifts, hers were the stronger, and she often knew exactly what he was thinking. She received messages all her life, and during the latter part of it she helped many people with tarot readings.

Although it is the norm for twin souls to share tastes in such important things as music, literature, art, and décor, they also normally (as we have just seen with Christine and Bruce, and Rose and Danesh) complement one another. David used to write poetry and was also gifted at drawing, but it was nevertheless he who (like Bruce) was the scientific, practical one, while May (like Christine) was more gifted artistically. May loved décor and David could execute everything she wanted; she regularly published stories in magazines under a pseudonym, and he helped by editing her drafts. When their children were young, they shared most of the work of caring for them, and he also helped regularly with the cooking. So, all in all, I feel that May and David were the quintessence of a mature twin soul couple.

4

Teaching One Another Lessons

The love of God cannot be described. But it can be felt as the heart
is purified and made constant. As the mind and the feeling are
directed inward, you begin to feel His joy. The pleasures of the senses
do not last; but the joy of God is everlasting. It is incomparable!
—PARAMAHANSA YOGANANDA

Society on this Earth would not work if we were all at the same level of evolution. We clearly need to have people around with varying abilities and interests to perform all the necessary tasks in the world and, if during our time here we mixed only with our own soul group, we might well be frequently absorbed in fascinating and rewarding discussions, but we might also be twiddling our thumbs a lot of the time rather than learning our lessons.

The woman in my next pair would not wish to be described as an "old soul" (which she says implies a wisdom that she does not feel she has), but she is aware of having lived very, very many lives on Earth, starting in Lemuria, and nowadays she is feeling more than a little world-weary, and yearning to return permanently to her soul group on the other side. Sathya Sai Baba says to his followers that he gives them what they want in order that they will "want what I have come to give"—i.e., Liberation—and I am personally convinced that there are many people here at present who are on their last earthly lives. My next subject is one of many I have met who are determined not to come back. In her case, there is no obvious reason why her soul partner should not (assuming he wants to!) also be able to "clear off for good." One of many things that they have in common is an addiction to work—to help others and the planet—and such a desire is normally indicative of an advanced soul.

Eleanor and Joseph

"You just cannot imagine the pain," said Eleanor, "when Joseph and I were at the same conference for a whole weekend without saying a single word to one another! He seemed to have turned almost overnight from the sweetest man in the world into someone unbelievably cruel. Of course, I later came to appreciate more and more the extent to which it had all been my own fault for pestering him, but I had just been so depressed at the thought of our losing touch altogether; and I think he exaggerated in his mind what I was asking for. In fact, all I wanted was, say, an annual exchange of Christmas cards containing some brief news, and maybe a lunch together once a year or something. However, thanks to everything I've learned since that distant day, I realize now that he was teaching me the thing I most needed to learn—the thing that probably only my twin soul *could* teach me, since I had stubbornly refused to learn it from anyone else. . . .

". . . I've come to terms with it all now. If people like Robert Schwartz[35] are right, no doubt Joseph and I planned the whole thing together before I came in, but at the time I couldn't imagine I would ever be able to get over the pain."

Eleanor had been a deprived child—not materially, but emotionally. She was the oldest of a large family, which entailed a great deal of responsibility before she was really old enough for it, her parents had little time for her, and her father's idea of bringing up children was in any case totally Victorian. "Seen but not heard" would be putting it too kindly: she was made to feel unacceptable simply when seen. However, one very positive thing that her father did for all his children was provide a foundation of a belief system. He made sure they were well educated in Christian schools and insisted on regular church attendance. Eleanor is still grateful for the firm belief in God that this gave her. However, what was much more difficult for her, was to believe in God's love. She believed in it intellectually but, never having experienced human love, she found it impossible to *feel* it.

---

35.   See the book by Robert Schwartz, *Courageous Souls: Do We Plan Our Life Challenges Before Birth?* (USA: Whispering Winds Press, 2007).

As Eleanor grew into her teens, she withdrew ever more into herself, hiding upstairs in books or in her homework. When her father did see her—at mealtimes or when she was washing the dishes, which he insisted was her job—he only had critical things to say. Her hair was too long, or untidy, or she was too fat, or her skirt was too short, or her shoes needed cleaning. Or she hadn't cleared the table properly, or she was too extravagant with the hot water. The list seemed endless, and she felt that she could never do anything right, however hard she tried. Worst of all, her father made her feel that no eligible young man would ever look at her twice. On top of all this, her mother, who was always busy looking after the younger children, was too scared of her husband to stand up for Eleanor.

So her only escape was into books or into a dreamworld. In her dreamworld, she would leave school for university (in her family, this was not optional), and there—or more likely very soon after she had graduated—she would meet her Mr. Right. She would know him the moment she set eyes on him. He was tall, not particularly good-looking, but with a kind face that revealed his gentle nature, very gentlemanly in manner, sensitive and considerate, highly intelligent, and an Oxford graduate. This last measure made it more likely that they would meet after obtaining their degrees, because she did not believe she could get into Oxford.

On leaving school, Eleanor went to Manchester University, and later trained as a social worker, partly because her Christian upbringing had instilled in her a firm feeling of obligation to do something useful in the world. Well, Eleanor's Mr. Right did in due course appear, *exactly* as she had imagined him, which is an example of the fact that we generally plan the most significant events of each of our lifetimes beforehand. However, there were a couple of obstacles. Eleanor was already in her forties and had long given up hope of matrimony when they met, and, more importantly, Joseph was already married with a growing family.

They met at a conference connected with Eleanor's work, and the feeling of instant recognition associated with twin souls was unbelievably strong for her. Eleanor just knew the very moment that she set eyes on him that he was the "ideal man" she had been waiting for all her life. And, what's more—unlike any man she had previously felt attracted to—he appeared to notice her, too. As one of the conference organizers, he was pretty busy the whole weekend, but at one meal they happened to sit next to each other, and when they conversed, she had a very firm feeling that he was endeavoring to impress her. During that meal, Eleanor noticed Joseph's wedding ring, which might have been the end of the story, but the conference became an annual national event that they both attended (along with other professional conferences).

They lived in different cities, but these regular meetings gave them the chance to become better acquainted. The more often that Eleanor met Joseph, the more sure she became that the attraction was mutual. Initially she felt dreadfully envious of the old friends and acquaintances whom he always greeted with a kiss, feeling that she would never be worthy of such a privilege, but after a couple of years or so she found herself also being greeted in this way. Or rather she didn't, because of her conviction that the kisses he gave *her* were delivered much more meaningfully than any of the others. Once, when they happened to bump into one another when no one else was in sight, he even kissed her on the lips. She says that this felt so natural that she didn't even realize what he had done until afterward! On another, completely unforgettable occasion, not only was Eleanor greeted with a kiss, but when they said "goodbye" at the end of the weekend, Joseph gave her a real bear hug. This, for a woman previously so starved of love, was one of the most powerful experiences imaginable. She describes it as "simultaneous ecstasy and agony," saying that on the one hand it felt like being in heaven—like coming home—but on the other hand it was hell because she knew it could neither last nor be repeated very frequently. In fact, it never was repeated, and Eleanor feels sure the reason was that for him the agony felt even stronger than the ecstasy.

And so Eleanor's introduction to true love led her into what she saw as an impossible situation. Since Joseph was also a committed Christian, she knew that he would never contemplate divorce or adultery. (Nor would she want him to.)

Eleanor had always been somewhat prone to bouts of depression and, while the occasional brief encounters with Joseph gave her some moments of joy, she sometimes wondered if they were worth all the accompanying agony. On balance, however, she decided that for someone who had for so long regarded love as beyond her grasp, these precious meetings were much better than nothing. The problem was that, rather than working to find other worthwhile things in her life and on making the friendship seem less important, she allowed herself to become overdependent on these little fixes and began to worry about how she could stay in touch with Joseph if their work contact were to cease.

Despite the emotional problems caused by her upbringing, Eleanor was never without good friends she could rely on. When one of her closest friends was going through a difficult marriage breakup, she found a very helpful astrologer, so Eleanor decided to consult him too. Since she had already deviated from her conventional upbringing by going to a homeopath, this seemed to be a fairly natural next step.

The astrologer was a deeply spiritual man who had studied the question of relationships from the spiritual perspective for many years, and he was also extremely psychic. When one of their meetings happened to take place on Joseph's birthday, the astrologer used these birth details to establish that the two of them were twin souls. This was naturally a completely new concept for Eleanor, who had never before thought about the possibility of reincarnation. However, hungry for more information, and encouraged by the astrologer (who rapidly became a friend), she started to read books about reincarnation and other spiritual matters. Books about Edgar Cayce helped her particularly, since they showed her that belief in reincarnation was not incompatible with Christianity. Then she made an appointment with a regression therapist whom I will call Moira.

This therapy proved invaluable, particularly for curing the headaches that homeopathy had not helped. Moira was also very knowledgeable about the different types of soul mates. Eleanor found the whole subject enthralling, and then felt greatly consoled by the thought that she would inevitably come together with Joseph again, even though it could not be in this lifetime. In fact, she became very excited by this idea and longed to share it with Joseph—especially since her psychic astrologer friend had confirmed her intuitive feeling that he was not totally happy with his wife.

This desire to share the information was (for obvious reasons) not easy to accomplish, and in any case Eleanor could not imagine that Joseph would be open to such novel ideas. So she decided to prepare him for the knowledge that he was her twin soul by lending him a couple books, one on Edgar Cayce and one on astrology. Her father's upbringing had made her very scared of men, but the attention she had received from Joseph had greatly increased her confidence, and, encouraged by Moira, she decided to give him her little parcel surreptitiously the next time they met. She included a note explaining that she would like him to read them as an introduction to "something important" that she wanted to tell him. Joseph made it very obvious that he was curious, but he had often complained of being overworked, and at their next couple meetings he gave Eleanor no indication of having made time to read the books.

This was frustrating because Eleanor, who had begun to tire of social work, had now started to train in Reiki and in

crystal healing and was aspiring to move into a healing profession full time. Everyone she met in these new circles told
her that she needed to find love inside herself rather than
depending on a man to give it to her, but she thought that was
impossible. Try as she might to get closer to God, she never
felt any response from him, and the one thing that put her
off changing her profession was the thought of her occasional
meetings with Joseph coming to an end. She did not want to
ask for anything more, but the thought of losing touch altogether seemed unbearable. "He might even die and I would
have no means of finding out," she said to herself woefully. "I
know that twin souls tend to be telepathic, but I can't believe
that I would ever be able to contact Joseph's spirit."

So, once again encouraged by her therapist, Moira, who
felt that clarity in the relationship would be beneficial to
both sides, Eleanor decided to take drastic measures. Her
first step was to write a brief summary of all that she had
learned about twin souls, and her second step, at their next
weekend conference, was to persuade Joseph to go off to
a pub with her so that they could talk alone. She was not
encouraged when he told her that he would have to return
her books since he was not going to find time to read them,
but she felt nevertheless that the evening went off well, and
they embraced tenderly when they said "good night" and she
handed him her precious envelope. Her intention was, after
he had read what she had written, to find another occasion
to discuss how they might be able to keep in contact after
she had given up working in the same field as he did.

However, as Joudry and Pressman[36] comment, "A man in a distinguished position, married, and with a family, could understandably be thrown into turmoil when suddenly confronted with the other half of his soul. In such a case there may be refusal to acknowledge the twinship." This is undoubtedly what happened here, because when they next met a few months later, Joseph was unprecedentedly cool toward Eleanor, and her subsequent letter pleading for another meeting in order for her to explain what she wanted received a negative, very pain-inflicting reply. This was only a couple of months prior to the conference at which they did not even acknowledge one another's presence.

Eleanor' grief after that weekend was even more intense than it had been when she received the letter, and she confided the whole story to a good friend she had made in her crystal healing course. This woman was a devotee of Sathya Sai Baba, and Eleanor's tears prompted her immediately to lend her a couple of books about the avatar. Eleanor was enthralled with the topic and, shortly after reading the books, she had a dream about Baba that convinced her that He was calling her to India. Well, her father had died some years previously, her mother more recently, and Eleanor knew that she would inherit a tidy sum. She decided to pay off her mortgage, keep some money in reserve to tide her over while she got established in her new healing profession, and buy a ticket to India. In fact, her crystal healing friend

---

36.   Joudry and Pressman, *Twin Souls*.

had already put herself down for an organized pilgrimage to Baba's ashram a few months later, and she was delighted at the prospect of Eleanor joining the pilgrimage as well.

In the meantime, Eleanor read every book about Baba that she could lay her hands on and, while still feeling the pain of Joseph's "harsh treatment," she began to see, as she recounted above, what his role had been. She had had good therapy from both a homeopath and a regression therapist, she had made some halfhearted attempts at doing inner-child work to help her with self-love, she had gone on going to church regularly, but none of this had really done the trick. In this particular lifetime, she now realized, it had taken her twin soul—the other half of her self—to really force her, by not offering her the love she was clamoring for, to go *inside*. Inside to that place where both God and love reside.

The rest of Eleanor's story resembles the stories of so many people whom Sai Baba has called. This does not mean "happiness ever after," or a problem-free life, but what it has meant for Eleanor (like so many others) is an ability to feel divine love as the only type of love that really matters, a new sense of purpose, an understanding that there is a good reason for everything that happens in life, and faith and trust such as she would have previously regarded as unimaginable. She is now happily absorbed in her work as a healer, goes fairly regularly to Sai Baba's ashram, looks at other men now and again without bothering too much about a potential relationship, and prays for Joseph daily. But otherwise she thinks of him only occasionally. Above all, she is thankful to know who her twin soul is, and grateful to him for the painful but fruitful lesson that he gave her. Also, Eleanor believes that she may have taught Joseph one or two things. Even though he remains, as far as she knows, a committed practicing Christian, before they stopped communicating, he gave her a couple of indications that he was opening his mind to her way of thinking; and she thinks and hopes too that she taught him something about just how much he could be loved by a woman.

Finally, Eleanor has found out through her regression work and meeting clairvoyants that, way back in Atlantis, she had a clandestine relationship with Joseph when he was married to somebody else and they were colleagues teaching at the same institution. In that life, he cared more about his reputation than her feelings, and she was more devoted to him than she was to God. She knows of one or two other lifetimes that they have shared happily, but feels that this Atlantean life has the most bearing on her present one. For we are given challenges each time and, if she as Eleanor is to break free from this pattern, she needs to avoid letting her pain destroy her and instead offer it to God and make use of it for helping others who may be suffering in a similar way. Eleanor appreciates too that she is much better off than those who have not yet found any sort of spiritual path.

Things Don't Get Easier!

Happiness is an interval in between two pains.
—SATHYA SAI BABA

No, getting together with one's twin soul does not necessarily make life any easier—especially if, as was the
case with Kathryn and Martin, one has been left penniless
and homeless following a divorce.

Kathryn and Martin

It was ancient Egypt. The woman I now call Kathryn was, at
the age of only about twelve or thirteen, put by her parents
into the temple of Rameses III to train as a priestess. This
was known as one of the color temples, since color was one

of the main methods of healing used in it, and Kathryn, who had a very acute eye for color, was singled out early on for special training as a healer. She pioneered some new ideas in addition to using the Atlantean methods that she had been taught, and people came from far and wide to benefit from her treatment.

Martin's family in that life was, like Kathryn's, well-to-do, and he was also taken for training as a priest at a young age. Having a talent for administration, he rose rapidly to a high position in the Rameses III temple and, although not all the Egyptian priests were celibate, it did not occur to him initially to contemplate matrimony. He and Kathryn were, however, trained together as adepts—those who, on leaving their bodies at night, went to the help of souls who were passing from Earth to the other side (on this subject I recommend the Egyptian books of Joan Grant, and particularly *Winged Pharaoh*)[37]—and the memory of the out-of-body work that they did together at night soon filled Kathryn with the desire to be together with him by day as well. So she took steps to become better versed in his spiritual interests, and Martin then began gradually to recognize his twin soul in the form of this attractive young woman.

After they were married, they found that everything that each of them did was enriched by the other's energy. This caused the respect from those around them to increase still further, with everyone sensing their combined energy

---

37.   Joan Grant, *Winged Pharaoh* (Columbus, OH: Ariel Press, 1985).

as something from which strength could be drawn by those in need. Shortly before he died, Martin gave Kathryn the most beautiful piece of lapis lazuli, saying to her, "Keep this forever as a symbol of our eternal love." When Kathryn was dying a few months later, she made sure that the stone would be buried with her, and, having seen it clearly in a regression in her present life, she hunted for a while for a duplicate. However, once she and Martin had finally come together again, finding another lapis diminished in importance to her.

Although from a purely romantic point of view, Kathryn and Martin's present-day story has a happier ending than Eleanor and Joseph's, there are nevertheless certain similarities. Kathryn's family background was also a difficult one. Like Eleanor, she took quite a long time to find her path, but (rather as Joseph's rejection forced Eleanor to search for love inside herself) meeting her twin soul was the main trigger for the radical change that Kathryn needed to make in her life before being in a position to realize her true purpose.

Kathryn's two older sisters had been despised by their father, while she, as "the pretty one," was the apple of his eye and was expected to succeed where all the rest of the family failed. She was even expected to marry before the sister who was quite a few years older than she was. She is highly intelligent and, in contrast to her siblings, seemed to have been born full of self-confidence. Nevertheless, the expectations laid on her were still a big burden. Consequently, when her eldest sister married at a comparatively late age, Kathryn inevitably felt some pressure, and this was no doubt one of the factors that caused her to enter an undesirable marriage to a man who was very good-looking, but had *all* of her father's worst characteristics and none of his good ones.

Kathryn found out, when she eventually managed to break free from Carl, that she had fallen for him in many previous lifetimes and that he had always abused her. However, even though Carl has massive karmic debts to Kathryn, the two of them cannot be described as karmic soul mates, because (even though Carl feigned it initially) there has in this life been no real love between them. Kathryn simply got trapped, as so many of us do through our multitudinous lifetimes, in a repeated pattern.

However unhappy a woman is in a marriage, it is rarely easy to escape when there are (in this case three) children to support and the whole family depends on the husband's income. It was Kathryn's lack of independence that enabled Carl to carry on being brutal to her for many years. She embarked on several different trainings but, until she eventually completed a massage course, the difficulty of running a household single-handedly rendered her unable to complete any of her studies. But it was thanks to the massage training that she met Martin.

Kathryn and Martin's families lived in the same small town and their sons went to the same school, but it was with Diane, Martin's wife, that Kathryn first became acquainted. They met through the school, and became reasonably friendly fairly quickly despite the fact that Kathryn found Diane distinctly odd and difficult to like. Martin was at the time—no doubt due to tension in the marriage as well as pressure of work—suffering with a severe neck problem, so when she learned about Kathryn's massage practice, Diane immediately suggested that he go to her for some treatment.

The treatment was very effective, but—even more importantly—the twin-soul recognition was, as usual, instantaneous. Martin (who also had a difficult past-life connection with Diane) had realized very soon after his marriage that she had quite serious mental-health problems. However, being an extremely caring and upright man, he had made a vow to himself always to look after her. This became increasingly difficult as his family grew, with Diane contributing nothing at all apart from very big demands on him, and when Martin first met Kathryn he had more or less reached the breaking point. But despite the mutual attraction, they resisted it for as long as was possible. Kathryn felt immediately that Martin and his wife seemed a curious match, but initially had no reason to think he was unhappy in the marriage.

For several months, Martin came regularly for treatment, and they talked about many things besides his physical problems, gradually finding that their empathy and common interests were incalculable. The strong, mutual attraction was unbelievably painful for Kathryn, but her professionalism was impeccable and she treated him like any other client. On the evening when she suddenly found herself in Martin's arms, Carl had shouted at the children particularly brutally, and Martin had left his house with Diane screaming after him because he had not finished redecorating the living room. Confiding in each other seemed like the most natural thing in the world, and falling into each other's arms made them realize what they had been missing all those years.

But is divorce ever easy? Martin repented immediately and told Kathryn that he had better not come for any more treatment. And, when Kathryn nevertheless, without mentioning Martin's name, plucked up the courage the very next day to tell Carl that she was leaving him, Carl proceeded to put every possible obstacle in her way. Kathryn's main problem was, of course, financial, since her massage work only brought her a very tiny income, but the twin-soul connection suddenly gave her a determination and strength that she previously would have thought unimaginable. Within a very short time, Kathryn and the children were in a cheap apartment and Carl was forced to put their house on the market.

Of course Kathryn hoped desperately that Martin would decide to file for divorce too, but at one point she had so little confidence that he would ever do so that she allowed herself to get involved with another man (very likely a companion soul mate), whom she believed would be a truly caring figure for the children as well as a good support for her. Now she and Martin met rarely—bumping into each other occasionally if Diane was too sick to pick the children up from school—and the pain when he spoke to her really coolly was no doubt as intense as Eleanor's when Joseph rejected her friendship. In both cases, these men were coping with the situation by cutting themselves off from their feelings—something men tend to be rather better at than women.

But, apart from giving her real love, the main thing that Martin had done for Kathryn was to help her to become aware of her full potential. Not only had he treated her in a caring and gentlemanly way—a thing that she had never once experienced with Carl—he had also encouraged her to qualify in other healing fields besides. Martin had been reading about different sorts of therapies, and he immediately recognized Kathryn's talents and made suggestions as to things which would interest both of them. This, they found out later, stemmed not only from their shared Egyptian life, but also from an African life in which she had been the village shaman and he the village chief and once again her husband.

In the little spare time that she had, Kathryn ardently pursued further study. She read numerous spiritual books, realized that she and Martin were twin souls, and became convinced that they could do wonderful work as a team. She even put this into a letter to Martin, which she managed to give him at the school gate, but he refused to follow up, partly because of his loyalty to Diane and partly because he believed that he could not afford to give up the career that had enabled him to support his family from the first day of his marriage.

Kathryn decided to try to move on with her life, too. Without trying to hide her feelings for Martin from her new suitor, Robert, Kathryn allowed that relationship to develop—

and even moved to a different town to put some distance between herself and Martin. But then she met a clairvoyant who assured her that her destiny in this lifetime lay with her twin soul, so she decided to be patient, telling Robert she was far from ready to make a commitment. A huge blow came when the house sold and Kathryn found that she got nothing at all because of the debts that Carl had accumulated. Carl had to be hounded for child support, and Kathryn found herself working a number of odd jobs, at times almost day and night, to keep the children from starving.

In the end, love got the better of Martin. Kathryn had given him her new address just before she moved. One day, more than three years later, when his work happened to take him near her new abode, he decided to drop in to see how she was faring. After that, nothing could stop things taking their natural course, and Martin's decision to file for divorce did not tarry too much longer. Kathryn had by this time become interested in Sai Baba, and she was yearning to visit his ashram. A sudden little bequest from an aunt made it possible for her to pay both their fares to India, and the trip made just as big an impression on Martin as it did upon her.

The now-deceased John Hislop, author and well-known Baba devotee, was asked why it was that many people, after coming to Baba, were stricken with all sorts of diseases or problems, however hard they were praying and striving toward liberation. Hislop remarked that people often said to him that their life beforehand had been quite straightforward, whereas now that they had found Baba they seemed to have nothing but trouble. His reply was that Baba had explained to him that, although it was not essential to go to India to see him, it was best to have his direct *darshan* (which, as I mentioned before, means "seeing and beholding the Lord and receiving his blessing") because this brings an acceleration in one's spiritual life. For the true spiritual aspirant, an avatar can speed up the working out of karma, so that someone who has been to the ashram will often find that a whole series of difficult things suddenly start happening; they can be plunged straight from one karmic crisis into another.

Thus it appears to have been for Kathryn and Martin. Even though their journey to Puttaparthi was a nightmare, with one calamity after, they both felt it all to have been a million times worth it. Martin's divorce went through shortly after the trip, but Diane somehow succeeded in getting such a competent lawyer that she was awarded their house in the settlement.

So now the two of them were together, blissfully happy to be so, but with nowhere to live! Trusting that they *would* be taken care of (Sai Baba says that he never allows his followers to go without either food or shelter), Kathryn blew most of the rest of her aunt's legacy on a truly wonderful wedding with all the members of both families present, but then they had to really sit down and think what to do next. Since Martin was now considered too old to be granted a new mortgage, and since the children were only partially off their hands, the only possibility seemed to be a rented house near the school Kathryn's youngest child was now happily enrolled. And, much though they both wanted to be able to work together full time, they could not see any way of coping without Martin's continued income.

Just as in Buddhism the only path to Liberation is seen as being through total acceptance of what *is*, so Sai Baba enjoins us to say, "Yes, yes, yes to everything." He says that everything —troubles, suffering, sickness, death—must be regarded as a gift from God. Like the remedies prescribed by the doctor, everything that happens is for our good and is a sign of his love. Kathryn and Martin both truly believed this, but it was far from easy when the children were going through a series of karmic crises, which included both serious illness and accidents. All of Kathryn's children had so much anger against their father that they decided to cut ties with him completely, but giving them the support that they needed was extremely draining. Martin's children, too, empathized with him over the separation, but Diane went to a great deal of trouble not to make their lives easy either.

Nevertheless, by the time several years had passed, Kathryn had become well established in her new career and widely recognized in several types of healing circles. She led successful workshops, always finding Martin an invaluable source of support and using him to bounce off ideas during her preparations, but this type of work rarely provides a reliable income, and rents have a nasty habit of rising frequently. Martin would love to be able to give up his work to join in with hers full time, but so far that has not been possible. Kathryn is the most wonderful optimist and rarely doubts that her Life Plan is to continue the valuable work that she loves so much, but, while her and Martin's trust continues and their love deepens, the notion of owning their own home and working together in the healing field remains for the time being a dream.

6

Same-Sex Relationships

*For many an individual entity those things that are of sorrow are
the greater helps for unfoldment.*
—EDGAR CAYCE, READING 3209-2

In their otherwise truly excellent book,[38] Joudry and Pressman make the astounding assertion that twin souls are
always of opposite sexes. They give no substantiating evidence, and one of my many aims in writing this book is to
disprove this assertion. Rita Rogers,[39] on the other hand,
does recognize the fact that twin souls (soul mates to her)
can be the same sex, but the implication she makes is that the

---

38.   Joudry and Pressman, *Twin Souls*.

39.   Rogers, *Soul Mates*.

love that they feel for one another will inevitably cause them to be homosexual. While not doubting that *some* twin-soul relationships might in a given incarnation be gay ones, I dispute the notion that this may be necessary. We saw in the first chapter that the Pink Twins were definitely twin souls, and now I have another story of two women who believe themselves to be that, but who are neither related nor gay.

Mary and Susan

When she had only just arrived at her new boarding school, at the age of thirteen, Susan saw the fifteen-year-old Mary across a room and immediately said to herself, "That person is going to be very important in my life!" They quickly became very close friends, which is not of course surprising for a pair of twin souls, but is unusual for girls in their early teens. Later in life, a two-year age gap seems negligible, but fifteen-year-olds normally tend to feel superior to and above mixing with younger girls. This pair, whose interests were virtually identical, bravely defied convention and were more or less inseparable through the remainder of their school years.

Mary in particular had a very difficult upbringing. She describes her family life as chaotic, since both her parents were constantly having affairs, and they finally separated when Mary was sixteen. Her mother was an artist, and she describes her father as "very eccentric and excitable." She was always close to her younger brother, but never had an adult to relate to. Nor does she relate to the stepbrother and stepsister she has from her father's third marriage.

Susan's family was comparatively more conventional and stable, but her life was also hectic because she was always terrified of her mother. She did have a good relationship with a nanny, but of her three siblings, the only one she has ever been close to is her youngest sister.

Both these women are very artistic, and both have always been spiritual seekers. They were very religious during their teens, and they both came under the influence of a high Anglican priest, to whom Mary introduced Susan shortly after she had left school. The first thing that Mary did after leaving school was to go into the Wrens (the Women's Royal Naval Service) for a while. Then she went to art college in London, where Susan joined her the following year. They were always together through most of their training, and Mary comments, "I feel complete with her. We have everything in common. We're like one person."

Due to her very difficult background, Mary used to think of herself as the one with problems, but later in life Susan shared her many difficulties. Mary was the first to marry, by several years, and she sees the failure of her marriage as the result of her emotional problems that left her ill-prepared to handle a satisfactory relationship. She says that as she and her husband grew apart, they agreed to a trial separation, but that he then quickly fell in love with someone else. After many years of "working through her stuff," however, she came to realize that she had really always loved her husband very much, and after the death of his second wife, she was, when I met her, becoming much closer to him again and hoping for reconciliation. Susan, on the other hand, never divorced, but says that she and her husband do no more than coexist in the same house.

When Mary met Hugh, he was studying for the Anglican priesthood, but he later abandoned that in favor of another career, and at the same time both Mary and Susan gave up going to church and started pursuing alternative spiritual interests. For a few years, they met rarely because Mary and Hugh moved to the north of England, but even when they had little contact, they were developing in exactly parallel ways. Once they did not meet for three years, and when they did, they found that they had both been studying Gurdjieff and becoming interested in alternative medicine.

However, since twin souls are nevertheless separate individuals, there will inevitably be certain differences between them. For these two, one difference is their attitude toward children. While Mary has always been close to her two children, and in her later years moved back to London in order to be near to them and her grandchildren, Susan, despite bearing a family of six and always doing motherly things such as baking bread for them all, claims to not have really taken to motherhood and is close only to her youngest daughter. Another difference is that Mary has always been more gregarious and less self-sufficient than Susan.

Both have kept up their art throughout their lives. When Mary married soon after graduating from art college, Susan moved to another London college to study stained glass and, while never needing to work since her husband is very well off, she has always painted at home. Mary has also always kept up her painting, and for many years taught art.

When Susan had a nervous breakdown, it was a minor secret until her youngest daughter eventually told Mary about it. Mary was of course very distressed at the thought of her best friend having been suffering on her own, but realized Susan was trying to protect her from the anxiety. However, once she found out, she helped pull Susan through it. After that difficult time, they were again able to have a lot of fun together regularly and go on trips together. The most memorable of these was to see Mother Meera, the Indian avatar[40] in Germany.

I have for many years been fascinated by the whole question of why certain gurus and avatars draw certain people to them and not others. As I made very clear in my first book,[41] my own spiritual destiny in this lifetime lies with Sathya Sai Baba, whom I also knew in his previous incarnation as Sai Baba of Shirdi. After meeting a number of people who had been to see both Mother Meera and Amma ("the hugging avatar"), I felt a desire to do so as well, and eventually achieved both these ambitions. I found each of these occasions a very moving experience, but feel no need at all to repeat either. On the other hand, repeated visits to Sai Baba's

---

40.   The Sanskrit word *avatar* means "divine descent."

41.   Merivale, *Karmic Release.*

ashram in Puttaparthi are a compulsion for me, which I assume is because of my strong connection with him. Maybe I have no previous link with either Amma or Mother Meera, whereas I feel sure that Mary and Susan must both have had a past life in which they connected spiritually with the beautiful woman who is now incarnate as Mother Meera. This would explain why they were even more moved by meeting her than I was.

Mary, who, after doing a great deal of spiritual reading, became convinced that she and Susan were twin souls, had this confirmed by a clairvoyant. She has further been told in a reading from another clairvoyant of two previous lives in which she and Susan were also very close, and in both of these they were both men. In one, they were political prisoners, and in the other they were working together as priests in Tibet. Mary finds the Tibetan lifetime particularly relevant because, even without ever having read anything about it, she feels she knows the country. She says that she has sometimes had an inner vision of being high up in very steep-sided mountains, looking out of a monastery window over a deep valley filled with sharp blue light. And Susan has been deeply involved in the Arcane school of the teachings of Alice Bailey, which were channelled through a Tibetan.

All in all, we clearly have here another quite evolved couple, who may well be ready to fuse very shortly.

Separation for Growth

Your pain is the breaking of the shell that encloses your under-
standing. Even as the stone of the fruit must break,
that its heart may stand in the sun, so must you know pain.
—KAHLIL GIBRAN, *The Prophet*

Since reunification with our other half is our ultimate destiny, and since twin-soul partnerships are seen as the ideal, it is hard to fathom that twin souls who have found one another in a particular lifetime should sometimes see fit to separate. However, contrary to Joudry and Pressman's asser-tion, this undoubtedly does happen from time to time—for varying reasons. The French writers Anne and Daniel Meurois-Givaudan, who wrote numerous books together, and whose definition of twinsoulship I have quoted, are certainly twin souls, yet they are now living apart and writing independently.

Who am I to hazard a guess at their reason(s)? I only know that in 1996 Daniel moved from France to Quebec, where he is still producing approximately one book per year as well as lecturing in numerous places. As for Anne, the Internet is at present delivering no update on her, but the last time that I went into a bookshop in France, I did notice one book that she had written on her own. Perhaps the explanation is a very simple one: that they have completed all the work they came to do together this time round and are now working out karma with other people.

I have met a few people who were once married to their twin soul, but here is the story which best illustrates the idea of separating for growth.

Olivia and Patrick

On their wedding day, Olivia first realized that Patrick had a drinking problem. She explains: "He got drinking with his brothers and didn't want to go off on the honeymoon!" From that point on, his drinking got steadily worse, until one night, when their second child was about three months old, he came home so drunk that he beat Olivia up, prompting her to take refuge with some neighbors. Patrick was horrified the next morning when he realized what he had done, but that did nothing to make him try to change or to seek help.

Olivia was quite precocious in that she started dating boys when she was eleven, and Patrick came into her life when she was only fourteen. He is two and a half years older than she is, and at school had quite a reputation for running a protection racket against bullies. This intrigued Olivia, so she persuaded her brother, who was at the same school as Patrick, to introduce them. Their first meeting was with a group at a local restaurant, and Olivia, who says that there was an instant feeling of familiarity, felt attracted to him immediately. It was not long before he started walking her home but, unlike her, he is quite shy and never talks much. At first she saw his guardedness as a challenge—to find out what was behind the façade—but she says that their communication was always mainly "on a different level" than normal conversation.

She is the more spiritual of the two, which will probably come as no great surprise to those in the habit of attending New Age–type workshops, which always have noticeably more women. (Here, let me hasten to add that while I have had the privilege of meeting many very spiritual and intuitive men, women are generally more intuitive and tend to take the lead in spiritual development.)

Olivia and Patrick were both the third child in the family, but, whereas her background was a comfortable, happy one, his was more difficult. His family are Cypriots and moved to England when Patrick was eleven. His father's pay for a job in the Royal Air Force camp was inadequate for bringing up five sons, so his mother supplemented the family income by running a corner shop, which made it hard for her to be there for Patrick. He is tall, dark, and rugged—quite a contrast to Olivia, who is short with a typically English complexion—

and at school his great passion was rugby, while her interests have always leaned more toward the arts and people.

Olivia has found through regression a previous life that she sees as relevant to their current relationship—a lifetime in a farming community around the sixteenth century, when Patrick was her father. (Such a relationship is unusual for twin souls, but the Cayce saga gives other examples of this.) In the regression, Olivia found herself giving birth at a very young age and under very unpleasant circumstances. Numb from the waist down, surrounded by figures in dark garments with large cowls, she left her body during the birthing process and fled across a field of ripe green to a farmstead with a wall and a large gateway. Looking back, she saw that the building she had left was a monastery, realized that she had been banished to the care of the monks because of her pregnancy, and wanted to understand the reason. So she traveled on toward some houses with half doors, and saw a woman standing there whom she recognized as her mother. Not realizing that she was out of her body, Olivia was distressed when her mother failed to see her, but went on into the house. There, sitting in a chair was her beloved father, whom she immediately recognized as Patrick in her present life. Olivia then became aware that it was by him that she had got pregnant and that that was the reason for her banishment. So Olivia says that, having failed in that life as her father to provide her with a home, Patrick was given the opportunity to pay that debt this time around—and failed once again.

Courtship through their teens was fraught because of their different social personalities. While Olivia was a social animal who enjoyed mixing with people of both sexes, Patrick was very possessive and could not tolerate her receiving any sort of attention from other boys. Although Olivia never gave them any sort of encouragement sexually, Patrick would often misinterpret their intentions and even get aggressive toward them. They learned about sex together when she was only sixteen, and her parents turned a blind eye, even though they had a strictly religious outlook on such matters. Olivia believes that this was because her parents were aware of the depth and strength of the bond. Because of this too, when Patrick went off to university, Olivia's father paid her fare to the same city so that she could be near him. She supported herself there by working as a waitress and, when the need to complete her own education brought her home again, she stayed in doing needlework during the evenings because Patrick did not like the idea of her going out. Her parents thought that she ought to have some social life, but she says that she felt "grown up and condescending to her friends who were not in steady relationships."

Between leaving school and getting married at twenty (as soon as Patrick had obtained his degree in engineering), Olivia took a job as a housemother in a school for children with cerebral palsy, and she says that this experience was invaluable in fostering her innate interest in caring for people and in molding her later career in healing. He joined the RAF (Royal Air Force), and his first assignment was to

Germany. This was where their two children were born, and where Olivia was forced to take refuge with neighbors following her first bad beating.

The neighbors were so concerned about what was going on that they actually drove Olivia to the gates of the camp to see the medical officer, but she could not bring herself to go in. "The conflict," she explains, "was so great: my injuries against his career and the dependence of the children. Looking back now, I really wonder how I stuck it for so long, but when you're married to your twin soul it's incredibly hard to leave. The bond is so strong!" And so she went on enduring physical abuse for twenty years.

Earlier on I gave the yin/yang symbol to illustrate how twin souls fit together. That shows how we were in the beginning and how we will be again when we are ready to return to the Source, but in between, owing to our "going off the rails" and incurring bad karma, many distortions can occur.

In such cases, we can see that the two halves do not match— that they will no longer fit neatly together inside the circle. More often than not, when each half has become as distorted as this, no meeting occurs on Earth, but when they do take place, the pain is indescribable. Imagine from the illustration how painful it must be when the spikes on one partner dig into the other, and the pain is increased by the knowledge that one's other half really *ought* to fit. Eventually, the outline can be smoothed back into shape, but it takes time—sometimes many lifetimes. Sometimes one partner's shape will be less jagged than the other's. In this case, Patrick is the one who still requires extra smoothing, but Olivia is spiritually aware and, though painful for her, she understands that it will happen eventually.

The drinking and physical abuse were not the only things that made Olivia's twenty years of marriage so very difficult. Patrick has an excellent brain, but tends to be arrogant and an intellectual snob, which she always found immensely irritating. Also, she finds him excessively left-brained, while she is more rounded intellectually, with wider interests and more feeling for people and for the arts. Since Patrick spent so much time in the RAF Officers' Mess bar, Olivia's life in Germany centered almost entirely on the children. However, she was born a seeker, which quite early on in the marriage led her into yoga.

After they had returned to England, Olivia managed, with difficulty due to Patrick's possessiveness, to train as a yoga teacher. She says that it was only this, plus meditation and the support of friends and of her daughter, that enabled her to keep going through incredibly difficult times. Since so much of what Patrick earned was spent on drink, housekeeping was an immense struggle and, though she knew that he often said good things about her to others, he failed to express to *her* appreciation for anything she did, and constantly criticized and ridiculed her.

At one point after their return to England, a friend she was giving yoga lessons to was training as an Aura Soma therapist and, since Olivia was fascinated by this too, her friend brought her bottles round one evening and gave Olivia a reading. Aura Soma, which was brought through by the now-deceased Vicky Wall, consists of beautiful bottles in two colors (oil on water) and the choices that a person makes of the bottles reveal an uncanny amount about her character. As soon as Olivia had been given her reading, she felt impelled to call Patrick into the room to choose his four favorite bottles. It was early in the evening and so he was quite sober, but he rather pooh-poohed the whole thing and walked out without waiting for the interpretation of his choice. However, the two women immediately realized that his choice had been almost identical to Olivia's, who says that this made her suddenly face up to what she had always known deep inside: that she and Patrick were twin souls. This realization helped her to understand why she had been unable to leave the marriage for so long, but it also forced her to appreciate the necessity of breaking free of Patrick, at least for the remainder of her present lifetime. She knew that staying with him was seriously holding back her spiritual development, and she also knew that she was ultimately the person who could help him the most, but that the suffering he was inflicting on her was rendering her totally ill-equipped to do this.

When Olivia made the decision to file for divorce, Patrick had taken early retirement from the RAF, Jeffrey, their son, was in the Army, and Caroline, their younger child, had just left school. Over the next four and a half years, Patrick proceeded to put every obstacle that he could think of in the way until the divorce finally went through. His first ploy was to try to get the two children to speak for him in court. In order to avoid that, Olivia decided initially to go for separation under the same roof. They had by now returned to their hometown and taken out a mortgage on a house. (The original idea had been to buy a house with Patrick's RAF annuity, but too much of that disappeared into drink!) Olivia's parents were relieved at her decision, since friends had long alerted them to the situation, and so they gave her what little financial support they could scare up. Olivia embarked on studies in various alternative therapies, living in just one room and refusing either to cook or clean for Patrick. She says that, with both the children away, the house became a black hole in which she was the only light.

It is hardly surprising that, in this situation, some trouble that had started with Jeffrey's birth suddenly flared up again and caused Olivia's uterus to burst. She reckons that she could easily have used this as a means of departing from such a difficult life, but realizes that she still had work to do here in the field of healing, so she made an amazing recovery. Eventually she succeeded in earning enough money to leave the house and rent a place, which may well have helped in getting Patrick finally to let the divorce go through. Olivia says that, besides the financial aspect and the difficulty of separating from one's twin soul, one reason she took so long to get away was her determination not to incur any bad karma in the process. Another difficulty for her was that both their children, obviously appreciating the strong bond between their parents, felt that they should have stayed together. Patrick's "Leo pride" was severely wounded once he had realized that her only reason for leaving was *him*, and so he continued to disrupt the proceedings, refusing to answer lawyers' letters.

The divorce, when it was finally achieved, was a huge relief, but was not the end to Olivia's difficulties. Though their daughter has made a highly successful career and is now happily married, their son has left the Army and has unfortunately taken up his father's habit of excessive drinking. Furthermore, after giving several years of dedicated service to Aura Soma, Olivia was made redundant in a "clean sweep" that they decided to make, and so she is now struggling to establish herself as a therapist entirely on her own. Even though Olivia had acquired several certifications, it is not easy to make a living in this way. However, she is very determined, and she appreciates that her redundancy, though a huge shock at the time, pulled a "cushion of complacency" from underneath her, thus forcing her to become even stronger in learning to stand alone.

Also, she knows that, though Patrick at present shows no sign of overcoming his drinking problem, her development will help him a great deal in the long run. While not wanting to excuse his behavior completely, Olivia appreciates that his background was less advantageous than hers was for molding his character. When his mother died very quickly of stomach cancer when he was only thirty-two, he was completely devastated. He told Olivia that one of the things that distressed him most was never having hugged his mother or telling her that he loved her. She then had to convince him that he did not need to feel guilty, since his mother should have instigated demonstrations of affection. She comments that becoming part of her family, who are very loving, was a good learning experience for Patrick, and she still continues, for the sake of her own family as well, to do all she can to remain on friendly terms with him. (I find it truly amazing what some brave souls take on for their learning!)

When I asked Olivia what she feels was her purpose in choosing to marry her twin soul, she gave various reasons, one of which was to please the brother who had introduced them, and another that it was a means of escaping from her family and having an independent life over in mainland Europe. (She comments that third children in a family have particular difficulties!) She further believed that what she had to offer him, both domestically and socially through her greater experience with people, would help him in many ways and improve his career prospects. "Love, lust, passion, Mother Nature's drive to find a strong genetic pool," were also, she says, "a strong part of it," and furthermore she is aware that her two children, whom she describes as "strong, special, individual, and loving souls," chose both of them as parents, for their life purpose and karmic agreement. She says that she "fell into the trap of self-delusion" in her desire to uncover Patrick's mask, but that "curiosity can kill the cat" since there wasn't that much behind it after all.

Looking back now, Olivia appreciates that she learned from the marriage the lesson of self-sacrifice, as well as "more than I could have anticipated about myself and my inner strength." And she recognizes that her difficult years with Patrick prompted her to embark on the yoga and well-being lifestyle that she has found to be so lifesaving.

It is all too easy (perhaps especially for outsiders!) to imagine twin-soul relationships as the most blissful, but in reality, many of us, in many lifetimes, can find love more easily and satisfactorily with someone other than our twin soul. Olivia is now hoping very much to form a much more fulfilling relationship than she had in her first marriage, and she has recently made friends with a man whom she is sure is a companion soul mate. As I mentioned earlier, companion soul mate relationships are often the most comfortable, and to further illustrate this, here is another picture:

Here you can see that the two halves, although they do not actually belong to one another, can come very close to fitting each other perfectly. Edgar and Gertrude Cayce were a very good example of this, but I also know companion soul mate couples who share many interests and work together very well as a team. Well, Olivia's new friend is an art historian and art dealer, and he has suggested that they write a book together about color in art. Clearly her qualifications in color therapy will be invaluable to him in such a project.

But there is a lot more to this new relationship than work! Carl Gustav Jung said that in each lifetime we all need to go through each stage of life—childhood, adolescence, maturity, and old age—but that it does not matter in which order we do them. Olivia has come to realize that, because of her early relationship with Patrick, she missed out on adolescence. As a result, following many years of celibacy, she is now, at sixty-three, beginning to find some of the real enjoyment in life of which she was previously deprived. I have just taken advantage of a journey northward for a birthday party to make a detour to visit her in her new abode, and it was rather like meeting a teenager. Excitedly she showed me photographs of her handsome lover, and she even got me to listen to his voice on her cell phone.

At the moment there are difficulties because they are of different nationalities and living in different countries (they met on the Internet). He, however, is not short of cash for fares to England, and is even contemplating buying a house in her area to retire to. So let us hope that Olivia will finally find the joy in a relationship that she deserves! Her case is a very good example of one of the theses of this book: that meeting one's twin soul does not always make for a bed of roses.

8

Impossibility of Being Together

For how does one cleanse the mind? By the pouring out,
the forgetting, the laying aside of those things that easily beset and
filling same with pure, fresh water that is of the eternal life,
that is of the eternal goodness as may be found in Him . . .
—EDGAR CAYCE, READING 1620-1

We have already looked at a case (that of Eleanor and Joseph) where being together was not in their Life Plan this time around, but where there was an obvious reason for their meeting. This undoubtedly happens frequently. I know of a young woman who was very shy, and self-conscious about never having had a boyfriend, but who met her twin soul while attending the same university. They quickly became friends and dated each other for a while, which greatly increased her confidence, but when she went off to start a job in another town, the relationship died a natural death. Their meeting had clearly served its purpose, and in this lifetime they probably each had karmic issues to work out with other people.

But some twin-soul relationships that do not end in marriage can be a great deal more painful. Imagine, for instance, recognizing your twin soul, feeling the strong attraction, but then discovering that he was gay! This is the case with my next couple.

Penny and Ronald

The meeting between these two happened quite naturally, since they were living on the same apartment block in a large English city. Penny's feeling of attraction to Ronald was instantaneous and they quickly started having very deep conversations, but it was not long before she realized that he was living in a gay relationship. Neither this, however, nor the fact that she is seventeen years his senior, prevented them from developing a deep friendship. Even early on, they were not only meeting daily, but also talking on the telephone up to four times a day.

Penny and Ronald have many things in common, of which the most notable is, perhaps, very high intelligence. Both are scientifically minded as well as being artistic and creative and, believing for a while that they had some important work to do together in the field of healing, they embarked together on a research project.

Though brought up in different countries, they both incarnated into extremely difficult circumstances, and as a result, both have felt a need for therapy to help them out of problems. Penny, who is dyslexic but a gifted artist, comes from a very rigid, perfectionist background in which she was never allowed to express herself physically or given love demonstratively. Her mother, who was a strong disciplinarian, urged her husband to discipline his daughter as well, even though this did not come naturally to him. She found throughout her childhood and early adulthood that she was never able to get on with both her parents at the same time, and nowadays her relationship with her widowed mother is distinctly strained.

Back then, schools in England (and elsewhere) did not recognize dyslexia as they tend to now, so Penny did not realize how bright she really was until she was in her late twenties. Therefore, it is hardly surprising that she had an eating disorder (which she says still leaves her with a tendency to be overweight), and that she had two disastrous marriages. Penny's first husband, who is now dead, was bisexual but had a preference for men, and her second husband was also repeatedly unfaithful to her.

Ronald was born in South Africa during a very difficult period for white people, and his mother taught him to lie as a defense when they were being persecuted. Though he has been working on overcoming this habit, Penny has found not knowing when he was telling the truth to be a problem on many occasions. Despite the fact that his father left home when he was only five, Ronald has always felt responsible for both his parents—particularly because they lost a number of other children either through miscarriage or very early death. He now has a good relationship with his father, but is unable to see him very often since he still lives in Africa. His mother, on the other hand, has several serious health problems, and she uses these manipulatively to limit her son's sense of freedom. She is a rather selfish individual and very possessive of her only surviving son. Penny says that his mother displays more jealousy of his women friends than she ever has of his male partners. For example, before their research project had been able to get very far, Ronald's mother intervened to put a stop to it!

Ronald was sent to boarding school when he was only nine, and sometimes his parents failed to communicate with each other about him—so that on occasion he did not even know who, if anyone, would be collecting him for the holidays. There were constant arguments over his care, and he used to pick up his mother's anger and resentment and keep it stewing inside him for hours on end. He also says that he always felt like an ugly duckling because his mother was so beautiful.

Much more serious than Penny's eating disorder, Ronald was at one time so addicted to alcohol and cocaine that he developed serious liver problems. But he is of a strong character and, as well as having undergone hypnotherapy to help him to give up smoking and paying off all the debts incurred by his drug habit, he has worked hard on various self-healing methods. He says that his all-around ability has been his salvation, but that this is also hugely confusing.

Now in his thirties, he is not yet completely clear where his path in this life lies. For a while, he worked very successfully as a theater director and though he was for a time still doing some acting on occasion, his mother's demands kept him far away from London, where most of the work in that field is to be found. He was married for a time, in an attempt to appear "normal," but nowadays, after coming through one or two extremely difficult and painful relationships, he prefers to be quite open about his gay orientation.

Besides sharing most of their major interests, Penny and Ronald had in common an awareness of a need to work on the problems they still carried from childhood. I met them (separately) for therapy, when Penny was already reading Alice Miller, and they both found John Bradshaw's work on the inner child[42] to be useful, but Ronald unfortunately did not persevere with therapy.

Penny, who was brought up mainly by a series of au pairs, hardly saw her parents as a child. When they went to the theater, she would leave notes on her mother's pillow saying, "I miss you," and sometimes these touching notes would have little drawings on them as well. She knows that her creativity was always there, but she was made to feel invisible because her pictures used to be put away in a drawer rather than being displayed. As for Ronald, despite his mother's now overbearing attention, he says, "Sometimes I feel that I am my only friend."

---

42. Bradshaw, *Homecoming*.

We have seen how telepathic twin souls can be with one another, and Penny and Ronald are no exception. After he had moved away to be closer to his mother, who is so dependent on him, they continued to communicate regularly, and often their text messages or telephone calls would more or less coincide. On a few occasions when they met again, they performed channelings together. One in particular—when Penny's deceased first husband appeared with very personal messages for them—was so powerful that it brought them both to tears. These experiences were perhaps too intense for Ronald to feel able to deal with. Penny, on the other hand, has more recently been soaring ahead spiritually, studying with a master based in Switzerland, and learning a great deal. Thanks to that, she has gained an understanding of the workings of the kundalini, realizes that hers had started to be aroused during the powerful experiences that she and Ronald had together, and has learned to control it.

The astrology of twin souls probably merits a whole book, but I am not qualified to do that. Penny, however, consulted two highly reputed astrologers, both of whom were convinced about the couple being twin souls and also thought that they would eventually come together in this lifetime. One astrologer even pointed out that they each had an asteroid in their chart that bore the other's name! The second astrologer thought that they had been together in their most recent life, caring for the sick, but that some great tragedy had prevented them continuing the relationship. He felt that they needed to meet again in this life because of the loss they had suffered previously, and that their potential to work as a team was tremendously strong; but he also pointed out that love did not always need to be expressed sexually.

Can that, however, ever be easy for someone who is feeling a strong physical attraction to another person? And such attraction is especially natural when the person concerned is the other half of one's being! Penny is strongly spiritual, and also very loving. Having felt deprived of love both by her parents and, in turn, by the two men she married, she has a totally understandable desire for a loving and fulfilling relationship. Ronald was able to give her the former, but not the latter, because he feels physically attracted to men. He admits to feeling the connection with Penny just as strongly as she does, and also recognizes the nature of the twin-soul bond, but he is—at present at least—afraid of losing an aspect of his identity if he commits to her. Also, although he is in some ways extraordinarily old for his years, he is quite conscious of the large age gap between them.

Despite Penny's inevitable difficulties caused by her feelings sometimes getting in the way, they made a real effort to achieve a truly meaningful and worthwhile working relationship, even after his mother had put a stop to the pedagogical project. However, after Ronald had made a sudden decision to put his energies into opening a restaurant, Penny found that she never knew where she stood, that he seemed to be "all over the place," and that there was no consistency between what he said and what he did. He also expressed negativity about the master with whom she was planning to study in Switzerland, despite the fact that she had not told him even so much as the man's name. (He claimed to have received negative information about him in meditation!) She therefore decided reluctantly to sever the connection, at least for the time being, and to get on with the work that she felt called to do on her own.

Meanwhile, Ronald was in the early stages of a new gay relationship that he claimed to be very happy about, but Penny's decision clearly proved to be traumatic for him. After a silence of two or three months, Penny felt concerned and sent him a rather special gift, for which she expected some acknowledgement. When this did not come, she telephoned, and found him flustered, accusatory, and hostile. He told her that the severance had been so traumatic for him that he had not even opened the present. There is nothing at all surprising here: for the previously mentioned couple, Joseph and Eleanor, when Joseph found he was afraid that Eleanor was asking for more than he felt able to give, it was easier to express hostility than indifference. The bonds between twin souls are so strong that, when something is blocking the expression of love, likely reactions are anger, frustration, and confusion.

Before I had entered the healing and therapy fields, I was involved for many years with organizations that give aid to the Third World. The aim of people in both these professions is to work themselves out of a job! In the case of Joseph and Eleanor, it can take a long time for underprivileged communities to become so self-sufficient. For Ronald and Penny, people vary immensely in the length of time that their healing takes, but it is always a great joy to the therapist to find himself or herself no longer needed. When I last spoke to Penny, while still empathizing with her pain over Ronald, I was truly delighted to hear about her progress. Not only had the master in Switzerland (who has become a close friend) agreed to train her as a yogini, but she had also found her soul group among her fellow students. The valuable research that she had embarked upon with Ronald is now exciting a number of people, and she even had the possibility of doing an innovative doctorate in it. This shows there was clearly a purpose in their meeting, even if she has to continue suffering the pain of separation.

Following the distressing telephone call that Penny made to Ronald after sending him a present, a friend of hers, whom I will call Amy, decided to talk to him. This call proved to be a bit more satisfactory in that Ronald admitted to Amy that the trips to Switzerland were more negative for him than for Penny—the opposite of what he had said before she had started on her new training—and, although he had refused to give Penny his new telephone number (he had by now moved in with his partner), he was keen to have Amy's number. Their birthdays are only about a month apart, and Penny told me that this year, when Ronald's came around, she decided to send him a one-line e-mail, simply saying, "Thinking of you; missing you." When her own birthday was approaching and Amy asked her what she would like for it, her reply was, "What I would most like is a phone call from Ronald."

Amy waited until the day of Penny's birthday and then telephoned Ronald in his restaurant. He claimed (though Penny found this hard to believe) not to have remembered the significance of the date, and his "happy birthday" e-mail arrived a full two days later. This was of course painful for Penny and, when she decided to phone him herself and he was too busy in the restaurant to be able to talk, he agreed to phone her the next morning. This time he reacted as though everything was fine, talking enthusiastically about the success of the restaurant. But twin souls are rarely able to deceive one another, and Penny was not convinced that he was as happy as he claimed. Personally I suspect that, whereas she persevered in therapy until she had seen real improvements, he chose instead (as many of us do) to numb his pain with work. Penny told me that he talked at length about his own activities before asking anything about hers, and that he seemed to be trying very hard to impress her. When she finally did get a chance to have her say, Ronald was clearly very surprised about her progress and her new relationships. He had probably been imagining himself to be a vital part of her whole work enterprise.

Since that last conversation there have again been many months of silence, but the future of this couple, either separately, or ultimately in a joint working relationship, is very far from being bleak. One of the astrologers that Penny consulted picked up on her desire to rise above darkness and difficulty, saying that she most certainly had the potential to do this, and she has now obviously done so. Following the instability and confusion of her earlier years, she has regained control of her life and achieved tremendous insight. Her moon is in the house of spirituality, and I am sure that she can now only move further and further in that direction. Twin souls always catch one another up spiritually, and whatever Penny is doing for herself at the moment, she is doing for Ronald as well. Biologist Rupert Sheldrake's observation that a butterfly flapping its wings in Australia affects people in the Northern Hemisphere is even stronger for twin flames—two halves of the same being.

As for Ronald, the same astrologer saw him as a man of great faith, spirituality, and vision, with strong healing abilities. He said that Ronald had the courage to challenge the status quo, a powerful ability to communicate, and that, though he can be opinionated and arrogant with his views, he desires to give, to serve, and to demonstrate something to the world. Maybe all this is not incompatible with running a restaurant, or maybe in time he will move further away from his mother. In any case, mothers do also die. Although she knows that her soul group is doing valuable work together, Penny feels that there is at present a gap there that Ronald could fill very well. But whatever happens, they are undoubtedly a pair of old souls, whose combined light is something for the world to look forward to.

Though one partner being gay is also an impediment for the next couple I am about to chronicle, this is obviously by no means the only thing that can prevent a full relationship developing between twin flames who are incarnate together and acquainted. In my youth, long before I had begun to think about these matters and was still a good Catholic, I had a close friend, even younger than myself, who was extremely spiritual, and we attended religious meetings together. We both made friends with a priest who was involved in our organization, but it rapidly became clear that my friend's relationship with him was of a totally different nature from my own. They were very deeply in love, and now with hindsight I can see clearly that they must be twin souls.

Since he was completely committed to the priesthood and to his chosen career as a missionary in Africa, and she was also a very good Catholic, there was no chance of these two expressing their love sexually, and when my friend confided in me about her pain over the whole thing, I sensed how deep and how spiritual were the feelings on both sides. My friend did ultimately marry a wonderful man (no doubt a companion soul mate), but she and the priest have always remained close, and he has visited the family many times while on leave from Africa.

It remains to be seen whether the astrologers Penny consulted were right in thinking that the two of them would ultimately make it together this time around, but our next couple are certainly even less likely to do so.

Sally and Paul

Sally was a cellist, and her long-held dream was to play in one of the world's great orchestras. After winning a competition, she received an invitation to audition for the Berlin Philharmonic. It seemed too good to be true, but she excitedly booked a flight to Berlin on the appointed day. However, just as she was driving into Heathrow, she clearly heard her friend Paul's voice in her head saying, "You mustn't board that plane." What could she do? She knew that she must obey the voice, yet her whole career was at stake. If she telephoned Herr Scheckel and told him the reason why she could not come that day, he would surely write her off as a lunatic and tell her to forget about the job! Still cogitating, she drove slowly into the long-stay car park and then simply sat in her car for a while, perusing the score of her favorite Bach cello suite. Eventually she said to herself, "I'll just have to miss the flight. I'll blame it on bad traffic conditions and pray that I can be given a seat on the same flight tomorrow."

A couple hours later, after the person on the Lufthansa desk reluctantly changed her ticket, Sally was wondering whether to check into a nearby hotel or drive all the way home again, when she suddenly heard a massive explosion followed by panicked screaming. Then she saw flames in the sky and watched as the wreckage descended. "Now I understand," she exclaimed to herself. "Thank you, my darling Paul!" Too shaken up to even think of driving home, she walked straight to a nearby hotel and got a room. Then she walked back into the terminal and saw that the Lufthansa desk was completely surrounded by people and that all its staff were busily making telephone calls. The call that she had attempted to make to Herr Scheckel from the hotel had not got through and, since there was obviously no point in attempting to talk to anyone in the airport, she went back to her hotel and telephoned her mother, who screamed, "Sally, is that really *you*? Thank goodness! I've just seen on the television news that a Lufthansa flight crashed immediately after taking off from Heathrow. I was sure it must be your flight!"

Sally's mother, despite being a devout Methodist, was interested both in healing and in the paranormal, so Sally felt quite comfortable in explaining exactly what had happened. This was by no means the first time that she had heard Paul's voice when he was miles away. Their communication goes both ways—on one occasion she had written Paul a letter telling him firmly not to buy the motorbike that he was keen on, and enclosing the extra money he would need to buy a car instead. Three weeks later, an acquaintance of Paul's had bought that same motorbike and promptly had a near-fatal accident. An analysis had shown the bike to be faulty, and the garage owner who had sold it was severely prosecuted.

All this happened some years before the advent of cell phones. Herr Scheckel was driving back to his office after his lunch break when he heard the news of the airplane crash on his car radio. Being sure that it was Sally's flight, he suddenly remembered that she had given him her mother's phone number "in case." Great was his relief when, once back in his office, he was able to speak to Sally's mother, and he also told her that the following day would have been an impossible one for Sally to be auditioned, whereas on Thursday he would be able to meet the flight himself and give her lunch before taking her for the audition.

Once Sally rescheduled her flight, she secured a voucher for two nights in her hotel and then spent most of the next day practicing her Bach suite. She had a comfortable flight, a delicious lunch with Herr Scheckel, and the audition went so well that she secured a position with the Berlin Philharmonic Orchestra, which she retained for some years until ill health forced her to retire.

Sally has been told by a clairvoyant that she and Paul were once priest and priestess in one of the great temples of ancient Greece. Both celibate, they worked very well in combination, performing a great deal of healing work. A few centuries later, however, when Paul was a distinguished personage in a high position in the Italian church and several years her senior, he was largely responsible for thwarting her desire to become a nun, deeming her to be "unsuitable." This broke her heart initially, but she had an unqualified admiration for Paul, and several years later, when she had found her vocation as a wife and mother, she felt extremely grateful to him. Often it is only our twin soul who can steer us onto the right path in a given lifetime.

In this lifetime, Sally and Paul first met when she was only fifteen and he thirteen. They lived only a few streets apart in a relatively small English town and, despite the age gap, which always seems larger at that time of life, they

formed an immediate friendship and became almost inseparable until Sally went off to the Royal College of Music in
London. Paul, who is equally musical, went two years later
to Cambridge to study philosophy but, after floundering for
a while, came back home for a rethink. He was at Sally's
house daily as soon as the vacation had started, and she did
her best to advise him, suggesting that he should follow his
heart and follow her to the Royal College of Music. When
he replied that he did not believe that he could ever succeed
as well with the piano and flute as she did with the cello, she
encouraged him to think of teaching music.

Sally's teenage feelings of attraction to Paul had by this
time developed into a deep, mature, feminine love, but she
realized fairly soon that there was no chance of her senti-
ments being requited. One day she plucked up the courage
to ask Paul if he had met any attractive girls during his time
at Cambridge, he responded by looking very nonplussed
and mumbling something vague about his college being an
all male one and there not being any opportunity. (Women
only began to be admitted to men's undergraduate colleges
at Cambridge University in 1972, and Paul is now in his sev-
enties.) A few days later, he came back to see Sally and said,
"You're the only person I can talk to about this. I started
wondering recently whether I might possibly be queer." Sally
says that, despite her initial distress, she realized not long
afterward that she had always known deep down that Paul
was homosexual. She further says that it was thanks to that
that, rather than expressing any sort of shock, she was able

straight away to be a real support for him. The climate at the time was rather different than nowadays, and so it took some years for Paul to be able to drop his use of the word "queer," which reinforced his negative feelings about himself, and declare himself openly as gay. He has had a number of different partners, and has never quite found what he feels to be true love, but Sally has always been the first person he introduces to a new partner—and the best person at consoling him after a heartbreak.

Personally I have no doubt that the causes of homosexuality are numerous, and I am sure that few people, if any, still go along with Plato's assertion that homosexuals are souls who were not originally hermaphrodite and whose "other half" is consequently of the same sex. I have regressed hetorosexuals to previous lives as homosexuals, and I have homosexual friends who were heterosexual in previous lives. I know someone who has found a life that she had in Greece as a gay man, when she says that she never matured. She believes a certain amount of immaturity to be the norm with homosexuals, and she points out that, since a child's first love is always the mother, a man will always have an extra step to take towards heterosexual love.

For the reincarnationist, homosexuality could be karmic (the consequence of having been homophobic in a previous life), or it could be the result of having spent a succession of lives as one sex and consequently having difficulty with suddenly being the other sex in a new life. Joan Grant gave another possible reason for it: the result of a decision to avoid childbirth after suffering intensely giving birth in a previous life or number of lives.[43]

A number of years ago, a priest psychologist of my acquaintance had an article in the highly reputed English Catholic journal, *The Tablet*, in which he stated that all the homosexuals he had ever met had a difficult relationship with the parent of the opposite sex. Sally agrees that this is often a factor—it is clearly a probable factor in the case of Ronald—but Sally feels that Paul also suffered from "over-mothering" on account of being an only child.

Paul eventually graduated from the Northern College of Music, and he has used his good degree in a variety of ways, including teaching. Sally has never married, but music is her life, and a very rich one it has been too. Although her health has been poor for some time now and she no longer has the strength in her arms that she had when she played in an orchestra, sometimes she and Paul enjoy meeting in her home and playing together. They also share other interests, including spiritual ones, and it would not surprise me at all if they were almost ready to take off from the world together and make the final fusion.

---

43.   Joan Grant, *Speaking from the Heart: Ethics, Reincarnation and What it Means to Be Human*, edited by Nicola Bennett, Jane Lahr, and Sophia Rosoff (London and New York: Overlook/Duckworth, 2007).

Guilt and Confusion

I have been here before, But when or how I cannot tell;
I know the grass beyond the door, The sweet keen smell.
The sighing sound, the lights around the shore . . .
But just when at that swallow's soar
Your neck turned so,
Some veil did fall—I knew it all of yore.
—Dante Gabriel Rosetti, "Sudden Light"

O ver the course of our many incarnations—in fact during single lifetimes as well—it is very common to get trapped in repeated patterns, and it is only when we have become aware of the pattern that we are able to free ourselves from it. This is one of the many ways in which deep-memory-process/regression therapy can be so useful, but sometimes people get the information they need from a clairvoyant past-life reading. Kathryn wanted for a long time to understand what had caused her to marry Carl, who abused her so badly for sixteen years, and she wondered for a time whether she had a karmic debt to him. Finding out that he had already abused her many times in the past, and that in her present lifetime she had fallen yet again for his good looks and his superficial charms, enabled her finally to cut the ties that she had had with him forever.

The beginning of Jane's story is not dissimilar, in that in her present lifetime her first marriage was to someone who had a habit of beating her when they were man and wife in the Wild West.

Jane and Vijay

"One day," Jane told me, "we were standing opposite each other and I just looked at him. I found myself looking deep into his eyes and I was overcome by this incredible feeling of 'I know you.' It's impossible to describe, but there was a sort of timelessness about it. It was as though we were looking straight at each other's souls with a sense of having known one another for ages and ages, eons and eons. Neither of us said anything. Time just stood still for I don't know how long. Eventually we came back to reality and the present day, and realized that we were just standing there in the kitchen; but it was a really strange experience for both of us."

Jane's life this time has been far from easy, and the famous English clairvoyant, Edwin Courtenay, explained in his reading for her that this was because she was coming near to the end of her necessary incarnations and had chosen to pay off a large number of debts. She had a difficult childhood, married young, and had a daughter, Ruby. This marriage was happy at first, but failed when she got pregnant a second time very quickly and her husband, Bernard, did not share her joy at the thought of another child. She feels that it may have been partly Bernard's attitude that caused her to miscarry, but nevertheless they parted without too much animosity and nowadays they are good friends and have always shared in the care of Ruby.

When Jane fell in love with Will, who was an old school friend, he was also divorced, but her new in-laws were hostile to her from the start. Will's father is a vicar, and the parents disapproved of Jane's interest in spiritualism as much as they disapproved of her being divorced. The first time she visited them, they put on the video of their son's first wedding, and they apparently turned a completely blind eye to the fact that Will was also divorced!

Edwin Courtenay said that, in the previous life in which Will constantly beat Jane, she was rescued by her twin soul, Vijay, who was black, and so they had to run away together to avoid recrimination from a prejudiced society. In fact, interracial marriage is another pattern for this twin-soul couple, who are this time around English and Indian respectively. Edwin Courtenay further told Jane not only that she had absconded with Vijay in Greece, when she had been the wife of a senator and he a slave, but also that there had been other lifetimes in which their match had been an interracial one that was frowned upon by those around them.

When Will and Jane married in their present life, he was running a business in their home county of Devon. He accepted Ruby, and Jane eventually bore him two sons. The pregnancies and births were difficult, however, and she also suffered a number of miscarriages. She regretted never having had the opportunity to realize her academic potential and so, after a few years of marriage, she started studying for a degree in psychology. However, before she had been able to get very far with that, Will suddenly got an urge to move to Spain and dragged the family off with him. Jane, who was not sorry to move farther away from her in-laws, quickly decided that the sun had a lot of appeal for her, and so they leased their house in Devon and rented an apartment in a small town on the Costa Blanca. Before long, the rental of a laundry service came up and they decided to take it on. This was extraordinarily hard work in the summer, the height of the tourist season, and they found it much more difficult to make ends meet in the winter.

Will, who had begun to get interested in healing, taught himself to do acupressure and massage. This proved to be very helpful to Jane, who was suffering from various physical problems, and so he decided to supplement their income by offering treatments to some of the guests. The resort was quite popular with English people, and I myself made friends with the couple when I took my family's laundry to be washed when we were on holiday there. (At that time, I talked more to Will because of our shared interest in healing; Jane was working very hard in the background.)

Vijay, who is a Sikh from the Punjab, also went to this seaside resort in search of work, and he got himself a post in an expensive Indian restaurant situated on the same street as the laundrette. His marital history was a sad one, alas not totally uncommon in that society. To be sure, arranged marriages are often very successful, especially in a country such as India where there are excellent astrologers and the parents heed their advice regarding the compatibility of their respective offspring. In Vijay's case, however, the couple did not meet before the wedding day, and they took an instant dislike to each other. She looked so tiny and frail that Vijay (who is quite well built) was afraid she would break if he touched her. Neither felt any desire to consummate the marriage, but after a month, an aunt accused Vijay of not being a man, so he proved her wrong by engendering two daughters.

Being a conscientious man and a devoted father, Vijay stayed with his family for a number of years, even though the marriage was totally unsatisfactory for both parties. Then, when he felt that his daughters were old enough to leave, he decided to come to Europe, hoping that eventually he would earn enough to bring the daughters over to join him. Interestingly, it was Will, not Jane, who first got to know Vijay, and after making friends with him, he made use of the friendship in a rather odd manner.

One day when Will was giving a treatment to a young English vacationer, Jane needed to go back to the apartment for something, and she went into the bedroom. Immense was her horror when she observed the erotic way in which her husband was performing the "massage," and she rushed back to the laundry feeling extremely upset. Neither said anything to the other afterward, but it gradually became clear to Jane that Will was having an affair with the young Caroline, and that he was borrowing Vijay's apartment for the purpose.

Vijay is not the type of man who would normally condone adultery, but Will had spun such a convincing yarn about being abused by his henpecking wife that his kind heart was touched, and he lent Will a key to his apartment while he was busy working in the restaurant. The funny side of the story is that Jane in due course confirmed the picture painted of her by turning up in a rage at Vijay's place when he happened to be at home while Will was with Caroline. She commented to me, "You tell me that a first meeting between twin souls is normally a memorable occasion. Well, I was slapping Vijay around the face and screaming at him to send my husband back!"

Caroline's holiday was coming to an end, and Will did indeed come back. He realized that he had made a complete fool of himself and, since she believed him to be genuinely sorry, Jane forgave him and they made a fresh start. After only a few months, however, Will suddenly announced that he had had enough of running a laundry service and wanted to return to England and think about his next move. Although she would have liked to be able to continue with her degree course, Jane was by now feeling settled in Spain, the children were settled in school and learning Spanish fast, and in any case their house in Devon was on a long-term lease. So, since Will was so insistent, she decided to let him go off for a while and live with his parents while thinking about his future. She still loved him despite his recent infidelity and trusted that he would return before too very long. As for Will, he did not want to leave her completely in the lurch, so he enlisted Vijay's help with the laundry service whenever he could spare the odd hour during his time off. Vijay welcomed the extra hours of work since his pay in the restaurant was very poor.

Subconsciously, Jane must have known that in this lifetime she needed to learn to stand up to Will—something she had failed to do when she had been married to him previously. So she did this initially by not tolerating his adulterous behavior, and then by staying put in Spain, which she believed to be the best option for the family at that time. As for Vijay, he once more took up the role of rescuer, even though Jane did not at all appreciate it at first. She recognized that she could not do all the work in the laundry single-handedly, and so for some months she put up with Vijay's presence at her side. But, since she knew no Gujarati and his English was extremely limited, she made little attempt to communicate with him.

Far from having any thoughts of a new relationship, she was continuing to hope that Will would decide to return to Spain. However, Will eventually announced that he wanted to become a student and obtain some qualification; consequently, he would have no money to send to his family. His parents, delighted to have their dear son back, were perfectly happy to support him and apparently not the least bit bothered about his deserting his family!

Jane was distressed, to say the least, but still determined somehow to make a success of the relationship—and still convinced of her genuine love for Will. Vijay had, of course, by this time changed his view of her, and was extremely sympathetic to her predicament. He had become fond of all three children, who also liked him, and he continued to play his part at the laundry whenever he had some free time, supporting her gently and quietly. Then the Indian restaurant suddenly closed and, since it was a busy time for Jane, she suggested that he come and work with her full time.

One of the fascinating things about this couple was that, because of the language difficulty, they communicated—at this stage at any rate—mainly by telepathy. When I was again on holiday in the vicinity of the laundry, I heard Jane's tale of woe, and made the acquaintance of Vijay; but I found his limited English a real problem and had to get Jane to translate for me when we were all together. And it was at just about this time that the twin-soul connection was made! Jane's telling words about it were quoted at the beginning of this story.

After that, events just had to take their course despite Jane's feelings of guilt and confusion; the twin-soul love inevitably expressed itself sexually. In their beautiful book on twin souls,[44] Joudry and Pressman say, "If twin souls meet and one or both are already married, then there could be a conflict between the man-made law of marriage and the spiritual law of attraction. But while laws made by man take little account of the heavenly, the spiritual laws have regard for the earthly. The divine agency that directs the movement of souls is not likely to bring twin souls together in such circumstances as to break any true moral code." Well, in this case Vijay's marriage (if one can really call it that) had long since ended, and though Jane was loyal to Will, he was not fulfilling his duties either as a husband or as a father. Nevertheless, she felt torn apart by her strong feelings for Vijay, combined with the love she believed herself to still have for Will and her sense of responsibility toward him.

At this point, my role as a therapist came into play. I had already embarked on my first training course in regression, and had been studying the whole question of twin souls and soul mates for quite a while, so was very willing to listen and give what advice I could. Since, however, I did not yet feel sufficiently confident in regression therapy to offer it as a possible solution for such a major dilemma, I suggested that Jane seek a reading from Edwin Courtenay. In his reading, besides giving the information about Jane and Vijay's shared past, Edwin told her that they were twin souls, and that she had no karmic debt to Will (rather the other way around). This helped Jane get over the guilt and confusion, and she

---

44.   Joudry and Pressman, *Twin Souls*.

soon decided to file for divorce and to start sharing her life with Vijay. This does not mean that she had no qualms. After all, Will was the father of her two young sons, and she still felt bound to him in other ways, too. But when she told Will that she was prepared to sacrifice the relationship with Vijay for the sake of their family unity, his response was weak and indecisive.

The divorce did not prove to be much of a problem, but marrying Vijay took a great deal longer. This was because of his insecure status as an immigrant in Spain. While they were exploring various options, I acted as interpreter for them on a visit to a lawyer. He explained that, in light of the racist attitude to immigration still prevailing in Spain (as, alas, in so many countries in Europe), qualifying for a civil wedding would take a very long time. He said that the simplest solution would be for them to become Catholics and get married in church, which they were willing to do to avoid the risk of Vijay being deported. However, the local priest I spoke to on their behalf said that they could only be married in church if they first underwent a course of religious instruction. Since Vijay is a Sikh and Jane's spirituality is hardly in line with traditional Catholicism, this seemed more than a little farcical. Also, Jane and Vijay knew little Spanish and the priest spoke no English!

But when relationships have been preordained, no civil laws can prevent them from unfurling. The concept of twin souls as opposed to other soul-mate relationships was a new one to Jane, but when Edwin Courtenay and I explained the whole thing, it all rang bells deep within her. So often, as we have seen, there are similarities in the backgrounds of twin-soul couples, and Jane then told me that to each of them their youngest brother was special and that these two brothers had the same birthday. Also, one of Vijay's daughters was born in the same year as Ruby, and Jane arrived on the Costa Blanca on April 1, 1994, which was the very same day that Vijay had left Amsterdam for Andorra (prior to his move to the Costa Blanca). At one point, before the two of them had become emotionally involved, Vijay (who is a truly excellent chef) was offered a really good, better-paying job in a restaurant in another town. However, just as he was set to move, he suddenly said to Jane, "I don't think I should go." And without in the least knowing why, Jane replied, "No, I don't think you should either."

In the end, they decided to persevere with pushing for a civil wedding in Spain, doing all that they could to either get around or cut the red tape which can cause such endless and frustrating delays. Whenever my family and I were there, Jane was always very tied to her work but, since she wanted to discuss her problems with me, we managed to arrange a time for us all to go out for a meal together. It was the school holidays and all Jane's children were in England. To enable Jane and myself to talk privately for a while, we started off the meal at separate tables, which meant that my husband, David, and our younger son were sitting with Vijay. Although David took an instant liking to Vijay, he found communication difficult due to his limited English. However, as soon as we had finished eating our paella, I suggested that we sit together for the dessert. David, who had not taken any interest in the concept of twinsoulship during my previous attempts to explain it to him, suddenly understood what I had been talking about. He exclaimed to me afterward, "They're like one person!" David was also amazed at how communication, which had been so difficult a few minutes earlier, became easy the moment that Jane and Vijay were sitting together.

Eventually the necessary paperwork was completed and they were able to get married, which ensured Vijay's continued residence in Spain. In the meantime, the possibility of opening another Indian restaurant came up, and this had much greater appeal to Vijay than continuing with the laundry service. Jane was also quite happy to make the change, and in due course they found themselves able to take out a mortgage on a little house in the area. At this point, Ruby was going through a very difficult teenage period and Jane was extremely worried about her future, but the boys were doing well and she felt that they would be all right in Spain for a while longer. The last time that I met the family, I thoroughly enjoyed a meal in their Indian restaurant. I heard all about a wonderful trip that Jane and Vijay had managed to make together to India. She told me that Vijay would have dearly loved to have another child with her, but she was put off both by her difficult gynecological history and by various health problems.

Then we lost touch for a few years. My holidays in Spain were replaced by pilgrimages to Sai Baba's ashram, we were incredibly busy relocating to a different part of England, and one or two e-mails that I tried to send to Jane bounced back. So I assumed that she had changed her e-mail address and failed to remember to tell me. I meant to send a letter, but somehow life was always too full. However, writing this chapter prompted me finally to try to get in touch with them by telephone. When I tried the cell phone number that Jane had given me when they moved into their house in Spain, a voice in Spanish told me that it was no longer valid. So then I phoned the restaurant number, which I fortunately still had, and got Vijay's voice—in excellent English—on the message service giving the opening hours of the restaurant.

I phoned again a bit later and had a very good conversation with Vijay. He told me that Jane had moved back to England a couple of years previously for the sake of the children's education, and also that he was now in the process of selling the restaurant because business there had become very poor. He explained that Spain was getting more and more expensive, and that tourists were now finding cheaper holidays in such places as Turkey. But he sounded just like his normal, calm, accepting self, told me proudly about what all the different members of the families were up to, and gave me Jane's new cell phone number. He said that his older daughter had qualified as a teacher in India, and that the younger one was learning sewing, and—most proudly of all—he told me that Jane had just become a manager in her job in England.

Well, I remembered from Jane's reading from Edwin Courtenay that she had previously been mother to the same three children and been unable to care for them adequately because of extreme poverty. Edwin Courtenay had consequently been sure that looking after them all would be her number one priority, and so a move to England for the sake of the children's education made sense. I was, however, left wondering about their present status as a couple until later the same day, when I was able to talk to Jane after her return from work.

She was obviously really blooming! She recounted how a second trip to India, this time with the children, had changed them all radically for the better. Ruby, who had previously been completely lacking in motivation, had upon their return immediately knuckled down to work and got herself a place at a British university to read for a degree in English and Spanish. Jane herself had set her heart on a proper career, which she realized she could only achieve in England rather than in Spain, and in any case she saw no future for her sons in Spain. John, the older one, is dyslexic, which the Spanish school had been incapable of dealing with properly, but now he has found his niche in a mechanics school in a major English city, and Joe, the younger one, who is very bright, is also undoubtedly better off at school in Britain.

As for Jane's own career, lack of funds had prevented her from continuing with the degree course that she had started in Devon, but she had made a plan for combining training with work, and that very day had started in her new post as head of human resources in a major company. Now she has given herself another five years in which to become a freelance management consultant, with the option of working only when she wants, and for a large salary. She has also just bought her own house in a convenient location for both her own work and for the boys' schools, and only a short train ride away from the university where Ruby is studying.

When I asked Jane about the present situation in regard to her marriage with Vijay, she replied without a trace of bitterness that they were still very close, talked daily on the phone, but that they had grown apart. This she attributes partly to the fact that, at forty-five, she feels really young and sees him as "old" in comparison (he is ten years her senior), and partly because his imperfect English makes it difficult to have "really deep conversations" with him. Her own work and her children's futures are her priorities now, and she cannot see Vijay being able to settle in England when he has finally closed the restaurant. So my personal belief is that this lifetime has been for them a preparation for a future one when they will be able to come together more fully. They may well decide that they have done with the difficulties caused by interracial matches, and that union will be easier if they incarnate in the same country—or at least the same continent!

What had already struck me when talking to Vijay before I telephoned Jane was his tone of total acceptance of the situation (the word "resignation" sounds much too negative), and the way in which he clearly puts what is best for Jane first, even though it necessitates physical separation from him. That is a sign of real love. Perhaps—I venture to posit—love that only twin souls are able to give to one another. (We shall see another example of this in the next chapter.)

As for poor Will, it appears that he has had a number of nervous breakdowns and is still living with his parents. When they first arrived in England, both the boys made a real effort to renew contact with him, but they were not well received, so they have decided that they would prefer not to see him any more. Sometimes people choose a parent for a particular lifetime simply for the genes it will give them and/or due to a certain piece of karma with the person concerned, but then obtain their real parenting elsewhere. Vijay certainly gave them both some good fathering for a while, and now it is perhaps time for them to learn to stand on their own. We have already seen that in certain lifetimes twin souls come together just for a period in order to achieve certain things, and there is no doubt that in this case the whole family has benefited from the relationship.

The Cords Can Never Be Broken

Always remember that nothing can quench Love, nothing can withstand it. Perfect Love casts out all fear. Love dissolves all guilt. Love makes the world go round. It is Love that will bring peace and unity to the world and nothing else can do it.

—Eileen Caddy

Joudry and Pressman's book on twin souls[45] is in most ways truly excellent, and so I find it more than a little surprising that they say that if one partner strays from a marriage, the couple are certainly not twin souls. No doubt this would be true if it were a couple such as those we looked at in the first two chapters, i.e., those evolved souls who are coming to the very end of their incarnations. Human nature being what it is, however, I have found no evidence to suggest that

---

45.   Joudry and Pressman, *Twin Souls*.

those who are with their twin soul will inevitably be impervious to temptation. The man of our next couple is dead now, but when they were together, though they loved each other deeply, each strayed from the marriage.

Alison and Ian

Alison came to me for therapy six months after Ian, her ex-husband, had died, when she was in a transition stage of her life and going through a period of difficulty in relationships. In the first regression, she went straight into a life in Egypt in which she was the first wife of the Pharaoh, whom she loved very dearly. Sadness came quite fast, however, when she found herself no longer the number one wife. The Pharaoh took not just one, but gradually several additional wives and, though he still came and slept with her occasionally, they failed to express their love for each other satisfactorily, and she was left for the rest of that whole life confused, bewildered and heartbroken. The Pharaoh died at forty-five, and she at a great age after many years of loneliness.

Immediately before we went into this regression, Alison had been talking with regret about another relationship that had just ended. Nevertheless, I somehow felt intuitively not only that the Pharaoh and Ian, Alison's deceased ex-husband, were the same man, but also that the couple were twin souls. Consequently, when I took her into the Bardo after her death, I asked her to ask her spirit guide what was the nature of their relationship—karmic soul mate, companion soul mate, twin soul, or something else. Alison herself knew little about the twin soul concept at the time, yet the answer came clearly and immediately: "twin soul." And, when the Pharaoh appeared to her after her death, she recognized him straight away as Ian.

Although she is highly intelligent, family circumstances forced Alison to leave school at sixteen and, not being quite sure of her next vocation, she applied for various jobs before deciding to train in nursing. She was shy and did not do very well at job interviews, but at one of them, Ian was on the interview panel and, without being fully aware of it consciously, he recognized her from their shared past as "the woman for him." Although the recognition was not at that point mutual, and the circumstances obviously prevented Ian from starting a relationship with her, this is another interesting case of someone who had clearly incarnated with the intention of meeting his twin soul. (You remember Graham Courtenay and also Eleanor?) Despite his instant recognition of Alison's true worth, he did not feel able to offer her the job when all his colleagues were expressing preference for another, more outgoing, candidate. This was clearly part of Alison's Life Plan since, if she had been offered the job with the firm concerned, she might not have found her vocation in the nursing profession.

Ian, who is about eight years older than Alison, is very intelligent as well and, although he had not been to university either, was working successfully in business administration. Alison says that at the job interview, when she was extremely nervous and not even sure she actually wanted the job, she did not really notice Ian. She was consequently very surprised when they met again several years later, he told her how he had never forgotten her from that interview. He said that, as soon as she had entered the interview room, he had felt his heart leap into his mouth and found himself more or less tongue-tied when trying to ask her questions. Fortunately, his colleagues unconsciously covered for him, and, besides the fact that she was not yet ready for him, this probably explains at least partly why Alison did not notice him at that point.

Alison is the oldest of four children, and her family was loving in reality, but had difficulty expressing their emotions. She now recognizes that her family background led her to attract men who have been emotionally closed, and it was her determination to break this pattern that made her bravely decide to seek therapy.

Alison's mother, who was always busy looking after the younger children, especially Alison's autistic brother, never had sufficient time for her; and her father, who had hoped for a boy first, did not give either of his daughters the attention and appreciation that they needed and deserved. This, however, did not prevent him from being rather overprotective of the two girls when they were growing up, making it difficult for them to experience normal teenage life.

Ian's family background is not dissimilar to Alison's, although he had only one younger brother. Even though they were not academically inclined and did not even think of suggesting that he apply to a university, his parents put a great deal of pressure on him to succeed. They also had a tendency to stifle the whole family's emotions. He did have one relationship with a girl when he was in his early twenties, but it did not last very long, partly because he knew deep down that she was not really the right person for him.

When the day finally came for Alison to notice him, she was busy working on a ward in a major teaching hospital, and Ian, who had become disillusioned with business and subsequently trained in hospital administration, had a junior position at the same hospital. He is as good-looking as she is pretty and, when one day they happened to pass each other in the corridor, Ian remembered her immediately from the interview, and she could not help noticing this "very striking figure." Her nurse's uniform enabled him to realize that she worked in his hospital and, being unable to recall her surname, he lost no time in making excuses to tour all the wards and track her down. In light of both the age gap between them and his "senior" position, she was flattered when he asked her to perform a certain task that would normally be done by someone more experienced, but also felt a little uneasy with his mildly flirtatious manner. This was partly because she had a boyfriend, Derek, at the time.

Derek was Alison's first boyfriend, and they had been courting on and off for six or seven years, but the relationship had never felt totally satisfactory to her and so, when Ian, after several months of mild flirtation, finally plucked up the courage to ask her out for the first time, she did not hesitate to accept. The attempts that Ian had made to form another relationship after his first failed one had been fairly abortive, and the invitation gave her the excuse she had—at least subconsciously—been looking for to break it off with Derek. Alison says now that, although the attraction was instantaneous and they got to know each other (as twin souls normally do!) very rapidly once they were courting, she felt all along that they were both holding back from each other their "innermost depths," and that this was always a serious impediment to real intimacy. However, only after Ian's death a few years ago from multiple sclerosis has Alison become aware of the extent to which they both feared opening themselves up wholly to one another.

Following the first regression that we did, Alison now realizes also that in the previous life as the Pharaoh and his first wife, their relationship was not dissimilar to this one. It was customary for Pharaohs to have a number of wives, but Ian had taken others less because of social pressure and more because of a lack of fulfillment in the relationship with her as his first wife. Their problems arose, just like this time— even though they truly loved one another, they had both had difficulty expressing it. She thinks that in both lifetimes his refusal to fit totally into the relationship, combined with her own lack of self-knowledge, were contributing factors to things going wrong. Very often do we need to make the same mistakes before we finally learn from them!

When Alison and Ian decided to get married this time around, it was only after she had changed her mind about it several times. Both their families were reasonably happy with the match, but she often felt frustrated by what she saw as his lack of consideration toward her family. Her relation-ship with both her parents improved after she had qualified as a nurse, and her younger siblings also held her in high regard, yet when they visited, Ian often behaved almost rudely towards them. Then, when she endeavored to point this out, he would go into denial and get annoyed with her. She feels that she made rather more effort to get along with his family, though this was not easy as she found both his parents rather strange and occasionally unwelcoming. Yet she freely admits now that, right from the start, she felt some sort of compulsion about getting into the relationship.

Since they had three daughters in fairly rapid succession, Alison gave up working for quite a long time but, now that they are all grown up, she has been happy to have a fulfilling profession. Her interest in healing now extends far beyond allopathic medicine, and she has managed in her spare time to train in both aromatherapy and reflexology as well acquir-ing Reiki. Since gaining the senior position on her hospital ward, she has been able to occasionally use all three healing methods on her patients, and also encourages the junior staff to open up to complementary therapies.

Another difficulty in the marriage was caused by the couple's differing attitudes toward raising the children. Although their philosophy of parenthood was mostly simi-lar—and they were both equally delighted with the arrival of each of their daughters—Alison wanted her girls to have what she had missed out on herself when she was young, but

Ian curtailed such opportunities by being what she regarded as excessively disciplinarian. This proved to be a cause of fairly constant friction between them, and Alison now feels that she could have made more effort to discuss the difficulties. Instead she says that she would "go off in a huff" and shut herself up in the bedroom, and that he consequently became increasingly resentful and "took it out on the children."

At one of these particularly difficult times, Alison fell for another man. Though she would not have admitted it at the time, with hindsight she feels reluctant to use the phrase "fell in love." The affair was caused more, she says, by "frustration with Ian, combined with a sudden desire to do things that I had been unable to do before committing myself to him." The man concerned, Clive, was a doctor, a family friend, and married himself to someone rather manipulative from whom he wanted to escape but was never able. Ian turned a blind eye, which at the time infuriated Alison because she felt that, if he had loved her deeply enough, he would have protested. When, however, she talked to him about it in the Bardo at the end of our first regression, he explained that he had been subconsciously aware of her need to tie up something karmic that she and Clive had not dealt with when they had been married in a previous life. In fact, she did this fairly quickly, once she had realized that Clive was never going to leave his wife, and that her love for him was more of an infatuation.

In the deep-memory-process therapy in which I have been trained by Dr. Roger Woolger, it is always after death, in the Bardo, that most of the real healing takes place. (Bardo is the Tibetan word for the in-between-lives state.) Since there are as many paths up the spiritual mountain as there are people to climb it, Woolger does not believe in being firmly directive with people he guides into the inter-life state, so what the therapist can do is to gently ask questions such as, "Where do you go next?" "Whom do you meet?" "What do they have to say to you?" Before I did this training I was under the illusion that one had to be strongly clairvoyant to be able to receive messages from the spirit world, but over the years I have learned that we are all "psychic" and that valuable guidance is always available if we are ready to open our minds to it. Alison was already firmly on the spiritual path before she came to see me, and consequently she was very open to what happened, but many a time I have had a client who has been amazed at the wisdom that has come through at the end of a session.

When they met in the Bardo at the end of her regression, Ian did indeed show a lot of wisdom. Alison was still holding some anger against Clive, and he told her that it was doing her no good, that it was time to let go of it, and that both of them had behaved badly at times in order to test her love. Clive, however, who had apparently been genuinely in love with her in the previous life but had failed to show it, had this last time just been using her as an escape from his marital relationship, whereas he, Ian, had appreciated the fact that she was always there for him, even during her affair.

Some time after Alison had ended it with Clive, Ian had an affair with Laura, another nurse at the hospital, while Alison was on maternity leave. Alison did not know Laura, but she got suspicious when Ian kept coming home rather late without a genuine explanation. When she first confronted him, he was unwilling to admit anything. Later, however, Ian had real regrets and explained to Alison that he had been seeing Laura because he felt that the two of them were not fulfilling each other as much as he hoped. He confessed only after Laura had tried to persuade him to leave Alison for her, which made him realize his true feelings.

This confession forced Alison finally to make hers about Clive. Ian then told her that he had indeed had suspicions, but that he knew Clive well enough to appreciate that he would never leave his wife and that the affair would consequently be short-lived. They then made up for quite a while and endeavored to do more things together, such as going to the theater and opera, but Ian still failed to get along with her family as well as Alison wanted, and they also started to have more problems over bringing up their now-teenage daughters. In fact, the middle one, Bella, became so difficult that Ian insisted on sending her to boarding school, which Alison found very difficult to accept.

They nevertheless managed to have some very good times together, and so it was a big shock to when Ian was diagnosed with multiple sclerosis. The illness often develops quite slowly, so he was not forced to retire from his job immediately, but both anxiety and the care that Ian increasingly needed were a strain on Alison. When he finally had to retire, he steadily became more and more demanding, expecting her to sit with him for long periods of time, which of course increased the strain still further. At times she got really depressed and, being tied to the house by Ian's disabilities, would try to console herself by listening to music. She had always been particularly keen on the Romantic composers, and she went through a phase that lasted for several months of listening to a lot of Tchaikovsky. After a while, however, she noticed that listening to Tchaikovsky's music actually increased her depression, so then she turned to Brahms and eventually Haydn and Mozart, all of which she found more helpful. Several years later still, she suddenly discovered Bach, and nowadays she recommends Bach as a "cure for most depression"!

During their conversation in the Bardo, Ian told Alison that after his death he had realized that he had been overdependent on her, and that he had in that life been supposed to learn to be alone but had not been very successful in that. It was truly heartwarming for Alison in the Bardo (and very moving for me!) to be told by Ian that she had done the right thing in often standing up for herself by insisting that she deserved to have a life outside of caring for him. She in her lonely Egyptian life had learned about acceptance and silence, but this time round she also needed to learn about caring for herself. He also told her that he had needed to learn strength, integrity, and honesty, and apologized for not

having expressed sufficiently his appreciation of those qualities in her.

When Ian died, Alison was, of course, thankful that he
was no longer in pain, but also felt a great relief to be free
of the responsibility. She therefore promptly suppressed her
grief and returned to her nursing. Her eldest daughter, Pam,
was by then away at university and Bella, who did not want
to go on to higher education, felt ready to leave school, and
so Alison encouraged her to come home again and look for
a job there. Alison was determined to take the opportunity
to make a new life for herself, and she says now that this
was why she did not admit to herself the extent to which all
three children were mourning the loss of their father. Alison
then endured a few years of problems with her daughters,
none of which is at all unusual these days. One or two of
them got into drugs for a while and the youngest one, Valerie, started rather precociously to be a bit promiscuous.

When she came for a second regression, Alison wanted
to look at her lack of self-forgiveness about the things that
she did not get quite right with her daughters. She knows
that she did her best under the circumstances, but, since Ian
had been so much more strict with them than she believed
necessary, she has sometimes wondered if she should not
have left him early on in the marriage for the sake of the
children. Once, for instance, he hit one of the girls severely
without good reason and, after Alison had challenged him
about it, he laughed it off. When Alison met Ian again in
the Bardo after her second regression, she told him that she

could not forgive him for having been overly severe with the children. He accepted what she was saying and understood, so some good healing then took place between them.

In the second regression, Alison found her shadow—a man who wasted his life, abandoning his family, and ending up on the streets as a drunkard—and she also identified all three of her daughters. Valerie was her (or rather his) mother, whom he had failed to respect because she had not stood up to his tyrannical father; Bella was a son she (then he) had abandoned in the earlier life; and Pam was his much-loved younger brother, who had taken over the care of the family after the man who is now Alison had moved to the town in search of work and failed to return. The fact that she had previously abandoned Bella when she was her son explains Alison's strong resistance to sending her to boarding school this time around and, even though there were difficulties once Bella had come home again, she is glad of having had (and still having) the opportunity to pay the debt from that previous lifetime by caring for and guiding her. Alison's big regret now with regard to her daughters is that after Ian's death, they failed to come together to create their own new family dynamic, and she believes that this second past life sheds some light on what went wrong this time. Alison found that the reason for the family's lack of connection was because they were all insufficiently aware of what Ian meant to them. However, the girls are all doing quite well now, and communication between the four of them is steadily improving. I have no doubt that both Alison and Ian have learned from their mistakes in past lives, and she is becoming better equipped to give her children the support that they need.

Another thing that Alison did after losing Ian to take advantage of her freedom was rush into a new relationship. Tom was an easy target since his wife had just left him and he was useless at looking after himself. He was less handsome than Ian, but he aroused her motherly instincts and fulfilled her sexually for a while. However, when she expressed her desire for him to seek a divorce and marry her, he refused to commit himself. As the affair dragged on, he started to take her for granted and Alison became more and more frustrated by his lack of commitment. Then one night, when she was beginning to think seriously about breaking it off, she suddenly had a dream about Ian, despite trying hard not to think about him. In this dream, they were courting again and he brought her the most beautiful bunch of roses. She woke up from it feeling extremely emotional, but, rather than letting herself have a really good weep, she got up and went off to work, hastily resolving to ditch Tom immediately, and look for someone who could better fill the gap.

Working full-time did not make this easy, but Alison had already planned a vacation in Mallorca for herself and Bella and Valerie. While they were there, the two girls found plenty of other youngsters with whom to mix all day (and all night!) long, which gave Alison the opportunity to have a fling herself. She says that she has always found Latin men attractive, and during that stay on Mallorca she met more than one who expressed interest in her. By the end of the first week she had settled on Pedro, who was just a couple of years younger than she was and claimed to be free. His English was far from perfect, but she had already picked up a bit of Spanish on previous visits and was keen to learn more. What is more, he told her that he had always longed to visit England and so, by the end of the second week, they had fixed a date a couple months later for him to visit her.

Alison returned home excited that she had at last met "the love of her life," and over the next weeks she and Pedro exchanged a number of postcards and telephone calls. Finally, the day came when she went to meet his flight, but it was a huge disappointment that he was not on it. She then went home in tears, cursing the "untrustworthiness of Spaniards," only to be greeted by a call from a distressed Pedro explaining in his broken English how he had missed the flight through "unavoidable circumstances." To her great joy, he promised to arrive at the same time on the very next day, and she then managed to rearrange her shift at the hospital to go to the airport a second time. Pedro did indeed arrive this time, and they spent a few fun-filled evenings together before a telephone call shattered it all. When she answered the phone, a girl's voice asked for Pedro, who then disappeared into the other room, but Alison was able to hear him obviously arguing heatedly. When she tried to question him about it, he was cagey, but another call came the very next day and also on the day after that. (This took place before the time had come for absolutely everyone to have their own cell phone.) Alison became increasingly sure that Pedro had been two-timing all along, but it took hours of questioning to force him to admit that it had been Maria Rosa who had caused him to miss his flight. Alison never actually discovered whether or not he was married to her, but she sent him packing straight away.

Alison says now that she is not sure which was stronger, her grief or her anger. One of the people she expressed her feelings to was Martha, a friendly colleague who had been able to step in for her when she had gone to meet the second flight. Martha was very sympathetic and promptly suggested that Alison accompany her to a Reiki healing course the following week. This, Alison explains, is what triggered her interest in studying alternative methods of healing, and, though she occasionally still feels a bit of anger toward him, she is also now grateful to Pedro for starting her off on the spiritual path. After that first Reiki course with Martha, one thing led to another, and Alison soon started meditating regularly and came to appreciate that she needed to learn to live on her own and to find herself independently of a man.

The meditation did not, however, work instantly. Alison found, as do many people, that she had to be very strong-minded and disciplined about it—especially since the first thing that happened when she started was that the depression she had suffered during Ian's illness returned. Fortunately, her friendship with Martha had deepened and so this time, rather than trying to smother the depression with drugs or Tchaikovsky, she talked about it, and Martha encouraged her to persevere with the meditation, assuring her that the surfacing of grief was a necessary stage in the process, and that the tide would turn in due course if she simply let the tears come and went with the flow.

Alison then found herself constantly torn between sitting with her pain and grief and trying to bury them with work, preoccupation with her daughters, and attempts at improving her social life. While putting her social life on the back burner, she believed for some time that, though both Derek and Clive were nothing but distant memories, it was Tom and Pedro who were the prime causes of her distress. When we talked about Pedro, she thought that she had probably had something karmic to work out with him—especially since the attraction had been instantaneous and very strong—but that she was not particularly interested in exploring that. Rather, after talking it through thoroughly, she feels indebted to Pedro now for having been the trigger for her starting seriously on her self-exploration and combining her innate interest in caring for the sick with older forms of healing.

Tom is a different matter, since Alison still feels that he could potentially have been a companion soul mate to her. He shares her love of music, they have the same taste in food, and she still feels frustrated by the knowledge that he was clinging to a false hope of one day being able to resolve things with his wife and consequently refusing to commit himself to her. But after she had persevered for long enough with regular meditation to get over her depression to a large extent, she began to find it genuinely helpful and to be able to let Tom fade into the background.

In fact, Alison had reached what she describes as a "plateau of stability," thinking mainly about her work, her family, and her spiritual life, when she started having a series of dreams about Ian. These varied a great deal in nature, with some of them being distressing, while others made her feel happy until she woke up and remembered that he was no longer around physically. Since we do normally leave our bodies when we are asleep, the likelihood is that at least some of these dreams were real encounters. Anyway, they triggered a number of mixed emotions in Alison, including guilt as well as grief, which she is still struggling to deal with. The discovery that they were twin souls helped immensely, since she found that it explained both her mixed feelings about Ian and her inability to cut the ties with him completely.

However, the first effect of these dreams was to give her a strong desire to embark on another relationship. The fact that she had sometimes had really good times with him when they were together made her, very naturally, yearn for love again, and also some of the dreams made her better able to understand the depth of Ian's love for her. She dug out and re-read all the letters that he had written her when he had occasionally had to go away for trips connected with his work, and these caused the first real surfacing of her grief.

Alison had still not made a great deal of effort toward making a good social life for herself, and in any case she was not interested in mixing with people who would not share her spiritual interests. So she decided to try Internet dating, which seemed to be quite good fun at first, but had led to another heartbreak. This was with a man called George, who was a few years younger than her and expressed a great deal of interest in the complementary healing that she practiced. He even taught meditation himself, so it was a big shock to Alison when she discovered after a few months that he had not been telling her the full truth about his own "previous" relationship. Since he lived some distance from her and it was easier for him to travel than it was for Alison, they met only in her town, so at first it was not difficult to hide the fact that he was still living with his wife Maggie. But by this time, cell phones had become the norm, and on one occasion when they were together George forgot to switch his off. Fortunately, her experience with Pedro had put Alison on her guard, and so she gradually extracted the truth about Maggie from him. She then went through an agonizing time while George was supposedly making up his mind about them. Alison and I met for the first time not long after he had finally decided to stay with Maggie. Since his expression of love and his promises had seemed to be genuine, she was deeply hurt by the betrayal, and when we did the first regression, George was much more on her mind than Ian.

The work that we did together consequently caused a huge shift of emphasis for Alison, and she is still very busy processing the whole thing. When it comes to emotions such as grief and guilt, and when people have experienced great loss, there are always innumerable layers to it all. Before we met, Alison had already dealt with the first layer, but the life as the Pharaoh's first wife opened up a deeper layer. Then, when she read through what I had written, she found it very difficult indeed, as doing so caused a great deal of grief to surface. However, making the corrections that, with hindsight, she found that she wanted, proved to be very therapeutic for Alison. She believes too that Ian is guiding her in the process, and I have every confidence that her life will now improve steadily. In fact, she still has time to make another, much more satisfactory, relationship, and Ian when she talked to him appeared to approve of this idea. So I wish her good luck in this, and I wish them both a happy final reunion!

The Pain of Separation

Live in Compassion today, as I did when I walked on this Earth.
It will show you the New World for which you long.
Then claim the gift of God that cannot change.
The Holy Mind of the Beloved is yours NOW.
—JESHUA BEN JOSEPH CHANNELED THROUGH
JAMES F. TWYMAN[46]

The desire to help others and the planet was normally
indicative of an advanced soul, as mentioned at the
beginning of chapter four. Now we have two further examples of couples who are clearly very evolved, and yet, despite
that, in both cases one of the partners has caused immense
pain to the other by leaving the marriage. It is not for me to
pronounce on the higher reason(s) for this (so often obscure

---

46. Twyman, *The Art of Spiritual Peacemaking.*

while we are still on Earth), but it does seem to me that—
superficially at least, and unlike Joseph in chapter four—the
two "defectors" still have more to learn than their partners.
Since, however, as the famous clairvoyant Edwin Courtenay
explained to me many years ago, twin souls always catch
one another up spiritually fairly rapidly, the main thing to
appreciate in these stories is the admirable way the two
abandoned partners have coped with their pain. I do not
even want to use the word "sufferers" for them, because it
seems more than likely that in both cases the two who have
caused the pain are in fact the ones who are suffering the
most. So all I can say to them is, "Good luck in your speedy
catching up!"

Steve and Zoë

"We met," Steve told me, "at a workshop on 'Discovering the
Western Mystery Tradition' and, following the instant recognition which almost invariably occurs when twin flames
first meet, our courtship was very fast indeed, despite
Zoë's fear of the intensity of the feelings." He went on to
explain that they both already believed in reincarnation, and
that they both recognized immediately not only that they
had known each other before, but also that they had studied such things as the mystery tradition together in previous
lives. Consequently, Steve's pain at the separation has been
intensified by the fact that they both believed for quite some
time that Zoë had succeeded in overcoming her fears con-

cerning the relationship, and that they would spend the rest
of their present incarnation together.

Steve started his professional career as a pharmacist and
then moved into teaching, and later into spiritual counseling,
for which he has a truly wonderful gift. Zoë also went into
teaching, but in her case it was less because of a love for it
and more due to pressure from her parents, for whom a conventional career was of the utmost importance. Their family
circumstances were very different. He was born and brought
up in London as a member of a large, joyous family in which,
he explains, he was allowed to develop as a human being with
no sense of pressure. Conversely, she was born into an upper
middle-class family in Yorkshire and was brought up with a
very strong sense of ambition, which caused her natural abilities to be put aside. Neither of them had any religious upbringing, but whereas Zoë's family was very materialistic, Steve's
was poorer and much more spiritually oriented. He says, "I
was brought up with love, but she inherited from her mother
a great difficulty in giving love, particularly to children."

For that reason Zoë decided right at the beginning of
their relationship that they should not have children, and
Steve acquiesced because of his great love for her. He says
that they both have memories of having felt more comfortable in past lives when their sex roles were reversed, and
he has conscious memories of a feminine past life in Egypt
when Zoë was his husband and their children were taken
away from them at an early age and brought up by the
priests. One of these priests is now Steve's sister, and the

two of them are paying karmic debts from that lifetime in their current incarnation. Both of the formerly Egyptian children are now Steve's sister's daughters, but this sister's disastrous marriage did not last very long—it was her failure to cope with the children which has sadly been the main cause of Steve and Zoë's separation.

Before Zoë and Steve met, she had a boyfriend I will call Roy, whom her parents approved of since he was an engineer like her father. Steve's profession of spiritual counseling, however, did not seem to them like a proper career at all, and her parents' disapproval was a constant blot on the marriage. (Zoë was, and still is, very much under the thumb of her mother, and she was unable to take Steve home with her to Yorkshire, even at such times as Christmas!) Yet, for a number of years, their mutual love was strong enough to withstand the difficulties, and when Zoë decided to give up teaching in favor of healing, Steve supported her throughout the training and the difficult process of establishing herself.

Her parents were, of course, horrified by her career change, and two further obstacles made it difficult for Zoë: the fact of Steve being so highly sought after as a counselor made her somewhat jealous, and the arrival of his nieces into their life. Steve explains that when he and Zoë first got together, they knew that they had a piece of karma to work out together that was related to responsibility, but they did not know that it would be connected to children. Although Zoë recognized the karmic debt she had to the two girls on account of her failure to bring them up when she had been their father in Egypt, she was, because of her difficult upbringing, unable to give them love in the way that Steve did. And her innate difficulty was compounded by the children's inevitable emotional problems caused by their parents' failed marriage.

To start with, Steve took to caring for his young nieces on weekends, but when his sister decided to move away from London, she enrolled the girls in a school in Steve and Zoë's neighborhood. This meant that the couple was forced into almost full-time care of the children and, while Steve's great love for them helped him cope with the situation, Zoë gradually found it increasingly difficult. Steve explains that she found her awareness of the karmic debt to be overwhelming, and that she saw in her sister-in-law a reflection of her own inability to cope and to be responsible, which further aggravated the difficulties. So, after four and half years of trying to deal with the children being too much in their lives, Zoë suggested that she and Steve live apart for a while. She was also influenced greatly in this decision by her mother who, according to Steve, has "never really grown as a human being, never allowed herself the beautiful opportunity of seeing the spiritual path, and whose purpose is to negate—both for herself and others—every opportunity of moving forward to happiness."

Steve's grief was naturally immense, but his strong spirituality combined with his great love for Zoë helped him accept the idea of separation, which he saw initially as temporary. However, just as Zoë's parents were greeting the decision to separate with alacrity at the same time as haranguing her for having "abandoned a good career for this healing nonsense," who should suddenly walk back into her life but Roy, the engineer ex-boyfriend! Although she has admitted to a friend of Steve's that she does not love Roy at all, Zoë lost no time in plunging straight back into a relationship with him. Then, before very long, feeling a need for security, she gave up her idea of setting up a healing center and moved in with Roy. Now she is working as a hospital secretary, and Steve is coping with his pain sufficiently to maintain friendship with her.

Being so deeply spiritual, Steve is also able to look very positively at the relationship. He recognizes that Zoë has some catching up to do on the spiritual front, but knows that twin souls always do catch one another up before too long, and he is confident that they will come together again— very likely the next time around. He further comments that he learned things from her when they were together, for instance consideration and gentleness—"a thing for which Aquarians are not noted!" In fact, as an Aquarian myself, I can appreciate his statement that they can at times be quite abrupt and direct, and he explains that this tended to be disconcerting for Zoë, who is a Cancerian. Let us hope that she learns what she needs to learn now from her secure, yet unfulfilling, relationship with the unspiritual Roy, and that she and Steve will consequently be able to work more satisfactorily together in a future lifetime. In the meantime, one cannot but admire Steve's ability to sustain a friendship with the woman he knows to be the other half of his soul, yet who has caused him so much pain in recent years. And, since I believe that we plan the broad outline of our incarnations, Zoë's background, which has caused the two of them so many difficulties, is no doubt teaching her certain lessons in how not to live life, and no doubt she will have benefited too from the time that she spent living with Steve and is still learning from his loving example.

Monica and Marcus

After putting down the telephone receiver, Monica stood motionless for what seemed like hours. Marcus' confirming the truth about his affair had sent her into total shock. The realization of what had been going on behind her back had been dawning on her slowly, yet she was still not fully prepared for the truth of her husband's clandestine relationship with a younger African woman, who had bore him three children. The effect of the shock was, she explains, to cause the left half of her brain to cease functioning properly. Not only did she suffer the intense discomfort of feeling that half of her brain was "dead" or "paralyzed," but the whole of one side of her body was also affected. The paralysis itself was not uncomfortable, but it meant that she only had one half of her brain with which to both survive emotionally and do the practical work necessary for securing an income and a roof over her head. The other half of her brain eventually got "overheated," which caused a burnout that is still in the process of healing.

Monica had already, at the age of eight, suffered the trauma of her father leaving her family ("the first sun that disappeared from my life"), and this had given her a fear of being on Earth[47]—a fear which expressed itself physically as well as mentally, and which affected one side of her body in particular. This childhood shock caused her a nasty fall, which slightly dislocated her hip joint and eventually, when she was forty-four, resulted in a slipped disc.

Monica then had to have an operation on her back, which went partially wrong and resulted in long years in which she was incapacitated and no longer able to participate in normal life. However, this very difficult time initiated for her a deeper spiritual search, and only much later did she realize that the inner searching, which had been so very valuable for her, was also the initial cause of the inner separation between her and Marcus. She comments that such a division happens to "so many couples when one 'goes on to the Path,' while the other does not." For couples, the woman starting off on a spiritual search is the most common scenario. Meanwhile the man pursues his male expression in the world without either having, or taking the opportunity, to go within. In Marcus' case, partly thanks to Monica's support, his career took him to the very top, but she explains that this stunted his emotional growth. And we have already seen what Monica's reward was for her support!

---

47.   For a discussion of how people often cope with trauma by detaching from their body, see my first book *Karmic Release*.

So Marcus' confession affected the part of her body that was already in difficulty, and it gave her a feeling of being in a constant state of pulling all her muscles upward, from her feet to her shoulders. Although she was experienced in working with energy, nothing she tried would bring the "dead" side back to life, and she described herself as having been a nervous wreck for fourteen months, until she was gradually healed by Sai Baba.

Because of her great love for her husband Marcus, Monica left a comfortable life in the Netherlands to follow him to Africa, where he felt he had a vocation to be of help with his engineering skills—bringing to very many people the essential element of life: water. Working together on a continent with so many needs, the two of them helped to build each other's mission for this lifetime—a mission of importance in the evolution of the planet—and, while Marcus worked tirelessly at putting his exceptional skill into practical use, Monica, while bringing up their son, developed her spiritual and artistic life and offered healing to people around her.

Twenty-five years in the tropics brought countless rich experiences, but also many hardships, and for Monica the greatest hardship of all was when she suddenly had to get Marcus into hospital following a heart attack. He suffered four cardiac arrests within two hours, and had to be reanimated because his heart went into shock. Monica supported him throughout his miraculous recovery, making use of her healing skills. Only light scarring was left physically, but the scarring on his personality was much deeper. She says that he subsequently became a different person in many ways.

Monica and I met in Sai Baba's ashram and rapidly became friends, at a point when I thought that I had completed this book. So, when she started recounting to me the sad story of her separation from the husband she loved so much, and a little voice in the back of my head kept whispering "twin souls," my rational mind refused to listen initially. First, I said to myself, "I've just finished writing that book;" and second I found myself thinking that I could not bear to face any more pain. After already hearing so many agonizing stories of twin souls who were not together, my heart ached at having no way of alleviating the pain that I empathized with so strongly. But Monica in due course made clear to me that Baba had revealed to her that she and Marcus were in fact twin souls who would be ready to fuse after the end of this lifetime. Baba is the soul of compassion, and what does "compassion" mean but "feeling with"? So of course I straight away found myself feeling with and for her. And once again, I'm sorry, Patricia Joudry and Maurie Pressman,[48] but you are mistaken here: twin souls who are married to one another can, and sometimes do, separate.

As we became acquainted, Monica confided in me further. When she realized that there was no turning back—that her husband's infidelity was irredeemable—she felt that she had no choice but to return to her native country

---

48.   Joudry and Pressman, *Twin Souls*.

and file for divorce. Her son was now grown up and living there, and she knew that she could make a new life through her art, music, healing, and writing. It was not, however, an easy choice because she had no income, and Marcus' earnings were insufficient to support two wives. Also, he refused to send her paintings to their country, and they might have brought her a little income to start with. Things were pretty difficult for her for the first couple years after leaving Africa. However, Sai Baba assures his followers that he never allows them to go without food, clothes, or shelter, and Monica has recently received an inheritance, which will provide for her needs for the rest of her life.

She explained to me that, when she first became aware of what had been going on behind her back, she did not dare to be in her body because of the incredible hurt, but gradually there were short times when she began to dare and then felt better for it; and now she says that the whole problem is improving as she gets stronger. In a recent e-mail she told me, "I have just come back from a wonderful life-affirming seminar in Atlanta, my first stepping out into the world. And the world liked me! So my step becomes stronger. I have to do a lot of physical activity: dancing, a little yoga, walking, cycling, and so on, to get the muscles out of that habit of pulling away in my left side." Now, following the amazing healing given her by Baba when she was last at the ashram, she is daring to be fully on Earth rather than withdrawing from life, and she has come to the realization that what she

went through was caused by her "other half" being quite literally torn off in such a cruel and sudden way.

Monica also told me that, besides having the consolation
of the two other great loves of her life—Jesus and Baba—
she had found some further consolation for her pain when a
psychotherapist explained to her that people who had a close
brush with death often subsequently "went off the rails." This
could make someone feel a need to do something such as
fathering more children in order to ensure his own continu-
ation in some sort of way. Monica recognizes that one of the
purposes of Marcus' staying on Earth, which would not have
been possible without her strong support, was to pass on
his lineage, to connect it with the African race—a race so
important both to the two of them and to the world, and
for whom Marcus has done so much through his many years
of work on that continent. In addition, through his work,
he is still providing clean water to millions of people on the
world's most needy continent.

Monica's love for her ex-husband has in no way diminished, but she says that she has grown to a deeper understanding of the basic greatness of what the two of them, as
souls, have done together in this lifetime and of what they
had decided beforehand to take upon themselves, both for
their own learning and for the benefit of others. She explains
that their task was "way greater than the outer life seemed
to express," and that having now separated "the real from the
unreal" (the unreal meaning the horrendous pain that she
had agreed to suffer), she has now "merged with his gran-

deur." She says, "And when this life has been fulfilled, he will join that experience with all that we already are, together, as a single being." Furthermore, she concludes that she feels at peace now and ready, even, for a relationship with a companion soul mate, because "having freed myself of the feeling of victimship and being able to discover the grandeur in what we did together, I am free to love someone else." So I pray that this will come about for her in due course.

Monica adds that her many years in Africa prepared her for what the larger world needs in these times of important changes in human consciousness. She says that her husband's gift to her has been to support her evolution mentally, emotionally, spiritually, and artistically, and that she is now beginning to express this in the larger world. Her gift to him was to support him in his career and now, even though they are apart physically, he is in a position of assisting and advising in a project that provides millions in Africa with the water of life. Knowing too the extent to which twin souls influence one another even when they are apart, she feels that he may now be catching up with her emotionally and spiritually as well. She says, "My zest for life is back. I am ready to step back on to the stage of the world! And I feel that the best way for us to honor one another now is to carry on making use of the talents and expertise that we helped each other to build up."

Monica's son is now engaged to be married, and she says that when she sees the two of them driving off together in their open sports car, "my heart is so happy because they are just like we used to be in our Peugeot," and she finds herself, to her own amazement, telling them happily how things were for her and her son's father in their early years together, just as if nothing had happened but his death. She feels that, hard though the end has been, theirs is a life that was meant to happen—a life of purpose and fulfillment. She now finds herself, by the grace of God, able to "separate the man, who was my husband and the father of my wonderful son, from the stranger he has become. I can talk about him and our joyful experiences together as if he had died, which in a sense he has—or at least an important part of him has died." In her most recent e-mail, she quotes Sai Baba's "Thought for the Day" of May 18, 2008: "Individual reconstruction is much more important than the construction of temples." She feels this to be the story of her life following her separation from Marcus, and she ends "I love him [Baba] so much!" So Monica's, my final story apart from the historical ones, is surely a wonderful example of forgiveness, hope, and courage that has its source in God.

Not Being Incarnate Together

The trees are singing my music. Or am I singing theirs?
———EDWARD ELGAR

I hope that I have by now made it quite clear that find-ing one's twin flame is not the be-all and end-all of any given incarnation. In fact, concentrating on that could be a complete waste of time, since the majority of twin souls are unlikely to be incarnate simultaneously. Not likely at all, according to Sandy Stevenson! In her book *The Awakener,*[49] she states that the twin flames of only about 4 percent of people who are on Earth at the moment are incarnate. If people like

---

49.   Sandy Stevenson, *The Awakener: The Time is Now* (Dublin: Gateway, 1997).

Edwin Courtenay and Celia Fenn are right (which I have no reason to doubt), the number of twin souls who are together on Earth is steadily increasing, but it will probably still be quite some time before the percentage becomes sizable.

But the fact of not being on Earth together does *not* mean complete separation. Edwin Courtenay told Kathryn, who had fewer incarnations than Martin, that in many of his lifetimes she had served him as a spirit guide. And my friend and colleague, Betty, who does a lot of psychic work, told me about an interesting regression she did in which she met her twin soul.

In the previous life to which Betty was regressed, she found herself as a Mounty in Canada, who had taken it upon himself to protect a widow and her children who lived in a house near his own. He was close friends with the local Indian chief and trusted him. Nevertheless, one day he returned to the widow's house to find it burned down, and he saw the woman's arm in the rubble. He was filled with the most terrible guilt, despite the fact that he had checked on the house only the previous week and found it to be all right. He was also very angry, since he felt let down by his Indian chief friend. The Mounty stabbed himself and, when he went into the Bardo, he wanted his body to be left so that the people could see what had happened.

The next Bardo scene in Betty's regression was very moving. The souls of all the Indians, and of all the white people who had been killed in the warfare, congregated in the valley, and she smoked the pipe of peace together with the Indian chief and was told that he was her twin soul. The chief then gave the Mounty the Indian name of Big Heart, and he filled Betty's heart with his own energy and made a pledge always to help her from spirit. So it looks as though Betty's twin soul has finished his incarnations and that they now work together on different planes.

After doing this regression, Betty remembered that, when she had been training as a medium with the London College of Psychic Studies, she had once been taken on a flying journey with an American Indian. When they landed, she was introduced to an Indian chief. She looked into his eyes, and there was instant recognition. Then the two of them were together with a group of braves, dancing around a totem pole. Gradually they all started going up and up, in a winding motion, right to the top of the pole. Betty likened it to the kundalini (the energy that is stored in our base chakra and which, as we develop spiritually, goes up the spine, through all the chakras in turn). So she is sure that this was the same Indian chief as in her regression—her twin soul.

For me, the beautiful quotation opening this chapter from one of my favorite composers sums up almost everything about the work that we do on Earth. How often have you listened to a piece of music that moved you deeply and wondered where it really came from? I am sure that Edward Elgar (and no doubt other great composers too) must have often felt that he was simply plucking his wonderful melody out of the air. Even though we are not often consciously aware of it, it is just the same when one of our spirit guides is communicating with us. In reality, the divisions between heaven and Earth, spirits and people in physical bodies are all *maya* (illusion). Once we become aware of this, and open ourselves to the world of spirit, where everything real resides, our lives become infinitely richer. So I thank Betty for sharing her moving story, and hope it will reinforce my argument that whether or not we are at present acquainted with our twin soul is immaterial.

13

Do Angels Also Have Twin Souls?

I myself will dream a dream within you—
Good dreams come from me, you know . . .
from those who share my dreams
I ask a little patience, a little humour,
some small courage, and a listening heart;
I will do the rest.
—CHARLES PÉGUY, GOD'S DREAM

Quite a few years ago, when I was regularly in touch with Edwin Courtenay before he had become so famous, he told me that angels sometimes incarnated, though not in very large numbers. (In fact he gave me an approximate figure, which I recall was in thousands rather than millions, who were incarnate as helpers on Earth at that time.) I was intrigued, but I always like to get such assertions substantiated and, not believing myself to be clairvoyant, I saw no means of doing that. Until—at least twelve years later—Donna came to see me.

Donna and Tom

When Donna telephoned me to make an appointment for a regression and I agreed to the following Monday evening, my husband thought I was making a big mistake because we were due to leave for a trip to Canada the very next morning. But something inside told me that I had to say "yes" both to her and to her friend Paul. I'm glad I did. Donna's story seemed relevant to this book, so after our return from Canada I went to see her again in her own home, which is in a town near to our own.

Donna, who was twenty-eight when we met, chose a difficult incarnation this time, and it became immediately apparent to me that she had come in as a healer. Her parents' relationship was disastrous, since her father was an alcoholic, and disappeared from the family when she was very young. Her mother could not cope with looking after her, and so she was adopted by her maternal grandparents, with whom she was very close until they sadly died recently. When her mother remarried, Donna went to live with them for a while, but returned to her grandparents when that did not work out. Her mother used to visit fairly regularly throughout Donna's childhood, and nowadays they have a good relationship. Donna always feels, however, that she has to be a mother to her mother. Her brother, who is about a year older, drinks too much and they have little contact, but she also has a younger half-brother, whom she describes as "lovely." When she went into the Bardo at the end of our session, she was told that this half-brother was a "star seed."

Donna had never heard of star seeds, but the interesting thing is that, on the airplane the very next day, I read about them in Sandy Stevenson's book *The Awakener.*[50]

Donna told me that at the age of seven she had been singled out as a healer by a Buddhist monk. Ten years later, he met her again, remembered her, and sent her off to acquire Reiki I and Reiki II.[51] After she left school, a short-lived relationship prevented her from finishing training as a nursery nurse, and then, following a second short-lived relationship, she tried in vain to settle in France before moving to Devon. She explained to me early on in our preliminary discussion that she did not feel like she belonged in England. However, in Devon she trained in beauty therapy and massage, and then worked there for a while before moving to the town she lives in now. When I asked what had brought her up to my part of England, she replied, "Because it was where my finger landed on the map," but she further explained that she could not see her present abode as permanent either.

Donna was just coming through an extremely bad patch, and was suffering intensely not only with her own pain, but also with that of people around her and the world in general. In a very short time, she had nearly lost her beloved rabbit Barney, the grandmother who had brought her up was diagnosed with terminal cancer, her mother was losing her

---

50.   Stevenson, *The Awakener.*

51.   Reiki healing was brought through to the world by a Japanese man named Usui.

home, and she had her own breast cancer scare. Fortunately, the rabbit pulled through his illness, but she was spending any time off that she could get nursing her grandmother. One of her chief motives in coming for regression was to obtain a little more clarity about her path in life.

I consequently suggested that we aim to get into her Life Plan. When performing regressions, one can always set out with a particular aim but, since the subconscious is in charge and knows what the person most needs to deal with, sometimes one gets taken elsewhere. In Donna's case, however, when I directed her to her most recent past life and then through the death and into the Bardo to look at what she had come in for this time, it was all 100 percent successful.

Donna found that her last life was during the First World War, and the house she was living in got bombed. She was not in the house at the time and, since the rest of her family got killed, her Canadian soldier lover sent her to live with his family. She then became a nurse, and Andrew, her lover, died in her arms. This did not deter her from her noble nursing work, and she made friends with another soldier, called Christopher, whom she recognized as Paul, the friend she had brought with her for a regression, and when Christopher died during the war under her care, he gave her one of his medals. At the end of the war, she married another of her patients, also called Christopher, whom she felt sorry for because he was so traumatized by the war. Her new husband Christopher had a drinking problem and once, when he was in a particularly bad state not long into the marriage, he threw Donna down the stairs while she was in the early stages of her first pregnancy and then cut her throat. After realizing what he had done, her husband Christopher told the neighbor who found her (whom Donna recognized as a friend in her present life) that it was suicide and, though finding the situation suspicious, the neighbor was unable to do anything because of Christopher's elevated position in their society.

As soon as I had taken Donna through her death in that life and into the Bardo, she found herself surrounded by angels, who told her that she was one of them and that she did not belong on Earth. This made perfect sense to Donna, who felt completely at home with the angels, and who had tried in vain to find a place in the world in which she felt that she could belong; I, of course, immediately remembered my conversation with Edwin Courtenay several years previously. Then, while reading Sandy Stevenson's book on a flight to Canada the next day, I saw that she also talks about the fact that angels do sometimes incarnate.

While Donna was in the Bardo, her deceased lover Andrew appeared to welcome her home, and she recognized him as Paul's friend Tom, to whom she feels very strongly attracted in her present life, but who has another partner. The angels they were with in the Bardo told the couple that they were twin souls. Donna was also able to ask the angels a number of questions concerning her present life, which they assured her was her last incarnation. Without giving any definite answers about her future, they also assured her that they were always there guiding her, and that all she needed to do was to trust that the decisions she made were the right ones. I then asked her to call her husband Christopher into her presence and see how she reacted to him. Her compassion for him in his state of trauma caused by the war was so great that she did not feel she had anything to forgive! At that point, I remembered Edwin Courtenay having told me that angels, being extensions of the will of God, did not accrue karma when they incarnated. Paul then had his regression and the two of them went home happily, agreeing that I should keep in touch with them as part of my writing.

While I was away in Canada, I pondered the question of whether angels really had twin souls. Since their line of evolution is said to be different from ours, I was unable to feel sure about it. Soon after my return, I was attending a fortnightly meditation led by a friend who lives in our town. Toward the end of the guided visualization, my friend took us up to the angelic realms, and I felt myself surrounded by the comforting presence of large numbers of angels. I was particularly aware of Gadrasiel, which Edwin Courtenay had told me was the name of my own guardian angel, and I felt his solidity, wholeness, and strength. (I had already received a picture of him during a previous meditation. He looks much more human than the normal pictures one has of ethereal-looking angels with wings!) This made it hard for me to imagine that he was only one half of a soul. So I put my question to him: "Do angels have twin souls?" The reply that came clearly was, "They split when they incarnate in order to enter fully into the human condition." The implication I got from that response was that, for angels to be best able to give help on Earth, they need to experience the pain and the joys of love in exactly the same way as we humans do. Please note that I am not categorically stating a case, but simply recounting my experience.

A week or so later I went to see Donna in her own home, where I also had the privilege of making the acquaintance of Barney the rabbit, her most cherished companion who lives with her like a housecat would. I told her about the reply I had been given in meditation, and she said it seemed to make a great deal of sense. What she had already told me about Tom when she came for the regression fit my concept of a twin soul exactly, and when we met the second time I asked a bit more about their relationship. Donna had met Tom's girlfriend when he had sent her to Donna for a massage. After meeting, Donna did not feel that she and Tom were ideally suited, so I wondered whether there was any chance of Tom leaving her for Donna. She replied, however, that shortly after our previous meeting, she had heard from a mutual friend that the girlfriend was now pregnant, so this information had enabled her to "put the whole thing to bed"—especially since she believed that Tom and his partner did really love each other.

Also, since the regression we did, Donna had reflected more upon the situation and she appreciated that Tom had come into her life in order to help her through a time of crisis. She had told him in detail about her problems, and he had been really strong for her throughout it all, being always at the end of the phone for her and also sending her text messages several times a day. She said that Tom had offered her sympathy, understanding, and support in a way that absolutely no one else could have done. They had commented to one another about the feeling they both instantly had of already knowing and understanding each other totally. Even though he has never given any thought to questions such as reincarnation, he said to her, "We have a strange connection. I feel as though I've known you all my life." Now that she was over the crisis period, they were no longer in touch, but Donna said that the knowledge she had gained from the regression—the realization that they were one and the same being and would inevitably come together again in due course—helped her to accept the situation and to get on with her own life of helping others.

Tom is a couple years younger than Donna, and they are both very loving, caring, generous people. She said that she felt whole and complete when she was with him. They are also both very independent, and they both shine when they go out and socialize. They like the same type of music, and are both keen to travel. His family background is, however, more stable and easier than hers, and she said that he grounded her. Donna then commented, "He's kind of like the stable side of me. I'm the flighty side—always wanting to move house or jobs—whereas he's down to earth, wants to buy a house and so on."

We met in November, and Donna was anticipating spending what she knew would be her last Christmas with her beloved grandmother. Her grandfather, too, was coming up on eighty, and she felt sure that he would not survive her grandmother by very long. So that would leave her free to go and work abroad, and her mother was coming to terms with the idea. She said that apart from her grandparents, only Barney was holding her in England at the present time. She had once had a fortnight's holiday in Gambia and had not wanted to come home again, but now she was looking at possibilities in Uganda or Rwanda. She had a strong feeling that she would like to help both children and chimpanzees in East Africa.

On the other hand, Donna had recently met a man who wanted to go and work in Cape Town. At that moment, the relationship was a casual one, but she did not rule out the possibility of it developing further. Alternatively, she said, he could simply be yet another person that she had to help. "People come into my life quickly and then leave equally quickly as soon as they are mended," she commented. Then she added, "At least it has the advantage that they distract me from thinking too much about Tom!"

Donna also told me various other very interesting things about her present life. She is clairvoyant and often makes accurate predictions (though she cannot do this for herself or those closest to her). When people come to the clinic where she offers massage, she feels inside herself exactly where in their body they are in pain. She uses touch, and can identify allergies, or tell if someone is ambitious. People of all ages come to her for treatment, and she knows intuitively when she needs to give them something more than what they are asking for. She dreams a great deal, and all her dreams are about helping people.

After 9/11, Donna did not sleep for a week because her house was completely full of souls needing to be rescued. Yet she says that she did not get tired at all! A few months later, a little boy who had died on 9/11 came back to thank her, and he told her that they had all crossed over and were now okay. (My teacher, Dr. Roger Woolger, who lives in New York State, was also told by clairvoyants in the United States, a few months after 9/11, that a great deal of work had been done to help the victims and that there was no longer any residue of trapped souls in New York.)

Though she is aware of not belonging anywhere on Earth, Donna feels particularly alien to England, despite the fact that she remembers places here where she has lived in previous lives. She finds the English too self-absorbed, and she says that her clients are always too busy, that they forget to love and do not have any family time. She feels drawn to the simpler life of Mother Nature such as can be found in Africa. She worries that society in England is changing rapidly and that there is "nothing left of life apart from paying bills." She herself comes up against it every day in her work, saying that people take from the therapist without giving thought to what they are taking. She believes that people are no longer appreciative of what they have, that there is more selfishness nowadays, and that there are more extramarital affairs. She finds that those of her clients who are compassionate feel drained, while the rest do not trust or respect their partners.

In conclusion, Donna said to me that honesty was rare in the younger generation; "Wartime made the older generation honest." And these, please note, are not the words of a fifty- or sixty-year-old, but a young girl of twenty-eight. Is it so hard to believe that incarnate angels are at present walking this Earth?

Twin Souls in History

The supreme state of human love is . . .
the unity of one soul in two bodies.
—SRI AUROBINDO

Since reuniting with their other half is everyone's destiny, it makes sense when we find that some of the noblest souls who have ever graced this Earth lived in the company of their twin soul. Joudry and Pressman[52] write about a number of famous couples, including the poets Elizabeth Barrett and Robert Browning, the great scientists Pierre and Marie Curie, protegée and mentor Héloise and Abélard, and the Indian mystic Sri Aurobindo and his spiritual partner,

---

52.   Joudry and Pressman, *Twin Souls*.

who was known as "The Mother." We could possibly refer to the latter two as avatars, which means "divine descent," for many Hindus believe that this couple were an incarnation of the Father and Mother aspects of God: Krishna and Mahakali.

Many people who were brought up in the Western Christian tradition see Jesus and Mary Magdalen as twin souls (as I do—here again I recommend Tom Kenyon and Judi Sion's book[53]; and also note the suppressed Gospel of Philip, which states that Mary Magdalen was the one Jesus loved the most and that he often kissed her on the mouth). The well-known Christian writer C. S. Lewis,[54] who was a Cambridge professor, married his American secretary at the age of fifty-eight so that she could remain in England following her divorce. The moving story of the love that developed between them once she had become terminally ill is told in the movie *Shadowlands*. Richard Webster[55] describes this couple as "soul mates," but I believe them to be twin souls.

The American author Elizabeth Clare Prophet was married to her twin soul, Mark Prophet, who was twenty years her senior. Both were prolific writers, and one of her books

53.   Kenyon and Sion, *The Magdalen Manuscript*.

54.   C. S. Lewis is best known for his book *The Screwtape Letters* and for *The Lion, the Witch and the Wardrobe* and the other children's tales of Narnia.

55.   Webster, *Soul Mates*.

is a little one entitled *Soul Mates and Twin Flames*.[56] In this she recounts how when, as a young girl of eighteen, she was searching for God and asking him to send her spiritual teacher to her, he sent Mark, who quickly recognized her as his twin soul. Being more concerned about finding her teacher than about entering into a relationship with a man, Elizabeth Clare asked God to confirm what Mark was telling her. She got her answer when she looked into a mirror and saw not her own reflection but an image of Mark Prophet! Then she realized that in finding her teacher she had also met her twin flame, but during their ten years together, the teaching was by no means one-sided. They founded a church and worked prodigiously together, but sadly Mark died of a massive stroke at the age of fifty-five.

But we have already seen that not all twin-flame relationships are fortuitous. Elizabeth Clare Prophet begins her book with an account of the tragic story of the film stars Jeanette MacDonald and Nelson Eddy, whom she describes as having been "trapped in the net of karma." Jeanette ruined both their lives by putting her career before love. Another film-star couple who must be at least equally renowned is Elizabeth Taylor and Richard Burton. After the famous clairvoyant Lilla Bek had told me that she believed these two to be twin souls, I looked into their history and what I found appeared to me to confirm Lilla's view.

---

56.   Elizabeth Clare Prophet, *Soul Mates and Twin Flames—The Spiritual Dimension of Love and Relationships* (Gardiner, MT: Summit University Press, 1999).

Elizabeth Taylor and Richard Burton

Renowned for a long time as the most beautiful woman in the world, Elizabeth Taylor was born in 1932, in London, to American parents. She was an only child, and she suffered from her earliest years from an overly doting mother, who also pushed her excessively, went everywhere with her, and, when Elizabeth was a teenager, always answered the questions put to the young actress by other people. She received her first movie contract at the age of nine, and she made the transition from child to adult Hollywood star very easily, first achieving prominence in *National Velvet*. Nominated for Academy Awards several years in a row, she finally achieved one in 1960 for *Butterfield 8*. Her second Academy Award, in 1966, was for *Who's Afraid of Virginia Woolf?* When *Cleopatra* was filmed in 1963, she became the first movie actress ever to be paid a million dollars.

Few people in history have been the recipient of such adoration from the general public, the target of such ridicule, or the subject of so much gossip. Much of Elizabeth Taylor's life has been characterized by constant battles with drugs, bad health, and weight problems, but it must certainly be her love life that has brought her the most fame. Her first marriage, at seventeen, was to Nicky Hilton, and this was very short-lived. She was then married to Michael Wilding from 1952 to 1957, and soon after that union ended she married Mike Todd, who died in a plane crash the following year. Taylor was hit very hard by Mike's death, but became, not long afterward, the "other woman" in the breakup of singer Eddie Fisher and actress Debbie Reynolds. She subsequently left Fisher in 1964 to marry Richard Burton. This first marriage of the couple lasted ten years (her record). After their divorce in 1974 they remarried the following year, but their second marriage only lasted for one year. Elizabeth was then married to Senator John Warner from 1976 to 1982, and her final marriage was to Larry Fortensky, a younger man, in 1991.

In 1981, when the movie offers had temporarily dried up, Elizabeth turned to the stage. In 1983, she and Richard came together again on Broadway to co-star in *Private Lives*, and she also made some appearances on television. After that there were a few more movies (for instance, *The Flintstones* in 1994). In 2001, she starred in the TV movie *These Old Broads*, and she retired from acting in 2003 after starring in more than seventy movies. But these are not Elizabeth Taylor's only achievements. She was awarded the French *Légion d'honneur* in 1987, and in 2000 the DBE (Dame of the British Empire); and following the death of her close friend Rock Hudson, she became a leader in the battle against AIDS. Thanks to her noble work in that field, she won the Jean Hersholt Humanitarian Award in 1993.

Superficially, Richard Burton's background has little in common with Dame Elizabeth's, since he was born (in 1925) the twelfth of thirteen children, into a poor family in South Wales; but upon closer inspection, the common features so prevalent in twin souls are clearly present. Besides achieving early success, they both had issues stemming from both of their parents. Elizabeth's father was a shadowy figure to her, while Richard's, who was a miner named Jenkins, was an alcoholic. Their maternal relationships were strained in entirely different ways. Taylor's rift with her mother took time to build up, eventually erupted when Elizabeth found her mother's possessiveness and dominance unbearable (and was ultimately healed). Conversely, Burton barely knew his mother, who died while giving birth two weeks before Richard's second birthday, and he was initially taken in by his eldest sister, Cecilia, who had recently married.

Later Richard was sent to live with an aunt in Port Talbot, where he rapidly became prone to addictions. By the age of eight he had developed a taste for beer, cigarettes, and rebellion—and, since his foster parents did not like his habits, he also became an accomplished liar. This last vice, together with his renowned voice, has been seen as an asset to his natural talent for acting!

Since the family was so poor, Richard was forced to leave school early to start work, despite his obviously high intelligence. One of his teachers, however—Philip Burton—came to his rescue in 1943 by taking him to live with him and sending him back to school. Just as Elizabeth's mother had had her own ambitions as an actress thwarted by her marriage, and transferred them totally and relentlessly to her daughter, so Philip Burton, recognizing Richard's innate talent, transferred his ambitions as an actor onto the boy—going so far as to make himself his legal guardian. The fact that Richard legally changed his name by deed poll from Jenkins to Burton is indicative of the strength of the bond between them.

From high school, Richard went to Oxford University for six months, intending to return and complete his degree after his stint in the Army, but this ambition was never achieved. (He later earned a place at Exeter College as an Air Force cadet, which obligated him to military service afterward, serving in the RAF from 1944 to 1947.) Nevertheless, during his brief period at Oxford, he made an instant success in acting and his rise to fame and wealth was rapid. Before serving with the RAF, he starred as Professor Higgins in a YMCA production of *Pygmalion* and earned fees doing radio parts for the BBC. After his discharge, he acted in London, earning his first film role in *The Last Days of Dolwyn*. On the set, he met his future wife in the young actress Sybil Williams. His first leading role was in 1953, in *The Robe*.

Richard and Sybil married in 1949 and had two daughters, Kate born in 1957, and Jessica born in 1960. He was already renowned for his womanizing, which he made no attempt to give up when he got married, yet he was strangely loyal to Sybil until his marriage to Elizabeth. The first time that they met, Richard failed to attract Elizabeth's attention, and the affair began with the filming of *Cleopatra* in Italy, when he replaced Stephen Boyd as the co-star. At the time, this movie was the most costly ever produced, and it was fraught with difficulties and hold-ups. The production started off in London, but that venue proved too expensive (as well as too wet!). Another notable delay in London was the result of Elizabeth falling so seriously ill that she needed a life-saving tracheotomy.

After Elizabeth and Richard had both gone to film in Italy, their affair lost little time in taking off, and the scandal was soon big news in the press. Richard, however, left Italy to return to his family when his younger daughter was diagnosed as autistic. Elizabeth then took an overdose, which had the desired effect of getting Richard to run straight back to her.

Despite Elizabeth's reputation as a "wrecker of marriages" and Richard's habitual lack of conscience about his infidelities, they both made a sincere effort to return to their respective spouses after the filming of *Cleopatra*. However, they both owned homes in Switzerland, so proximity proved too much for their willpower. Sybil finally agreed to a divorce in 1963.

When they were living together, Elizabeth and Richard were so possessive of each other that he gave up womanizing. However, his addictive nature was so strong that as a replacement for the extramarital affairs, he took to his other old friend: the bottle. After the first divorce from Elizabeth, Richard started drying out, but this was wrecked by a six-month affair with Princess Elizabeth of Yugoslavia. Throughout it all he never lost touch with Elizabeth, and they remarried in Botswana. In 1976, he divorced Elizabeth the second time in order to marry fashion model Susan Hunt, but she divorced him in 1982 after having failed to keep him dry. Later that year he got together with his production assistant,

Sally Hay, and in 1984 that couple had a six-month break together in Haiti. One more movie was finished in 1984, but Richard failed to finish *Wild Geese II* later that year when he died from a cerebral hemorrhage in Geneva. He was buried in Céligny, near Geneva.

In the movie, Cleopatra had obviously recognized Mark Anthony as her twin soul when she had first set eyes on him at the tender age of about twelve, and he told her too that he had been in love with her even when she had been married to Cesar. This was played out in real life: Richard's fortieth birthday present to Elizabeth was a $50,000 heart-shaped diamond inscribed with a promise of everlasting love—a promise that he kept despite his two subsequent marriages. When they separated, no one believed that it would be permanent, and David Jenkins, one of Richard's brothers, says in the biography that he wrote, "More than once Richard told me, in the confidential small hours, 'If I live to be a hundred, I'll always love that woman.'" During the time that Richard was with Susan Hunt, Elizabeth's telephone calls to him never ceased completely; and when older brother David Jenkins showed Sally, Richard's last wife, a magazine article saying that Elizabeth had been admitted to a Los Angeles clinic for treatment and drying out, she begged him not to show it to Richard, "or we shall be bloody flying out to see her." It was only Sally's feelings that kept Elizabeth away from Richard's funeral in Céligny, and she turned up at the graveside a couple of days later. His family gave her a warm welcome soon afterward in Wales, and Sally was put off at seeing her seated among them at the memorial service in London.

While Richard is often considered the greater actor of the two (with his signature baritone voice and range of roles), most people felt that Elizabeth's performances were enhanced by his presence. Off camera, while she was never an intellectual or a great woman of literature, under his influence she developed a liking for poetry. Like other twin souls I have studied, they were opposites in many ways—he punctilious, she slovenly and invariably late for everything— and living together had the probably inevitable effect of intensifying the many flaws that they shared.

So, sad though it is that Elizabeth and Richard failed to make it together properly this time around, it is on the other hand hardly surprising in the case of a couple so plagued by human frailty. Not only did they both suffer from addictions to sex, alcohol, and other temptations of the flesh, but he, despite his wealth and fame, could not bear it if she was earning more than he was, or if her name was put before his on the posters advertising one of their movies. Only when twin souls both have spiritual ideals, and always put the interests of their partner before their own, can their marriage be one of unison and harmony. Elizabeth and Richard both craved fame and wealth above all else, becoming victims of these once they had achieved them. But, as Melvyn Bragg puts it in his biography entitled *Rich*, "It is as easy to dismiss her as appearing spoilt, greedy, selfish, and mean as it is to dismiss Burton as seeming boastful, faithless, a poseur, and a drunk. Far too easy. For we must recognise that these two people were subject to seductive and ravishing opportunities, to strains beyond the comprehension of most, to temptations of the flesh, the press, the purse . . . " Bragg in fact—probably without fully realizing the implications of the phrase—even says in his biography of Burton: "Strange, in some ways unreal creatures, Burton and Taylor recognized twin souls."

However, we need never despair of anyone. Burton's drinking problem curtailed his life shortly before the age of sixty, but hopefully he will have learned from that as well as from his other weaknesses and be able to overcome at least some of these defects in his next lifetime. As for Dame Elizabeth, it is said that suffering is our greatest teacher. She has had a good share of that, but has clearly learned from it. Though she cast off most of her husbands as easily as she did her dresses, the divorce from Richard made her suffer bitterly. She said, "I don't want to be that much in love ever again. I don't want to give as much of myself. It hurts. I didn't reserve anything. I gave everything away . . . my soul, my being, everything . . . and it got bruised and hurt."[57] Mike Todd's tragic death affected her very severely too and, according to an article in the magazine *Hello,*[58] she met him in a near-death experience that she had just prior to receiving brain surgery. Apparently he told her that she was

---

57.   Kitty Kelley, *Elizabeth Taylor: The Last Star* (New York: Dell, 1981).

58.   *Hello,* 22 March 1997.

to carry on living, and her response, quoted in the magazine article, was, "And I *have* lived. If the knife slips while I am on the operating table tomorrow and I never wake up again, I'll die knowing I've had an extraordinary life." People who have NDEs (near death experiences) always appear to return to the world with increased faith, and Elizabeth said after hers, "The power of love is a gift from God . . . It's so easy to forget that life is a gift from God." The AIDS-related death of her friend Rock Hudson was also a great learning experience for her, and the article in *Hello*, describing her courageous determination to win the fight for life, said that she postponed the brain operation in order to be present at her sixty-fifth birthday fundraising show for the AIDS Foundation. An article in another magazine of the same date[59] claims that she "now shuns Hollywood parties and the glittering celebrity circuit in favour of fundraising." At the time of my finishing this chapter, she has just celebrated her seventy-fifth birthday. My local paper, (the *Shropshire Star*) had a photograph of her arriving at her party in a wheelchair, dressed in white and "dripping in luxurious gems," and described her as appearing to "be in better health than she has in quite a few years." Labelling her as "one of Tinseltown's most beautiful actresses of all time," it further named her as "still one of the ultimate golden girls of Hollywood." Since twin souls always catch one another up spiritually, her development in recent years will benefit Richard too.

---

59.   *Catholic Life*, March/April 1997.

It appears that she has no intention of a ninth marriage, so I wish them both the very best for the future.

Edgar Cayce and Gladys Davis

Edgar Cayce's quite remarkable life has been very well documented by various American authors,[60] so there is no need for me to write about it at length. He was a strong Christian from the deep South, who from a very early age took to reading the Bible right through once a year, but failed to realize his ambition of becoming an ordained minister. On leaving school, he worked in a bookshop, and later he became a successful photographer, though he never earned very much money from that profession. He fell in love with Gertrude Evans when he was only eighteen and she was only fifteen, and they had a blissfully happy marriage despite constant poverty and the other difficulties caused by the challenges of his work. They had three sons, though the middle one died as a baby.

Cayce found while he was still at school that he could learn everything in his books by sleeping with them underneath his pillow. Later he developed the amazing ability to put himself into trance and let spirit speak through him to give prescriptions for people suffering from a wide variety of ailments. These prescriptions became known as "readings."

---

60. For instance, Bro, *A Seer Out of Season*; Thomas Sugrue, *There is a River* (Virginia Beach, VA: ARE Press, 1997); Gina Cerminara, *Many Mansions* (Virginia Beach, VA: ARE Press, 1990); and Jess Stearn, *Edgar Cayce: The Sleeping Prophet* (Virginia Beach, VA: ARE Press, 1989).

Cayce never knew what he had said until after he woke up and it was all reported to him. He had no medical training whatsoever, yet doctors made use of his help for their most difficult cases, and his reputation gradually spread throughout the world. When the work grew too much for Cayce and Gertrude to cope with on their own, he hired as his secretary a very young woman named Gladys Davis, who came and lived with the family. From the time she was first hired until his death, she recorded all his readings meticulously.

One day a man called Lammers asked for a reading. When Cayce awakened, Lammers told him that the spirit speaking through the seer had given as the main influence on Lammers the fact that he had been a monk in a previous life. Learning that, while in a trance, he had suggested a previous life or incarnation, the religious Cayce was at first more than a little shocked. Gradually, however, through further readings made not only for clients but also for himself and his family, he worked out a whole philosophy of reincarnation that was in total accordance with his mainstream Christianity. Cayce also learned about twinsoulship though these readings, and gained the knowledge that Gertrude and he were companion soul mates while Gladys was his twin soul. The fact that they were all able to work so well as a trio, despite Gladys and Cayce's mutual feelings of attraction, is surely an indication of their high level of spiritual development.

Although the bulk of the thousands of readings that Cayce made over many years were medical ones, after the first "shocking" reading he made for Lammers, he also gradually became much sought after for the "life readings," which he made from reading the Akashic Records. When Cayce gave someone a life reading, he selected from his or her etheric records the previous lives that had the most bearing upon the present one, and people found this useful for such things as correcting past mistakes or rediscovering latent talents.

In *A Seer Out of Season*,[61] Harmon Bro gives a detailed account of the most relevant of Cayce's own past lives, so I will summarize them here. In ancient Egypt, Cayce was a powerful priest and leader named Ra Ta, who was influential in healing and interested in perfecting the body. He also pioneered good family life made with partners of choice rather than arranged marriages, aiming to set an example of this in his own marriage. However, a group of enemies plotted his downfall by persuading a beautiful dancer named Isris to seduce him, and she suggested to Ra Ta that they could between them create a "perfect child." The fruit of their liaison was a daughter named Iso. Although Isris eventually replaced Ra Ta's wife, she was the favorite of the Egyptian Young King, and so he banished Ra Ta to what is now Libya. He kept Iso with him, and she died in loneliness at the age of four. The readings made clear that Iso was now Gladys Davis (Cayce's secretary and twin soul), while Isris was now his wife Gertrude. The Young King was Gertrude's twin soul and now their older son, Hugh Lynn.

---

61. Bro, *A Seer Out of Season*.

In a much later life in France, Gladys (then named Gra-
cia) had a liaison with the English Duke of York, and got
banished to a convent after her lover abandoned her. This
time the tables were turned and Cayce, who was *her* son,
died at the age of five. Bro recounts that Cayce's least flawed
past life was as a Persian leader named Uhjltd in about 8000
BCE. That time Gladys (then Ilya) was his lover and queen,
and their child Zend was said to be an earlier incarnation
of Jesus.

Another feature of the Cayce readings was prophecy.
Among many other things, he prophesied with accuracy
both the world wars and the precise year of the first moon
landing, as well as much of the flooding, earthquakes, and so
on of recent years. (Some of the predicted natural disasters
have occurred while others have not, but I have great faith in
the power of prayer, and Sai Baba says that one of the things
for which he has come is to avert much of the catastrophe.)
Cayce also predicted his own return to Earth in 1998, in
which case he must already be at least ten years old. I wonder if he will marry Gertrude, Gladys, or someone else this
time around. I am putting my own money on Gladys!

Joan Grant and Esmond

Joan Grant, who was born in England in 1907 and died in
February 1989, lived from an early age on Hayling Island off
the south coast of England, and is well known for her "novels," which are in fact taken from what she called "far memory." Her mother was psychic, and Joan herself had as a very

young child numerous past-life memories—so much so that she resented finding herself "trapped in a baby's body." The beach and the sound of the sea at Hayling Island caused her to remember being a Greek boy training to be a runner on a hotter, brighter shore. When her nanny overheard her telling the garden boy that she used to be a "red Indian," she was severely reprimanded. Gradually she learned to keep quiet about her past, assuming that, like going to the bathroom, it was something everyone did but no one talked about. Only years later did she come to realize that not everybody had such memories.

Joan was also told as a child that little girls who swore got struck by lightning. Always having a desire for empirical evidence, she promptly disproved this to herself by going out on to the beach in a thunderstorm and yelling every swear word that she had ever heard at the top of her voice!

Thanks to a signing session of my first book[62] at the shop where I sometimes practiced my therapy, I made friends with a delightful couple called Leonard and Miriam, who got to know Joan well during the 1950s and 1960s. Children who are very psychic often see spirits as though they were quite solid, and Miriam recalls Joan talking about her difficult childhood, when she was unable to distinguish between people around her who were incarnate and those who were not.

Joan's earliest months were spent in her grandmother's house, near to the London Zoo. She was extremely fond of

---

62.   Merivale, *Karmic Release*.

this grandmother, Jennie, and after her death Jennie came regularly to visit Joan in her bedroom on Hayling Island, sometimes playing the piano for her. Later Joan got engaged but, being always very prone to psychic dreams, she realized that she was not at all in love with her fiancé after meeting Esmond, who (though she never used the term herself) is clearly her twin soul, in some of her dreams. She consequently incurred her parents' wrath by breaking off the engagement. Fortunately, she and Esmond met in the flesh on a skiing trip soon after the wedding had been called off. Esmond stared at Joan for a long time before saying, "It really is you. I have been dreaming with you for nearly two years. Do you recognize me too?" They got engaged almost immediately, but tragically, before a wedding could be arranged, Esmond accidentally killed himself while cleaning his shotgun. The fact that Joan subsequently married three times may well be an indication of how knowing one's twin soul can make it difficult for people to sustain another satisfactory relationship.

In view of Joan Grant's own life history, it is hardly surprising that the twin-soul theme is strong in her books. Her life as Joan is paralleled by that of the Egyptian Ra-ab Hotep, who also first met his twin flame, Meri, in dreams. In *Eyes of Horus,* Ra-ab Hotep, son of the Nomarch of Oryx, took longer than Joan did to meet his twin in the flesh, and while he was waiting, he told his father that the girl he had lined up for him was a stranger and that he hoped to meet the girl of his dreams. Meri, who described the two of them as "two petals of the same flower," assured him that when they did meet in the flesh, he would recognize her even if she was fat and ugly. In fact, she turned out be slim and beautiful, and their life as a married couple is a superb example of twin souls coming together in order to work for good.

Life as Carola powerfully describes a brief Italian life very full of tragedies and, though the book does not actually say so, it is clear that Carola's lover Alcestes is the same soul as Esmond. In chapter two I mentioned the cousins Raki and Piyanah of *Scarlet Feather*, and this book is simply bursting with beautiful definitions of twinsoulship. When they were young children, Piyanah's mother sometimes took them to sleep in the mountains when it was hot and, sleeping under the stars, she would tell them how "each star was a torch set in the sky by someone who had entered the land beyond the Sunset," and how "the larger ones were two torches that belonged to two people who loved each other very much, so we knew there would only be one new star when Raki and I were dead." When Piyanah is going through an endurance test she says, "Because of Raki I am stronger than the cold! He is my sun, my fire, my warmth; for love is stronger than cold, and separation and darkness . . . The light and heat that were part of Raki soaked into me and gave me my strength." Then later, during their marriage ceremony, the elder, Na-ka-chek, says, "Because you loved each other, you were able to love yourselves. Because you loved yourselves, you knew yourselves . . . To this love shall you pledge your oath . . . and each day you will say 'I love us both, the male and the female: I love myself, the male and the female: and with eyes that are open to that love will I see others, the male and the female' . . . This oath shall endure after your bodies return to dust . . . Raki and Piyanah are of one spirit on the other side of the water." Finally, nearer the end of the book, Piyanah says, "I tried to explain that I was a very ordinary woman, who had no magic except that she belonged to a tribe who recognized that man and woman are the right eye and the left eye, the left hand and the right hand, the left foot and the right foot, of a third, who is man and woman, and so greater than either."

Despite her marital difficulties, Leslie Grant, Joan's first husband, was clearly an important part of Joan's Life Plan because he was very supportive of her extraordinary psychic work. Her second husband was Charles Beatty (a nephew of Admiral Beatty of First World War fame), and they lived at Trelydan Hall near Welshpool. A client of mine put me in touch by e-mail with her friend Glenys, who told me, "My association with Joan goes back to my childhood in Wales. As a child I remember her as a very kind and generous person, though I was not aware of her far memory, etc., at that time. My father, who was a skilled craftsman with wood, worked on many projects with Joan and Charles at Trelydan. Sometime in the 1950s the marriage broke up and they both went their separate ways."

Joan's third marriage, however, to the distinguished psychiatrist Denys Kelsey, lasted until near the time of her death and they did a great deal of valuable work together. Glenys further told me, "My father was eventually asked to go to France to supervise a conversion to a house Joan and Denys had aquired in Collonges in the Lot valley. I was fortunate to stay with them at this time. If only my father were alive, he would be able to recount so many incidents, as he was close to Joan and admired her greatly. My last telephone conversation with Joan Grant was in the 1980s after my father died. She loved to talk of her time living at Trelydan Hall and of the people she had known in those days. Somewhere there is a wooden box made by my father as a present to Joan; it has a marquetry picture on it, identical to the dust cover of *Winged Pharoh*. Perhaps Gillian has it." (Unfortunately Joan's daughter, Gillian, is now also dead. She married the sculptor David Wynne; and Glenys' parents eventually bought the Dower House at Trelydan Hall, which, Glenys says, had already changed hands several times after Joan and Charles had sold it.)

My friend Miriam told me that, soon after they had first met, Denys took Joan to a three-day conference of psychiatrists. When it was over, she said to him, "You may want to end our association if I tell you this, but I have never heard so much nonsense in my whole life!" The marriage was nevertheless successful for many years, and they were pioneers together in past-life regression therapy,[63] which is how Leonard and Miriam first met Denys and Joan.

---

63. See Joan Grant and Denys Kelsey, *Many Lifetimes* (Columbus, OH: Ariel Press, 1997).

Leonard explained to me that, after they had just moved to Dorset in about 1958 and he was going through a difficult patch, someone sent him to a healer, who in turn sent him to a psychiatrist. The psychiatrist said that he was unable to help him, and advised him to go to Joan Grant and her husband for therapy. Initially Leonard's sessions were performed by the couple jointly, but later Denys worked with him on his own. Leonard says that, when he and Denys disagreed about something that had occurred either during a regression or their subsequent discussions, Denys would always consult Joan about it, and Joan usually said that Leonard was right!

Like Anne and Daniel Meurois-Givaudan, twin souls and joint authors of numerous books in French, Joan Grant obtained the information for her stories by reading the Akashic Records while out of her body. In Joan's case this evolved naturally from the practice of psychometry,[64] which she had embarked upon with Leslie's encouragement. Her first book, *Winged Pharaoh,* which is still regarded as her masterpiece, was considered controversial when published in 1937, but its material has since been validated by archeologists and historians. Leonard told me of an "unfortunate question" that he had once had the temerity to ask Joan: whether *Winged Pharaoh* had been edited. Joan, who was

---

64. Psychometry consists of holding an object and tuning in psychically to its history and that of its owner or previous owner(s). Joan Grant developed this ability to an exceptionally high degree.

quite upset at the idea, replied, "Not a word," and to prove it she produced her original manuscript! She also wrote about further lives in Egypt, and she always insisted that she never did any research and that she had previously known nothing about Egypt on the conscious level. Yet Egyptologists have been unable to fault her writing.

Miriam recounts an interesting story of an encounter that Joan had with another of her past-life acquaintances. During the Second World War, when people in power in Britain were concerned about Hitler's belief in astrology, Joan was working undercover to get a line on it. She was living in Albany, near London, and one evening during the Blitz, Joan was invited to a party of well-to-do people. She had an aversion to everything to do with the church and so, when she noticed another of the guests who was clearly a cleric, she immediately averted her gaze. Later, however, she looked at him again and decided that he looked familiar as well as rather nice. They got to talking, he volunteered to walk her home, and she invited him in for a drink in her apartment. When they stopped at a turn in the stairs, Joan looked at him and suddenly exclaimed, "You were my mentor in Egypt!" to which he replied, "I wondered how long it would take you to recognize me." Naturally, Joan then asked this man (who was the brother of George Bell, then Bishop of Chichester) why he had chosen a career as a cleric, and he replied that he had gone into the Church with the aim of converting people to ideas such as reincarnation. Needless to say, he had little success, but he and Joan remained good friends.

Leonard and Miriam lost touch with Joan and Denys when they moved to France in the 1960s, but they introduced me to their friend Elizabeth, who turned out to live even closer to me than they do. Elizabeth helped care for Joan after she had suffered a couple of strokes, while Denys was convalescing following a heart attack. Their friendship began when she went to Denys for therapy because, after years of caring for her invalid parents, after their death she was at a loss as to what to do next, and was also depressed at being repeatedly unlucky while house-hunting. Since her present life offered no clues to the root of her problems, Denys and she needed to look to the past, and there Elizabeth found out that most of her troubles were due to the bad habit of putting things off. She comments that lessons are likely to be repeated in successive lives until they are finally learned! Unlike Leonard, Elizabeth was unable to experience the couple working together since Joan was by then bedridden from her stroke, but her opinion of Denys' work is very high, and she went on going to see him after her therapy was complete. He taught Elizabeth some useful techniques for her work in victim support. She says that while Joan worked on inspiration and experience, Denys was more methodical. He had a great gift for getting at the root of a problem, but he was also intuitive and would live through a regression with the client.

Elizabeth had already had many interesting conversations with Joan before she volunteered to look after her. She says that the strokes had not affected her speech, and that she was still quite a formidable, as well as a fascinating, character. She talked endlessly to Elizabeth about people she had known, and she told her that she had always been the one who "bolted from her marriages." Elizabeth finds it a trifle strange that, though Joan's mother was also extremely psychic, she never really understood her youngest daughter, nor appreciated her quite extraordinary gifts. Elizabeth comments that a woman named Daisy, whom Joan identified as having been her mother when she was Sekeeta in Egypt (see *Winged Pharaoh*), was more of a mother to her in this life than was her own mother. It was to Daisy's home that Joan would flee for refuge when in trouble with her family, and her ashes are buried there, at her own request.

Denys, who was Dio the architect in *Winged Pharaoh*, was ten years younger than Joan in their most recent life, and he died in 2005. He did a good job of pulling her through her strokes, but when he was no longer able to care for her himself, there was, alas, irretrievable breakdown in their relationship. When they parted, her daughter Gillian moved Joan into a nursing home in Wimbledon that was staffed largely by Irish Catholics. Gillian and her husband, the sculptor David Wynne, and their four children, lived close by, and were often in and out. Elizabeth came when she could, and she also put Joan in touch with a London friend who shared her beliefs and could visit fairly frequently. Joan suffered from arteritis and found it very difficult to live with her limitations and disabilities, but during her last talks with Elizabeth, she had come to terms with them. She wanted news of Denys, as he did of her, and each wanted the other to know that there was no resentment, just a sadness that things had ended the way they had. Elizabeth, who believes that the divorce proceedings were not quite complete when Joan died, felt that the serious health concerns on both sides had much to do with their separation. She hopes that all the help they had been, both to each other and to others, over the years will stand them in good stead on the next plane of existence. Denys told Elizabeth that, though he would like to continue to be in Joan's orbit in a future life, he would not want to be married to her again!

Denys further told Elizabeth that Joan had immense healing powers, which she would use unstintingly when the need arose, although it could leave her drained. Elizabeth surmised that Joan had honed this gift through many lives, often at great personal cost. Joan believed that the physical body should be one's obedient servant, demanded a great deal of her own body, and found life hard when it could no longer do as she wished. Denys and she would always open their doors to anyone in real trouble and sought to heal the whole person. Their house was often home to someone with difficulties, and when Elizabeth was looking after Joan in Denys' absence, one of these acquaintances was a man who could perform the tasks Elizabeth did not have the physical strength to complete.

Denys described both Gillian, Joan's daughter from her first marriage, and Elizabeth as "safety spreaders." Denys, who had four children from a previous marriage, said that

Gillian was the linchpin of the family and very different from her mother, although equally interested in life and healing.

After Joan's death, Denys married Tilly, his secretary, and they moved to Switzerland. Tilly, who is Dutch and multilingual, did a wonderful job of nursing Denys through leukemia. He wrote another book, which, thanks to Tilly's hard work, has recently been published posthumously.[65] And an even more recent book consists of some of Joan's hitherto unpublished writings, edited by her granddaughter, Nicola Bennett, together with two other people.[66]

Joan performed soul-rescue work at night from a remarkably early age, when she was too young to understand exactly what she was doing, and she continued to have extraordinary dreams throughout her life. It is normal for the soul to leave the body during sleep, and the more evolved among us tend to use this time for performing useful work on the other side. The ancient Egyptians (see *Winged Pharaoh* yet again!) trained themselves to remember the work that they did at night, and very often this consisted of helping people who had just died to cross over—a task also performed regularly by shamans. Joan in her last life had clearly not lost the ability that she had had as Sekeeta.

After Esmond's death (which incidentally was not a total shock to her because Jennie, her deceased grandmother, had

---

65. Denys Kelsey, *Now and Then—Reincarnation, Psychiatry and Daily Life*, (Folkstone, UK: Trencavel Press, 2007).

66. Grant, *Speaking from the Heart*.

appeared and told her that she would not see him again),
Joan did not dream about Esmond again for quite a while.
When he did eventually appear to her in sleep—for a single
last time—he took her to another planet, telling her that he
had finished his lives on Earth and that he had had great difficulty in bringing her there.

Only a very old soul could possibly have had such an
amazing life as Joan Grant's, though Miriam, who is very
aware of Joan's frustrations during her final illness, wonders
whether she might need to come back at least once more in
order to better learn acceptance. Who are we to judge as to
when she will be ready to join Esmond on some higher plane,
or on a planet other than those known to us here on Earth?
But I cannot imagine that he has very long to wait for her.

Peter and Eileen Caddy

Even those who have not had the opportunity to visit Findhorn, in the north of Scotland, will surely be familiar with
its name. This world-famous ecological village was founded
by Peter and Eileen Caddy together with Dorothy Maclean.
The latter is still alive, but Peter died in a car crash in 1994,
at the age of seventy-seven, and Eileen at the end of 2006,
at the age of eighty-nine. Long before I read either of their
autobiographies, a clairvoyant of my acquaintance told me
that she believed the Caddys to be twin souls, which I confirmed after finally getting around to reading both these

books.[67] Their fascinating story is an outstanding example of a twin-soul couple coming together for an important reason and subsequently separating for good reasons. Both of their lives were as extraordinary as the story of Findhorn itself, which developed from a single caravan (in which the Caddys lived for several years with three young sons!), and these two books make enthralling, if often harrowing, reading.

"Sun and moon," "chalk and cheese"—this couple is the quintessence of polarity: he the larger-than-life, extremely masculine man, who spent the first half of his working life in the Royal Air Force, where he attained high positions and walked over 2,400 miles in the Himalayas; she the very feminine figure, initially rather shy, under the thumb of her first husband Andrew, and totally absorbed in rearing the five children she bore him, and then, after leaving this family for Peter, very much in his shadow until forced by his departure to stand on her own feet.

Eileen's early life in Alexandria was happy and full of love, but her difficulties began when she was sent to boarding school in Ireland and were compounded by the loss of both her parents by the time she was nineteen. She admits to having married Andrew for security, and his membership of Moral Rearmament, with its very strict code of conduct, caused him to give her a very hard time.

---

67. Eileen Caddy and Liza Hollingshead, *Flight Into Freedom and Beyond: The Autobiography of the Co-Founder of the Findhorn Community* (Forres, Scotland: Findhorn Press, 1988, 2002, 2007). Peter Caddy, *In Perfect Timing* (Forres, Scotland: Findhorn Press, 1995).

Peter's spiritual interests started when he was very young and, despite the ultramasculine image that he maintained throughout his life, he was extraordinarily intuitive and always acted immediately upon his flashes of intuition. One of these flashes caused him to jump into an unsuccessful marriage at an early age, but most of them bore the most amazing fruit. In fact, his first marriage did bear fruit in the form of two children (with whom he sadly lost touch for many years), but his second marriage gave him five years of happiness as well as, he claimed, a great spiritual teacher.

When Peter married his second wife, Sheena, they believed themselves to be twin souls but, after she had realized this to be erroneous, Sheena actually encouraged him to get together with Eileen! Poor Eileen was then subjected to a very strict regimen of spiritual education from Sheena, whom she was forced to look after in Peter's absence, and who treated her very unlovingly despite the fact that Peter had described her as the most loving person he knew.

Peter actually met Eileen through her first husband Andrew. They used to visit while working with the RAF, and he introduced her to esoteric subjects and dazzled her with his learning. They did not fall in love immediately, but Peter's "message from God" that she was his "other half" coincided with Eileen's beginning to pluck up the courage to defy Andrew over such things as wearing makeup and drinking alcohol (which both conflicted with his values instilled by Moral Rearmanant) when they went to parties.

Peter then made the first move, when he insisted on acting as "chaperone" on an occasion when Eileen needed to travel without her family, and then—as is so often the case with twin-soul encounters—things moved very fast. Peter explains: " . . . as it was late, she invited me to spend the night. We were both surprised by what happened then: a tremendous surge of love engulfed us both, overwhelming and uniting us, its intensity amazing us; it was something beyond passion, it came from the source of our beings, and we were able to celebrate it on every level." Eileen lost no time in confessing to her husband Andrew, but he was so angry that he forbade her to see their children again, and soon obtained a court injunction whereby she could have no contact with any of them until they had come of age. She did return very early on for one brief visit, which of course caused intense pain all around, but she knew in the depths of her being that it was God's will that she make her life with Peter. Her oldest child, Jennifer, was only fourteen at the time, so it is easy to imagine the pain that Eileen went through during her years of separation from the five children, and also Jennifer's difficulty in finally reconciling with her mother.

The three sons that Eileen and Peter had together were born in quite quick succession and, before being forced into unemployment and to live in a caravan on what ultimately became the famous site of Findhorn, they worked together in hotel management. This work was very taxing indeed, but extraordinarily successful since it was all done on the basis of God being fully in charge. In fact, this was the way that

Peter lived his entire life: Findhorn was built from the start on faith and trust. Each time that a new venture for it was proposed, the plans were drawn up, the cost was estimated, a request for the funds was sent heavenwards, and then the building materials and so on were all ordered. Invariably the exact sum of money required would somehow or other arrive just in the nick of time, at the very last moment!

Eileen's world-famous messages from God[68] started early on in their relationship and, being so restricted in a caravan with three young children, she gradually formed the habit of spending several hours meditating each night in the toilets that were communal to the whole caravan site. Once the Findhorn community had been firmly established, part of the daily ritual was Eileen's message from God relayed in the Sanctuary each morning. My friend François Reynolds, who is a counselor and a fellow Woolger graduate, has personal experience of life at Findhorn and of these meditations. During 1967–1971 he made visits there every three months and made great friends with the Caddys, whom he says were extraordinarily kind to him. Like many others, his story of how he came to Findhorn is fascinating. He told me that Eileen's daily messages from God were already going out all over the world for some time before she was told to put them into a book, and François was given one of the little leaflets by a friend who had just visited Findhorn. He put

---

68. *God Spoke To Me*, as well as other Eileen Caddy's other books, are published by Findhorn Press, Forres, Scotland.

the leaflet aside until his children had gone to bed, and then he sat down peacefully to read it. As soon as he did this, he noticed that the room was suddenly filled with the most wonderful, strong perfume, and it was this experience that made him realize that he had to go there. During the three years in which he was making regular visits there, François saw the community grow from twenty-four to about one-hundred twenty. He met many interesting people there, including the renowned David Spangler mentioned in the Caddys' autobiographies, and he found that many of them had been drawn to Findhorn by an experience similar to his own.

François explains that there was no traditional ritual or paraphernalia in the Sanctuary: the meditation simply consisted of going quiet inside. Then Eileen would come in and deliver her—or rather God's—message, and it was absolutely certain that what came through her was completely authentic. After receiving the message through Eileen, the community members would go into a longer meditation before sharing their thoughts, and during that time François would always find himself resonating to what Eileen had said. He told me that these morning periods in the Findhorn Sanctuary made him realize that his psyche was bigger than his physical body.

François describes Eileen as "the essence of surrender" and Peter as "the action." For Peter, despite his strong intuitive powers, relied on her channelled guidance, and for a long time never undertook anything new without first obtaining confirmation for it through Eileen. He would talk of the "power of manifestation"—a universal process that he accepted unconditionally—and he always acted on Eileen's guidance immediately. François recalls being at Findhorn when Eileen reported having seen a vision of seven chalet bungalows, and when he was up there again the following summer, these were already built and positioned on the site exactly according to Eileen's description. On this point, Peter said, "It was a perfect partnership."

Yet, despite the community's dependence upon her, the world attention that her messages were drawing, and her evidently strong character, Eileen remained in the background for a long time, never wanting to speak in public. Peter was ever the outgoing, confident one, receiving more and more invitations to speak in many different countries, while she was always in his shadow.

Major change dated from the night in which God told Eileen that the members of the Findhorn community had come of age and should therefore no longer depend upon her guidance with daily messages, but stand on their own feet spiritually. This was to affect Peter as well, since she was told that he too must stop asking for her guidance. He did not accept this news at all easily, arguing that all he ever asked for was "confirmation," but she stood firm in the instructions that she believed to have come directly from God. This proved to be the beginning of the breakdown between them.

In her autobiography, Eileen recounts how, in 1974, when the first cracks were appearing in their relationship, she had a vision. She says: "I was taken to the beginnings of time when humans were etheric beings with bodies of light. Peter and I were in one light body. Then I saw us split in two and Peter wandered his way and I wandered mine." This echoes all the quotations that I gave earlier. Then Eileen goes on to say, "My being became denser and denser and lived through lifetime after lifetime of tremendous suffering, pain, and anguish. I wandered searching for something I had lost, but I did not know what it was. I was a lost soul. Peter and I may have been brought together from time to time, but we did not recognize each other."

The first really concrete event to effect a real deterioration in their relationship was Peter's falling in love with a young Swedish girl who had joined the community. Although that particular relationship was never consummated, it caused Eileen immense pain—a pain which was soon increased still further when Peter went off to Hawai with a woman named Shari. That affair was fairly short-lived, yet it heralded not only his and Eileen's separation, but also his departure from Findhorn. Eileen's suffering was indescribable (though she did in fact describe it herself, and I strongly recommend a reading of her autobiography). She felt rejected and worthless, and her pain was most acute when Peter told her—contrary to a previous declaration—that he had never been in love with her.

The clairvoyant who first told me about the Caddys being twin souls was somewhat disparaging of Peter. She said that he had come to her when he was leaving Eileen for another woman (presumably Shari), and had refused to believe her when she told her that it was in fact Eileen who was his twin. Then this clairvoyant told me, "But after that, he left the new woman for somebody else, and then he died!" However, my much more recent reading of Peter's autobiography put a completely different light on it all, and I have to say that I can see God's hand in every aspect of the story.

First of all, a wife nightly forsaking the marriage bed for God would surely put a strain on any relationship, however strong was the husband's own love of God. Also, François comments, she had had a lot of children and was no doubt at that time less switched on to sex than he was. After they separated, Peter went to see a healer called Andrew Watson about an acute pain in his back, and he was told that it was caused by a deep hurt. This echoed what he had previously been told by other sensitives, but he was unable to trace the origin of this hurt until one day, in the Findhorn Sanctuary, he was suddenly overcome by intense sobbing. He then realized that the deep hurt came from the fact that his relationship with Eileen had not been expressed fully on the physical level. On returning to see Andrew Watson, Peter was told to do something to unblock his sexual energy without feeling guilty about it—so he went to Hawaii with Shari.

Apparently, much though Eileen loved Peter, she was not in that life the woman best equipped either to fulfill him sexually or to foster his feminine side. Equally, she needed to develop her masculine side, and this only became possible after their separation. For it was only after she had begun an amazing recovery from the intense pain and hurt that Peter's leaving her had caused that she summoned up the courage to accept speaking invitations and travel the world—not as Peter's shadow, but as a truly remarkable and strong woman. In a channelling performed by a close friend, an entity named John explained to her, "Behind the voice then is a source which is your true nature, which you are seeking to grow into ever more fully. For this reason, the patterns between you and your partner need to be broken and the energies between you dispersed." Eileen's story is an extraordinarily impressive one of total forgiveness which, she explained, was only made possible through her faith in God. She also claims to have found, toward the end of her long life, complete wholeness in herself.

It is clear too that Findhorn was planned on the "other side" and that its foundation depended upon the two of them working together. Concluding the description of her vision about their being twin souls, Eileen said: "Then I was brought into this lifetime and God said, 'Now is the time. I have brought you together to do a very specific work for me. You are to bring universal love to the many. *As one you can do it*'" (my emphasis). This being the case, questions abound about the reason for Peter's departure from Findhorn, but, just as Eileen needed to learn to stand on her own and to develop her masculine side, the community needed to learn independence and to stop relying on Peter, who was such an exceptionally strong character and always wanting to be in on all the action.

Concerning Peter's final departure from Findhorn, this same entity named John channelled, "His personal transformation is important for the community even if he must leave the community to do it. But if he does, then he goes in blessing and in protection, and the community will require your [Eileen's] presence." John also showed an understanding of the couple's twin-soul bond, since he explained, "You will continue to work with him on the inner, for you cannot affect the energies in the community without affecting his energies as well, so closely are they blended. The two of you together—not together as you have been, but as two wholenesses combining to manifest a greater whole—can help the community to place itself in a more stable position."

Peter's departure from Findhorn did not by any means entail severing contact with Eileen. Peter, who was ever kind, understanding, and gentle, did his utmost to avoid hurting her more any more than necessary. They corresponded regularly and, after Eileen's recovery from the separation, she bravely suggested, ten years after he had left, that they go on a speaking tour together. This was, however, not very successful, since he found her new assertiveness difficult to handle, and also, since her communication with God led her to forsake the marriage bed, it hit him very badly when she spoke in public about her nightly meditations in the toilet. A lesson for *his* assertiveness came when he had to give way to her on questions about Findhorn, since she was the one who was still living there! Their concordance after separating— surely another sign of their twinsoulship—became evident to me after reading their autobiographies, one immediately after the other. So often when couples have separated does one hear one story from one partner and a totally different one from the other, but this is not the case at all with Eileen and Peter's accounts.

After Peter's affair with Shari had ended amicably, he acted, at the age of sixty-five, on another, rather strange, "order from God" and married Paula, an American woman half his age. There was no attraction between them, but she simultaneously felt that she had received an order from God to marry Peter *and* to have a child with him. The fruit of this short-lived, not-very-happy liaison was a son named Daniel, with whom Peter apparently developed a much closer relationship than with any of his other children, even though the marriage ended. His last seven years were spent in a very happy marriage to Renata—no doubt a companion soul mate—in her home above Lake Constance in Germany. The fatal accident (in which both Peter's son Daniel and Jeremy Slocombe, Peter's ghost writer, were injured) occurred before his autobiography had been completed, so the last part of the book was written by Renata, who writes movingly about the loving relationship that appears to have brought them both—as total opposites—great happiness. She describes Peter as always seeing with "eyes of light," looking for the good in everybody and everything. Talking of one of the differences between them, she explains that, while she would see both the lighter and the darker parts of a person, he was always determined to see only the light and ignore the rest. He told her, "That is how I built up Find-horn—by looking for a person's talents and strengths, not to what may be lacking. That which you focus on becomes real." What a wonderful message for the world!

Though I have many friends who know it well, I myself have not yet had the opportunity to visit Findhorn, and obviously it is now too late for me to meet either Peter or Eileen in the flesh. However, following an order that I received from spirit while on a weekend led by the English shaman Simon Buxton,[69] I perform shamanic journeying on my own on a regular basis. My main purpose in doing this is "soul rescue"—helping souls who are earthbound to cross over to the other side. This may be either because they are unaware that they are dead or because of an attachment caused by some other reason. But occasionally, I make a shamanic journey with a different motive and so, before writing this section, I decided that I would like to talk to the Caddys themselves. I found them overjoyed at being together, and I am sure that they have completed their lives on Earth. Peter confirmed my notion that Renata was one of his companion soul mates, and said that they had fulfilled each other's needs for human love. He confirmed his visit to my clairvoyant friend when he was leaving Eileen, explaining that he had wondered briefly whether Shari was his twin soul, but that this was because he wanted an excuse for leaving when

---

69. I strongly recommend Simon Buxton's book, *The Shamanic Way of the Bee* (Rochester, VT: Destiny Books, 2004).

he found that Shari fulfilled him sexually more than Eileen could. He said that he never imagined either Paula or Renata to be his twin soul. As for Eileen, she said that in her last life she was paying a debt from an earlier time when she had put Peter before God, and that she had been selected by God as a messenger on account of being a very pure channel. The suffering that they went through in their last lives, and the forming of Findhorn, were things that they had both agreed to before coming in that last time.

St. Francis and St. Clare

Assisi, Italy, in the Middle Ages was home to two people who are perhaps the most famous spiritual "lovers" in the whole of history, but I wonder how many people have thought about the fact that they are clearly twin souls. When I was doing research for and writing my first book, I read a biography of Pythagoras shortly after having read one of St. Francis, and I was so struck by the parallels between their lives that I consulted my clairvoyant friend Edwin Courtenay as to whether they had been the same soul. His reply was not only that this was the case, but also that he (and of course St. Clare, with whom he has fused) was now the Ascended Master Kuthumi. Kuthumi is the master of the Fifth Ray and governs the balance of the elements, relationships, and interconnections. His connection with the elemental kingdom is, of course, much linked with his incarnation as St. Francis.

Francis was born in Assisi in 1182, the son of the wealthy cloth merchant Piero Bernardone, and in his youth he was very far from behaving like an angel. During the twelfth and thirteenth centuries, Italy consisted of several small states that were all waging war on one another, and in 1201 Francis was involved in an attack on nearby Perugia. He was taken hostage and imprisoned for months, but this did not change his inclinations. In 1205, however, he was due to take part in an attack on Apulia, when he had a dream in which God asked him who could do more, the servant or the master? He interpreted this to mean that he had been serving the servant, and so he abandoned his dreams of becoming a knight and returned to Assisi to care for the sick.

The following year, Francis received the famous message from the cross in San Damiano. That church was very dilapidated at the time, and while he was praying in it, Jesus spoke to him from the cross, and asked him "to rebuild my Church." Later Francis came to realize that Christ had meant church with a capital "C," but his immediate reaction was to sell some of his father's cloth and give the money to the priest of San Damiano to get the church repaired. His father was furious and at first imprisoned him in a cell. Then, when his father took him to the bishop, Francis renounced his father, all his possessions, and his privileged life in order to help the sick, lepers, and outcasts. He took the clothing of a poor farmhand, which in due course became the well-known brown tunic of the Franciscans.

It was not long before Francis had gathered a group of followers, and between 1210 and 1221, when he retired from governing the order into a life of prayer, contemplation, and fasting, he sent them out into the world to preach to the poor and humble. One day he decided to talk to the birds, and he found that they stopped to listen and that he was able to touch them with his tunic. From then on he made it his habit solicitously to invoke all birds, animals, and reptiles to praise and love their Creator, and stories abound about his extraordinary communications with animals.

Once he quieted a flock of noisy birds that were disturbing a religious ceremony. They kept completely quiet until he had finished his sermon! A rabbit that he freed from a trap kept jumping up onto his lap until he finally persuaded it to take refuge in a nearby wood; and when he was in a boat, fish would come near to listen to him. But probably the most famous story of all is that of the wolf of Gubbio. After it had been terrorizing the inhabitants, Francis got the wolf to make a pact with the people of Gubbio. They promised to repent for their sins and feed the wolf, and the wolf put its paw into Francis' hand as a sign of its agreement not to harm them. The wolf then lived among the townspeople for two years, going from door to door for food, and they were all very sad when it died.

In 1224 Francis was given the stigmata, which means that he had the wounds of Jesus on his hands, feet, and side, and these never healed until his death two years later. (Another well-known person who experienced this is the much more recent Padre Pio of Italy.) Francis was canonized in 1228, and the Franciscan Order spread rapidly throughout Europe.

St. Clare, who was born in Assisi in 1193, outlived Francis by twenty-seven years and, to quote from an article by Sister Frances Teresa, entitled "Lady of Light," published in the Catholic journal *The Tablet*,[70] during those twenty-seven years, "At every turn Francis filled her thoughts even though he was long dead." She emulated her mother's love for the poor and underprivileged of Assisi, and when she was fifteen she refused the marriage that her father wanted her to go through with. She first heard Francis preach only a few years later—in the Cathedral of San Rufino, which was next door to where she lived—and she was so taken by his enthusiasm and love of Christ that she vowed to meet him and learn the secret of his great happiness.

They had a few secret meetings and then, on Palm Sunday night in 1212, Clare escaped from home to the tiny chapel of Porziuncula in the valley below Assisi, where, surrounded by the friars, Francis cut off her beautiful hair and gave her the garb of a Franciscan. He then put her into a Benedictine convent, since it would not have been deemed proper for her to stay with them, and her family tried in vain to drag her home. To the family's consternation, Clare's sister Agnes joined her shortly afterward, but in 1226 (the year of Francis' death), their mother also joined the order.

Clare and her companions took up residence in San Damiano (where the crucifix had spoken to Francis), and the Second Order of Francis, which she founded, was often

---

70. *The Tablet*, 13 August 1994.

called the Poor Ladies of Assisi. The Privilege of Poverty, given to Clare in 1215 by Cardinal Hugolino, preceded various other papal privileges, and after the cardinal had become Pope Gregory IX, he gave in 1227 the care of the Sisters to the General of the Friars Minor, John Parenti. In 1247, the Rule of Innocent IV was made obligatory. By this time Clare was severely ill, but she continued to work on her own Rule of Life for the Sisters. (The original manuscript was found in 1893.) Clare's religious fervor never weakened for a moment throughout her years of sickness. It was said that she always came from prayer with "her face so shining that it dazzled those about her," and popes, cardinals and bishops often consulted her. She died in 1253, was canonized in 1255, and in 1260 her body was transferred to the church of Santa Chiara in Assisi.

In Clare's escapes from home and her secret meetings with Francis can be seen the elements of a chaste and spiritual love affair, much like the ideals of courtly love in Francis' beloved troubadour songs. But Clare saw in Francis someone who could lead her to espousal with Christ, while he often turned to her for advice and inspiration. "The Canticle of Brother Sun" was composed while Francis was encamped outside Clare's convent of San Damiano and, when he was torn between prayer and teaching, it was Clare who said to him, "God did not call you for yourself alone." After he had been given the stigmata, Clare made Francis slippers to protect his bleeding feet. When he died, his body was taken to her convent for veneration on the way to burial.

As Sister Frances Teresa said in her article in *The Tablet*, "Their lives ran parallel in so many ways . . . Each set out to be brother or sister to the whole world, cutting across all the divisions of society. Each of them was filled with a deep, tender love for Christ, for the Eucharist, for the poor and vulnerable." But twin souls also complement one another: while Francis encouraged the Brothers to move through the world, engaging in the lives of the sick and laboring class, Clare's community led lives of enclosure, contemplation, and mutual support. Nowadays these two great saints continue to serve as beacons not only for the religious orders that they founded, but also for a large sector of the Western world.

I should like, however, to conclude this chapter by turning from the West to the East.

Sri Aurobindo and The Mother

Joudry and Pressman have written very beautifully about these twin souls, but following a recent visit to Pondicherry, I feel called to elaborate a little bit further on their lives and so trust that Maurie Pressman will forgive me. (The deceased Patricia Joudry has already given me encouragement on another recent shamanic journey of mine!)

Akroyd Ghash Aurobindo was born on August 15, 1872, in Calcutta (now Kolkata), and at the tender age of seven he was taken to England for his education and lived there for fourteen years, initially in Manchester. He was a brilliant scholar and linguist and, after studying at St. Paul's School in London, he won a classical scholarship to King's College,

Cambridge, where he gained a First Class in the Tripos and
record marks in Greek and Latin in the examination for the
Indian Civil Service. When he returned to India in 1893, he
joined the Baroda Service, becoming eventually a professor
of English and finally vice principal of Baroda College. Having already mastered French, German, and Italian in addition to Latin and Greek, he learned, after his return to India,
Sanskrit, and several modern Indian languages.

The partitioning of Bengal by the British in 1905 caused
a great deal of controversy, and Aurobindo, who had already
begun to be politically active, gave up his position with the
Baroda Service and became the leader of a group of Indian
nationalists known as the Extremists. Unlike the more mod-
erate nationalists, this group advocated outright independence and was willing to use violence. Aurobindo was one
of the founders of the underground revolutionary Jugantar
party, and also the editor of a nationalist Bengali newspaper,
and he consequently came into frequent confrontation with
the British Raj (the British governance on the subcontinent).
In 1907, at a convention of Indian nationalists, he was seen
as the new leader of the movement, but his life at this point
was already beginning to take a new direction as the result
of meeting a Maharashtrian yogi, who persuaded him to
explore the ancient Hindu practices of yoga.

This introduction must have been Aurobindo's lifeline
when he was imprisoned in the Alipur jail for a year prior
to his trial for his activities. (He was eventually acquitted.)
He made use of his year in jail to work on his inner life, and

meditating on the Bhagavad Gita[71] facilitated his conversion from political action to spirituality. Aurobindo claimed to be visited in his meditations by the renowned Swami Vivekananda, a Hindu philosopher of great importance to Advaita Vedanta (the philosophy of nonduality). When he came out of prison in May 1909, he found the Nationalist party broken, and he strove single-handedly for a year as its sole remaining leader before coming to see both that the hour of such a movement had not yet come and that he was not destined to be its leader. Is it not nevertheless of great significance that, when Indian independence was finally declared, it was on Sri Aurobindo's birthday?

After his trial, Aurobindo started two new weeklies, one in English and the other in Bengali. However, since the British government could not tolerate his nationalist program, he finally found refuge with other nationalists in the French colony of Pondicherry. How strange it seems now to read that Lord Minto wrote of this great poet and mystic: "I can only repeat that he is the most dangerous man we have to reckon with!" He settled in Pondicherry in April 1910 without any idea of founding an ashram[72]—in fact he was even at first a trifle reluctant to do so—but gradually it

---

71. The Bhagavad Gita is one of the most renowned of Indian scriptures. It consists of a dialogue between Krishna and Arjuna.

72. The definition of the word *ashram* is "the house or houses of a teacher or master of spiritual philosophy in which he receives and lodges those who come to him for the teaching and practice."

began to grow naturally from the handful of disciples who were attracted to his practice of integral yoga.

Sri Aurobindo's twin soul was born Mirra Alfassa, on February 21, 1878, in Paris, of a Turkish father and Egyptian mother. She started to have profound spiritual experiences at a very early age and, when she first went to Pondicherry in 1914, she recognized Aurobindo as the master who had been guiding her spiritually for many years. Later she wrote, "Between the ages of eleven and thirteen a series of psychic and spiritual experiences revealed to me not only the existence of God, but man's possibility of uniting with Him, of realizing Him integrally in consciousness and action, of manifesting Him upon earth in a life divine. This, along with a practical discipline for its fulfillment, was given to me during my body's sleep by several teachers, some of whom I met afterwards on the physical plane . . . " And in her *Prayers and Meditations* she also recorded another very interesting early experience: "When I was a child of about thirteen, for nearly a year every night, as soon as I had gone to bed, it seemed to me that I went out of my body and rose straight up above the house, above the city, very high above. Then I used to see myself clad in a magnificent golden robe, much longer than myself; and as I rose higher, the robe would stretch, spreading out in a circle around me to form a kind of immense roof over the city. Then I would see men, women, children, old men, the sick, the unfortunate, coming out from every side; they would gather under the outspread robe, begging for help, telling of their miseries, their sufferings, their hardships. In reply, the robe, supple and alive, would extend toward each one of them individually, and as soon as they had touched it, they were comforted or healed, and went back into their bodies happier and stronger than they had come out of them."

Closely linked to her spirituality was Mirra's great love of music and art, in both of which she was very gifted. She studied at the Ecole des Beaux Arts in Paris, and at the age of nineteen she married Henri Morisset, who was a disciple of the painter Gustave Moreau. Their son André was born the following year, in August 1898. For about ten years she lived among the cultural avant-garde, mixed with such artists as Matisse, Manet, and Cézanne, and some of her own paintings were exhibited at the *Salon* in Paris. At the same time, however, her high inner realization and spiritual radiance soon began to attract many seekers, and in 1906 a small group named Idea was formed under her guidance and met weekly at the Morrisets' home. Besides spiritual topics, this group discussed occult experiences, of which Mirra had many.

Her first marriage was fairly short-lived, and Mirra later married Paul Richard, a well-known philosopher who was keenly interested in Western and Eastern spirituality as well as in the practice of Vedantic Yoga. He also had political ambitions, and it was an election campaign in 1910 which took him to the French colony of Pondicherry, where, wanting to consult an advanced yogi about the symbolic meaning of the Star of David, he met Sri Aurobindo. After Paul returned to France and talked to Mirra about Aurobindo, the two of them corresponded and she developed an ever-increasing yearning to go to India, which she had long felt to be her true mother country.

Her longing was finally fulfilled in 1914, when the couple embarked for India on a Japanese steamer. While approaching Pondicherry, she had a vision of a huge column of light in the center of the town. She said later that she had felt Aurobindo's atmosphere materially at a distance of ten miles: "It was very sudden, very concrete, an atmosphere of pure, luminous, light, so light that it lifts you up." The Richards met Aurobindo on the very afternoon of their arrival. The following day she noted in her diary: "It matters little that there are thousands of beings plunged in the densest ignorance; He whom we saw yesterday is on earth; his presence is enough to prove that a day will come when darkness shall be transformed into light, and Thy reign shall actually be established upon earth." Until the outbreak of war necessitated the Richards' return to France, the three of them met daily, and together they started publishing a monthly philosophical journal entitled *Arya*, with a French edition entitled *Revue de la Grande Synthèse*. The first issue appeared on Aurobindo's birthday and is described by Wilfried in his short biography of The Mother[73] as being "like a message of Light for the world which had just been precipitated into the

73.   Wilfried, *The Mother: A Short Biography* (Pondicherry, India: Sri Aurobindo Society, 1986).

chaos of the First World War." Aurobindo contributed many articles to this journal, in which he promoted his own interpretation of important Indian scriptures as well as writing about Indian philosophy, world history, and world evolution. These laid the foundation for his major works such as *The Life Divine, The Synthesis of Yoga*, and *The Human Cycle*.

Mirra knew that her place lay at Aurobindo's side, so the return to France was extremely hard for her. After a year, however, her husband obtained work in Japan, and during their four years there she made a deep study of its culture and religion. In 1920, to her great joy, she was able to return to Pondicherry, and she remained in India until her death on November 17, 1973. Paul Richard soon realized that she was now giving herself spiritually completely to Aurobindo and that their collaboration was something that he could no longer follow. Though he recognized Aurobindo as a great yogi and sage, he did not want to become one of his disciples and, after traveling further in India, he went to America, where he founded a Centre of Asian Studies.

Aurobindo himself gave Mirra the name of The Mother, and only after she had come to live there permanently did the Pondicherry community really grow and develop into a thriving ashram. In 1926 Aurobindo put The Mother in charge of the disciples' spiritual care as well as all the administration of the whole setup. In addition, she created the Sri Aurobindo International Centre of Education. The Pondicherry ashram broke with the long tradition of asceticism and renunciation in Indian ashrams, returning to Vedic times, when "integral life, fullness and prosperity, equality of the sexes and a life-affirming attitude were similarly cultivated by spiritual seekers," and sports also had an important role in the life of the ashram.

The Mother and Sri Aurobindo both spoke about their twinsoulship/spiritual partnership. She said, "When in your heart and thought you will make no difference between Sri Aurobindo and me, when to think of Aurobindo will be to think of me and to think of me will mean to think of Sri Aurobindo inevitably, when to see one will mean inevitably to see the other, like one and the same person, then you will know that you begin to be open to the supramental force and consciousness." And Aurobindo, who said, "The Mother and I are one and equal," elaborated on this thus: "The Mother's consciousness and mine are the same, the one Divine Consciousness in two, because that is necessary for the play. Nothing can be done without her knowledge and force— without her consciousness—and if anybody really feels her consciousness, he should know that I am there behind it and if he feels me it is the same with hers . . . "[74]

The Mother's role as head of the ashram was only the visible side of her work; she had another, wider existence on the inner planes, a fraction of which is recorded in her talks. Also, in his major poetical work, *Savitri*, in which Aurobindo recorded his spiritual experiences, he included some of

---

74.   *Sri Aurobindo and the Mother on Themselves, Part II*, compiled by Vijay, (Pondicherry, India: Sri Aurobindo Society, 1971).

hers. She never told him about the occult experiences of her early years, but when he went through a period of reading to her in the morning the passages he had written at night, she found them reflected in his poetry.

Aurobindo was a very powerful force throughout both the Second World War and Indian Independence, and when he left his body in 1950, it was deliberate, in order to be able to work better for a world that was not yet ready to listen to him. The Mother knew that he was influencing Earth events from the subtle-physical plane, and she said, "Sri Aurobindo . . . has not left me, not for a moment, for He is still with me, day and night, thinking through my brain, writing through my pen, speaking through my mouth and acting through my organizing power." She lived for another twenty-three years, until she was ninety-five, and one of her major achievements of these latter years was the foundation on February 28, 1968, of Auroville, which is described as "a universal township in the making for a population of up to 50,000 people from around the world." (It is regarded as twin sister to Findhorn.)

The concept of an ideal township devoted to an experiment in human unity had come to The Mother as early as the 1930s, and when in the mid-1960s the Sri Aurobindo Society in Pondicherry proposed to her that such a township should be started, she gave it her blessings. The concept was then put before the government of India, who gave their backing and took it to the General Assembly of UNESCO (the United Nations Educational, Scientific and Cultural Organization). In

1966, UNESCO passed a unanimous resolution commending it as a project of importance to the future of humanity. A very large area, just 10 kilometers to the north of Pondicherry, was given over to the project, and on that auspicious day some 5,000 people assembled near the banyan tree at the center of the future township for an inauguration ceremony attended by representatives of 124 nations, including all the states of India. The representatives each brought some soil from their homeland, and this was mixed in a white marble-clad, lotus-shaped urn now located at the focal point of the Amphitheatre. At the same time, The Mother gave Auroville its Four-point Charter.

The purpose of Auroville is to realize human unity in diversity. Its inhabitants come from some thirty-five nations, from all age groups (ranging from infancy to over eighty, but averaging around thirty), from all social classes, backgrounds, and cultures, and representing humanity as a whole. The population of the township is constantly growing, but currently stands at around 1,700 people, of whom approximately one-third are Indian. All of them believe that The Mother is still with them, constantly guiding their activities and encouraging the development of Auroville as a beacon of hope for humanity as a whole.

Today, Auroville is recognized as the first and only internationally endorsed ongoing experiment in human unity and transformation of consciousness. The community is also concerned with, and performing practical research into, sustainable living and the future cultural, environmental, social, and spiritual needs of humankind. The Green Belt, though not yet complete, presently covers an area of 405 hectares (about 1,000 acres) and stands as an example of successful transformation of wasteland into a vibrant ecosystem. Its further planned extension with an additional 800 hectares (2,000 acres) will make it into a remarkable demonstration site for soil and water conservation, ground water recharge, and environmental restoration. As the lungs for the entire township, the new development will complete the healing process that Auroville started several decades ago.

The Mother said at the outset that the soul of Auroville would be a Park of Unity, consisting of a temple surrounded by a lake and twelve gardens, to each of which she gave a name such as "Existence, Consciousness, Bliss, Light, Life." In March 1970, her chief architect, Roger Anger, presented to her a model of the inner chamber of the temple, along with five different models, from which she selected a slightly flattened golden sphere that she ultimately decided to call the Matrimandir. The foundation stone was laid in February 1971, and on November 17, 1973, at 7:25 in the evening—the very moment at which the Mother left her body—the concreting of the four pillars that support the mandir (temple) was completed. It contains the world's largest man-made crystal as a focus for meditation. At the time of this writing, the Matrimandir was not open to the public while improvements such as a marble staircase are being made to the interior, but it is most impressive to look at even from a distance.[75] The residents of Auroville are among the first to admit that its growth is slow, but my belief is that the reason is that it is ahead of its time; and I am sure that these two great souls (now no doubt fused once more into a single being) will continue to watch over its development.

---

75.   I recommend a glance at: www.auroville.org/thecity/matrimandir/ mm_conception.htm

15

Conclusion

What is a friend? A single soul dwelling in two bodies.
—ARISTOTLE

"Without a twin soul, no matter what you have, you feel incomplete," commented Carol in a recent e-mail. And she continued, "With the twin, one feels complete regardless of things missing in one's life. It's like a puzzle piece that fits into the correct space. I know this is where my place is, and I am eternally grateful to be a part of this privilege."

Whether or not we are in such a privileged position (and how many of us are?), it is clear to me that this is what we are all aiming for—whether we are fully aware of it or not. We might achieve it on Earth, or might need to wait until we have finished all our incarnations. Having established that twin souls or twin flames are clearly the closest possible type of soul mate, I feel that I should conclude by summarizing what are the distinctive features of twinsoulship to demonstrate how we, i.e. the ubiquitous man or woman on the street, might be able, if we want, to recognize such couples.

First of all, however, I want to stress that finding one's twin soul on Earth is far from being the be-all and end-all of any incarnation. Karmic soul mates can give great joy to one another while paying off a debt, and companion soul mates are, as we have seen, often the most comfortable relationships. If you are in a happy relationship, why bother to try to find out its exact nature? If, on the other hand, you are not in a relationship and looking for a soul mate, the advice that is always given is to focus on working on yourself, and then a suitable partner will appear when you are spiritually ready. (Besides the Joudry-Pressman book,[76] I particularly recommend Richard Webster's book on soul mates.[77])

So what is it about twin-soul relationships that make them so different from other soul mates, and how can we identify them? My answer to the second question is that it is by no means always completely straightforward. When I first became interested in this topic and felt rather green about it, I tended to rely on the assessment of clairvoyants, but

---

76.   Joudry and Pressman, *Twin Souls*.

77.   Webster, *Soul Mates*.

more recently I have come to the conclusion that even they are not infallible. Clairvoyants of my acquaintance claim to be able to identify twin souls by noticing their auras merge, and I assume that this was the case with Jack and Jill when they met Edwin Courtenay. However, Dr. Roger Woolger has been told by a clairvoyant that sometimes the auras of therapist and client can be seen to merge, so no doubt there are more factors than twinsoulship that can cause merging. Probably people who are extremely clairvoyant would say that there are other ways of identifying twin souls from their auras, but in any case, since not everyone has auric sight, this is not a means of identification that I can recommend generally. So here is a list of features that anyone could look for.

1. A very common feeling when twin first souls meet appears to be that of "instant recognition." I am not claiming that such recognition is unique to twin souls—in my previous book, *Karmic Release,*[78] I wrote about the instant recognition I experienced with a companion soul mate of mine—but I am sure that with twin souls the feeling is even stronger still.

2. Countless times during this study I heard words such as, "I feel complete with her," or, "He makes me feel whole." Carol even suggested "Whole" as the title for this book. She commented, "I am not sure if it sounds nice, since wholeness tends to be used and abused in so

---

78.   Merivale, *Karmic Release.*

many ways to commercialize and sell products these days, but for me it really is the word which best sums up the feeling of being complete when one lives with one's twin soul." What more could one say on this?

3. Certainly one of the most important features seems to be a tendency to be telepathic with one another. Elfie and Graham Courtenay showed this to a marked degree. May knew that she and David could not hide anything from one another. (Remember how David failed to conceal his serious illness from her?) And in Sally's case, the telepathic communication even saved her life!

4. Though one can always find exceptions, another feature that appears to be very common in twin souls is similarity in backgrounds. Even when they are of different nationalities (e.g., Rose and Danesh), they are often born into similar circumstances.

5. Similar tastes in all the most important things seems to me to be completely universal, and in many cases twin souls find when they first meet that they have had similar experiences in their lives up until that point.

6. The well-known clairvoyant and author, Lilla Bek, told me that, since the final return to the Source cannot be made alone—that we have first to fuse with our twin— twin souls who are preparing for the final fusion tend to practice fusing when they are out of their bodies at night. This can apparently often make encounters in

the flesh difficult and nerve-wracking—even embar-
rassing—for both parties. Certainly one or two of the
people I have talked to, who were not courting (Eleanor
in particular), spoke of intense blushing and trembling
as being a real problem when meeting with their twin.
Others, too, have found themselves completely tongue-
tied when confronted with their other half. It seems that
when one is preparing to do without it, and to communicate only by telepathy, the body can be a real encum-
brance!

7. Even when "romantic love" is not part of the equation,
the bond between twin souls is indestructible. Both
Olivia and Alison found themselves somehow forced
into the marriage almost against their will; and Patrick
still lives near to Olivia and calls on her regularly
despite not being welcomed cordially.

8. The quality and intensity of the love that can be observed
between twin souls are the strongest imaginable. Though
I criticize Rita Rogers for not fully understanding
the concept of twinsoulship, which I believe is mainly
because she ignores the important question of reincarnation, she does give some excellent descriptions of the
unique love that exists between what she describes as
"true soul mates." She sums up the strength of the recognition of the bond when she says, "You may be separated
from your soul mate for years and years but that love,
that feeling you had for the other person, won't die.

However hard you try to fight your feelings, by moving in with another person, by marrying them, by shutting your soul mate out of your life forever, not a day will pass without you thinking of them." (Remember how, in Rose's previous life, when she was a king and Danesh was his queen, but he sacrificed their relationship to save their people, not a day passed without the king thinking about his queen? And even Eleanor, who claimed after she had "recovered" to think about Joseph only occasionally, admitted that it did not take much to stir a memory of him and that, when such memories were stirred, the love she felt was just as strong as ever.) I am also in complete agreement with Rita Rogers when she describes this very special attraction as being "of the soul rather than the heart." She says that "the emotions stirred when you love someone with your heart, such as passion, infatuation, rapture, will all diminish in time. But the feelings that come from the soul will never fade because they are the feelings that are truest to you. Your soul mate, after thirty years together, may not drive you to passionate distraction in the way they did when you were first together, but you will have other, greater, deeper feelings for them. The love between soul mates is constantly evolving and deepening."

Although they are a wonderful description of twin-soul love, I do think that the last two sentences could also apply to other soul-mate partnerships. However, the unique twin-soul bond is summed up by other

things that Rita Rogers says, such as, "Once that connection is made nothing else matters to us." (She comments that he could be a hobo and it wouldn't matter!)
And then she explains: "The reason why we feel such
an affinity with our soul mate is that a higher, spiritual
force—the spirit world—has sent you someone with
whom you are spiritually compatible. You and your soul
mate will always be bound together because your souls
are alike. People say that it is like finding their other
half, in that until they met their soul mate they were
aware that something was lacking in their life. When
you meet your soul mate that gap is instantly filled."

9. When, on the other hand, a relationship between twin
souls does not take off properly, the consequent frustration seems to be quite unlike any other. Although
I disagree strongly with his assertion that it is karma
(rather than the fact of being two halves of a whole)
that forces twin souls to come together again eventually, the psychic medium Steve Gunn has very good
understanding and experience of the distress caused to
one partner when the other runs away through fear of
the intensity of the feelings. A large part of me has difficulty in recommending a book that does not appear
to have been proofread, and which contains a mistake
such as the word "phenomenon" being used as a plural noun. (A much more common mistake nowadays
is using "phenomena" as a singular noun. Would that
happen if Greek were still taught in schools? Not that

I studied it myself, but in my day the knowledge that Greek nouns ending in "on" in the singular ended in "a" in the plural somehow rubbed off on everybody.) Yet I can nevertheless strongly recommend Gunn's book *When Two Souls Connect* for his numerous cases of one twin soul feeling ready for a relationship with his or her (usually her!) other half and being unable to understand the reason why her partner fails to acknowledge the obvious total compatibility between them.

10. Last, but not least, is the fact that the pain sometimes experienced in twin-soul relationships (or nonrelationships!) is more intense than any other pain. Broken soul-mate relationships that are not twin soul ones can also cause great suffering, but I do not believe that there can be anything in the world more excruciatingly painful than connecting with your other half and then having to disconnect. (Our last case—Sri Aurobindo and The Mother—are hardly a model that the rest of us can hope to emulate.) In her autobiography,[79] Eileen Caddy writes harrowingly of the pain she suffered when Peter left her. Ann Evans and Monica are among the most spiritual people I know, yet the pain of their husbands' death (or pseudo-death) is constantly with them. When Alison was vetting her chapter for me, I had to wait patiently for a while because read-

---

79.   Caddy, *Flight into Freedom and Beyond* (Forres, Scotland, Findhorn Press, 2002).

ing what I had written caused so much grief to surface, and she needed to work through that once more and make a few amendments before feeling able to give her seal of approval. (She commented, however, that the whole process had been very therapeutic for her.) And Eleanor, who has had one or two other heartbreaks, says that the pain she felt over Joseph is the only pain that she can never forget. The only consolation for such pain that I can see is the certainty that there is always a lesson in it. Monica does not doubt that she has been made stronger by her pain, and Marcus' soul must at a higher level be aware of having done that for her.

Besides these ten, there may well be other factors one could look for in identifying twin souls, and intuition (my main reason for not accepting Jack and Jill as twin souls!) should not be ruled out either. I know, for instance, that certain astrologers who are very spiritually aware can recognize twin souls from their charts. This must clearly be a very complex question, as there seem to be no rules regarding twin souls' respective sun signs. Aries/Leo, Aquarius/Leo, and Aries/Pisces are just three of the examples of combinations that have come to my attention, and obviously the Pink Twins must have the same sun sign. The system of astrology that I myself do know a little about, and sometimes make use of in my therapy, is the Japanese Nine Star Ki, and that is based on the idea of support versus challenge (e.g., Tree supports Fire, while Fire puts down Metal, but Metal cuts down Tree). Which year someone who is destined to meet their twin soul chooses to be born in clearly depends on whether they want to either give or receive support from the relationship, or whether they feel in need of challenge. Kathryn, who is a Six Metal, supports Martin, who is a One Water, whereas Joseph, who is a Four Tree, would always challenge Eleanor, who is another Six Metal.

I have already mentioned dowsing as a means of finding out whether a relationship is of twin flames. For such questions, the most common method of asking is with a pendulum, and for that the dowser needs to have already established the "yes" and "no" movements. A simple way to do this is to write the two words down on a piece of paper, hold the pendulum over each in turn, and then observe which way it moves. (For many people "yes" is a circular movement while "no" is a straight one, but my pendulum does the reverse.) The only snag with using the pendulum is that total impartiality to the answer is essential. Consequently, when I first started writing and was aware that I often had a vested interest in the answer, I always consulted my acupuncturist friend, who is a very experienced and reliable dowser. Now, however, that I have moved away to a different part of England, he is no longer so readily available to me, so I have recently devised other means of using my pendulum.

For instance, when I met Sally and we were talking around the subject of twinsoulship, she felt sure that she did know hers, but was initially torn between the two great loves of her life. I therefore handed her a couple of identical coins,

asked her to decide without telling me which of them represented which of the two men, and then held my pendulum in
turn over each. As soon as we got the answer that it was Paul
who was her twin (the other man appeared to be a companion soul mate), everything began to fall into place for her.

After that, I devised another method of dowsing impar-
tially to use when on my own. I wrote "yes" and "no" on
two identical pieces of card, and now, whenever I want an
answer, I turn them upside down, shuffle them so that I do
not know which is which, and then use the pendulum to
pick the "yes" for me. Although I would still not count totally
on its reliability on questions to which I am far from indifferent to the answer, I normally trust this method because all
the answers I have so far obtained in this way seem to make
perfect sense. I can also strongly recommend Heather Bray's
book on dowsing.[80]

Now I should like to recap on my disagreements with other
writers on twinsoulship. While maintaining the beautiful Joudry and Pressman book to be a must-read, I would
like to restate my disagreement on four points: their claims
that a twin-soul partner will never stray from a marriage,
that twin souls are always opposite sexes, that they never
incarnate into the same family, and that meeting his or her
twin soul will never cause an upright person to stray from
a marriage. Besides Marcus, Alison and Ian both had affairs

---

80.   Heather Bray, *Keys to Wisdom* (UK: Butterfly Press, 2005).

with others while they were still married, even though Alison later found that she was unable to break the bond with Ian. We have also looked at the Pink Twins and at Mary and Susan, and I have heard of others whose twin soul was of the same sex. As for the third point, the Cayces' son Hugh Lynn is said to be Gertrude's twin soul; Rose and Danesh in a previous life both died while she was giving birth to him, and were brothers in another life; and Ronald was Penny's father in a previous life. Ekavir and Faatina are an example of the fourth point. These four points, dear Patricia Joudry and Maurie Pressman, are perhaps not very big quibbles, but nevertheless important, I think, if we are striving to obtain a full picture of the concept of twinsoulship.

I have already recommended Richard Webster's book, but I was very surprised to read in it the following: "As well as your soul mates, there is one twin soul searching for you. This twin soul is your other half, dating from when we were all whole. It is most unlikely that you will meet your twin soul in this incarnation. *It appears that your twin soul comes into your life when you are both experiencing your final life on this earth plane.* (my emphasis).

Dr. Michael Newton expresses the same idea in his first book.[81] In this book, he says that he is reluctant to believe in the concept of twinsoulship because the idea of only meeting up at the end of one's incarnations does not make sense to him. But neither Newton nor Webster gives their reason

---

81.   Newton, *Journey of Souls*.

for having this idea, and I am puzzled as to where they got it from. As Joudry and Pressman point out, the notion of the individual being divided at the start into masculine and feminine has been transmitted down through the ages by mystics, and they quote Plato's *Symposium*, when Aristophanes relates how Zeus struck the soul into two opposite halves, each to wander the Earth in search of the other. But I have not found in Plato's words any suggestion that their search will not be successful until they have finished their incarnations.

I have come across many people who know their twin soul, but who do not appear to be quite ready to depart from Earth for good, and my stories include several people who also know of previous lifetimes in which they were together. Besides that, I have many friends and acquaintances who I am sure *are* on their final incarnation, but who are either single or living with someone other than their twin flame.

Moshab, of course, in the Meurois-Givaudan book,[82] also talks about the fusion that occurs only after the final death, in his statement that such a union "seals the end of the pact which they needed to make with the world of flesh," but in this case I am not inclined to take Moshab's words too literally—I think he is referring to the final reunion rather than to periodic encounters. One reason I have for saying this is that the authors are themselves twin souls and yet have now gone their separate ways rather than apparently preparing to fuse. (And do I hear you asking, "How do you know that

---

82.   Meurois-Givaudan, *Chemins de ce Temps-Là*.

they are in fact twin souls?" Well, I was at one time in correspondence with Anne over the possibility of translating one of their books, and she confirmed the nature of their relationship. But I am sorry to say that I gave up on the translation! Having a degree in the language has not, alas, endowed me with the rare gift of being able to translate it beautifully into my own.)

Escape from *samsara* (the cycle of earthly lives, symbolized by the Buddhist wheel) is everyone's destiny, but many of us get trapped on the Earth planes for a long time by desires of the flesh. Sex is often the strongest of these, and I strongly suspect that some readers of this book will have picked it up at least partly on account of an interest in that. Yet those who regard sexual intercourse as vitally important have nothing to fear about leaving Earth's plane, because it appears that spiritual union is even more ecstatic! Rita Rogers in her book mentions the lucid dream of one of her clients in which she met her deceased husband: "She told me that while they were together they made love spiritually. 'It was the most fantastic feeling,' she said. 'It was as if we had merged.'" In their book on twinsoulship,[83] John and Diadra Price quote the great poet Rumi as saying "Lovers don't finally meet somewhere. They're in each other all along." We just need to realize this and, if we focus on God, all will be

---

83. John and Diadra Price, *Soular Reunion: Journey to the Beloved* (Boone, NC: Wings of Spirit Foundation, 1999).

well whether or not we are at present in a satisfying human relationship.

Even when we are not yet ready for fusion, the twin soul bond is recognized after death. As I explained earlier, in Africa or Tibet, whenever anyone dies, the soul is helped to cross over to the other side, but in our Western civilizations, where death has been a taboo subject for so long and not dealt with properly, many people get stuck in the astral realms. There are souls in the spirit world whose job it is to take trapped souls "across the river," but shamans tell us that, to accomplish this important task, these spirits need assistance from us here on Earth. I have been doing shamanic soul-rescue work on a regular basis since November 2004, when I attended a weekend on "Death, Dying, and the Beyond" led by the distinguished English shaman Simon Buxton. I had hitherto believed myself to be "not the sort of person who receives messages from spirit," yet on the first journey that we did with Simon, I heard in my head a very clear order to carry on doing this work on my own at home. To my amazement as well, it was very specific: "Every Friday afternoon!"

On one shamanic journey that I have subsequently done, I met a man who was riddled with guilt after having had an argument with his twin soul and thrown her under a train in a rage. (It appeared that the relationship had always been stormy despite their deep love for one another.) Riddled with despair, he had immediately killed himself, but was then unable to move on because of his guilt. I suggested that it was now time to forgive himself, and that he call for his twin to take him across to the other side. She, who appeared instantly when called, had obviously been awaiting that moment for a long time.

On another occasion, I encountered a man whose whole body was crawling with worms. Repugnant though it was to me, I had to start by brushing off all the worms, and it took a while before it became clear whether he was actually a man or a woman. Once the worms had all gone and the scene had become clearer, it was apparent that he was a middle-aged man and that his twin soul, a slightly younger woman, had been crouching over the body. This man had in his last life never believed in an afterlife and had been convinced that he would cease to exist once his flesh had all been consumed by worms. For me, it was rewarding to be able to show him that he now had a beautiful ethereal body, and to see him come to appreciate that there is, in fact, no such thing as death after all. What interested me particularly in this case (because it was by no means the first time that I had found myself in this work persuading someone that they were not really dead) was the fact that his twin soul was stuck in the astral realms too because she felt unable to move on without him. Once I had performed a little bit of therapy with the two of them, they were able to call on someone they loved whom they knew to be dead, and then to be led across to the other side together.

Rehearsing Benjamin Britten's *Choral Dances from Gloriana* for a concert with my local choral society, these words of William Plomer's leapt out from the page at me: "The ripest fruit hangs where not one, not one, but only two, only two can reach." Edwin Courtenay explains that, during the present difficult times, the world has need of twin-soul unions to bring in the extra strength of their combined light. The reason the world needs them to come together is that the combination of the two halves adds up to more than the sum of the whole. John and Diadra Price put it thus: "Their fully realized state of consciousness opens them to the creative flow of Spirit which always seeks to 'serve' in love, beauty, joy, and creativity. Their union of forces also multiplies and empowers them, far beyond the power of two individuals. It multiplies the power of ONE which contains within it unlimited, boundless, infinite numbers of creative potential."

We have looked at the ways of identifying twin flames, and also at some of the purposes of their meeting. Now, do I feel you wondering why, if one of our pair is always the masculine and the other the feminine, do we regularly change sex throughout our countless incarnations? Well, Joudry and Pressman expound beautifully the notion of how we nurture our own gender seed through our varying experiences of lives in both masculine and feminine bodies. I am sure we can all think of women we know who have very masculine qualities, and equally men who have feminine qualities (which does not mean being effeminate), but I doubt whether either outer or inner gender is actually indicative of the true gender of the person concerned. Astrology, for instance, can play a part in appearances: in the Nine Star Ki system, the numbers One, Three, Six, and Eight are masculine, and Kathryn

is a Six/Three, which means that she—an extremely feminine woman—is a double masculine, and that has given her a
great deal of drive to support herself through many difficulties; and my above-mentioned acupuncturist friend (a Two/
Nine), while being outwardly very masculine, also has lovely
feminine qualities, which give him a gentle strength.

So how do we tell which is our true gender? Can it be
purely intuitive? Personally I do not know, though I think that
good clairvoyants could normally give the answer. But does
it really matter? We need to make the most of, and rejoice in,
the body we have chosen in each particular lifetime. Once
we have finally rejoined our other half, our true gender will
doubtless become clear. In the meantime, our very big task at
hand is perfecting ourselves in order to be ready for a union
that will be much more blissful than painful.

And for that to happen, we need to have ironed out
the yin or yang shape perfectly, as I believe the Abraham-
sens, the Evanses, and the Pink Twins—and many others of
course—have done. When there are still jagged bits remaining, as with Patrick, they will dig in to the soul of the partner, causing her incredible pain. Richard Webster who, in
his book on soul mates, writes extremely briefly about twin
souls, says: "A twin-soul relationship is an unbelievably perfect relationship on every level. You and your twin soul will
connect with each other on the physical, mental, emotional,
spiritual, and soul levels. Most people connect with their
partners on one level, and some have no connection at any
level. Good relationships are forged if the partners meet

on two levels. Imagine what it must be like to be connected with your partner on all five levels."

My stories have demonstrated the full range of joy and pain in twin-soul encounters, but I hope that I have also made it quite clear that finding one's twin flame is not necessarily total bliss in any given incarnation. And we have seen that, whether it be joyful or painful, there is always a purpose in twin-soul meetings. In cases where the relationship goes wrong, or where the couples are not able to be together, the meeting still always has an important purpose. Olivia, Jane, Alison, Steve, Monica, and the Caddys have all been made stronger by their temporary union. Eleanor reckons that she would not have found God if her twin flame had not, by refusing to offer her the love she craved, forced her to go inside in the search; and Mary was able to pull Susan through her breakdown, which probably no one else could have done.

If it is at present only 4 percent who are incarnate simultaneously,[84] this figure will be steadily increasing now that we are nearing the end of an era. Where I cannot praise Joudry and Pressman too highly is in what they say about the state of readiness that we need to achieve when preparing for the happy reunion. This is summed up too in Elizabeth Clare Prophet's words: "A twin flame is not looking for someone to take care of. A twin flame is looking for your wholeness to complement his own or her own, so that, when you are

---

84.   Stevenson, *The Awakener*.

together as one complete Alpha/Omega circle, you can minister to life in need, to others who have not yet discovered the law of their oneness."[85] Richard Webster recognizes that "to be totally in tune with someone at every level is a joy that all of us will experience one day . . . " Plato, in describing the meeting of twin souls, says, "the pair are lost in an amazement of love and friendship and intimacy and one will not be out of the other's sight even for a moment . . . ," and John and Diadra Price quote the Gospel of Thomas 22, which says, "When you make the two one, and when you make the inside like the outside, and the above as the below, and when you make the male and the female one and the same, . . . then shall you enter the Kingdom."

But I have to end with the point that Ann Evans stressed to me so strongly. This is summed up in Moshab's words, which bear repeating over and over again: "Human love, in its attempt to re-create that unique vessel of the spirit, is beautiful, so beautiful. However, you must appreciate that this love is only a recollection; that it is nothing other than nostalgia for another love so much more beautiful. A love whose radiance is so immeasurable that not one of us can even begin to conceive of its true nature."

So please remember that, whether you are acquainted with your twin soul or not, *that* is what we all have to look forward to!

---

85.   Prophet, *Soul Mates and Twin Flames.*

Free Catalog

Get the latest information on our body, mind, and spirit products! To receive a **free** copy of Llewellyn's consumer catalog, *New Worlds of Mind & Spirit,* simply call 1-877-NEW-WRLD or visit our website at www.llewellyn.com and click on *New Worlds.*

 LLEWELLYN ORDERING INFORMATION

 Order Online:
Visit our website at www.llewellyn.com, select your books, and order them on our secure server.

 Order by Phone:
- Call toll-free within the U.S. at 1-877-NEW-WRLD (1-877-639-9753). Call toll-free within Canada at 1-866-NEW-WRLD (1-866-639-9753)
- We accept VISA, MasterCard, and American Express

 Order by Mail:
Send the full price of your order (MN residents add 6.5% sales tax) in U.S. funds, plus postage & handling to:

> **Llewellyn Worldwide**
> **2143 Wooddale Drive, Dept. 978-0-7387-1528-5**
> **Woodbury, MN 55125-2989**

Postage & Handling:

Standard (U.S., Mexico, & Canada). If your order is:
$24.99 and under, add $4.00
$25.00 and over, FREE STANDARD SHIPPING

AK, HI, PR: $16.00 for one book plus $2.00 for each additional book.

International Orders (airmail only):
$16.00 for one book plus $3.00 for each additional book

Orders are processed within 2 business days.
Please allow for normal shipping time. Postage and handling rates subject to change.

SOUL MATES
Understanding Relationships Across Time
RICHARD WEBSTER

The eternal question: how do you find your soul mate—that special, magical person with whom you have spent many previous incarnations? Popular metaphysical author Richard Webster explores every aspect of the soul mate phenomenon in his newest release.

The incredible soul mate connection allows you and your partner to progress even further with your souls' growth and development with each incarnation. *Soul Mates* begins by explaining reincarnation, karma, and the soul, and prepares you to attract your soul mate to you. After reading examples of soul mates from the author's own practice, and famous soul mates from history, you will learn how to recall your past lives. In addition, you will gain valuable tips on how to strengthen your relationship so it grows stronger and better as time goes by.

978-1-56718-789-2
240 pp., 5 ³⁄₁₆ x 8 $13.95

PRACTICAL GUIDE TO PAST-LIFE MEMORIES
Twelve Proven Methods
RICHARD WEBSTER

Past life memories can provide valuable clues as to why we behave the way we do. They can shed light on our purpose in life, and they can help us heal our current wounds. Now you can recall your past lives on your own, without the aid of a hypnotist.

This book includes only the most successful and beneficial methods used in the author's classes. Since one method does not work for everyone, you can experiment with twelve different straightforward techniques to find the best one for you.

This book also answers many questions, such as "Do I have a soul mate?" "Does everyone have a past life?" "Is it dangerous?" and "What about déjà vu?"

978-0-7387-0077-9
264 pp., 5³⁄₁₆ x 8 $12.95

LIFE BETWEEN LIVES
Hypnotherapy for Spiritual Regression
MICHAEL NEWTON, PH.D.

A famed hypnotherapist's groundbreaking methods of accessing the spiritual realms.

Dr. Michael Newton is world-famous for his spiritual regression techniques that take subjects back to their time in the spirit world. His two best-selling books of client case studies have left thousands of readers eager to discover their own afterlife adventures, their soul companions, their guides, and their purpose in this lifetime.

Now, for the first time in print, Dr. Newton reveals his step-by-step methods. His experiential approach to the spiritual realms sheds light on the age-old questions of who we are, where we came from, and why we are here.

978-0-7387-0465-4
240 pp., 6 x 9 $15.95

Bringing Your Soul to Light
Healing Through Past Lives and the Time Between
Dr. Linda Backman

What happens after we die? What is the purpose of my current life? Have I lived before?

In this unique and inspiring guide, Dr. Linda Backman answers these questions with compassion, objectivity, and more than thirty years of experience conducting traditional and past-life regression therapy with clients. *Bringing Your Soul to Light* includes a wealth of first-hand accounts from actual past-life and between-life regression sessions, offering readers a compelling and personal glimpse into the immortality of the soul.

Readers will discover the extraordinary universal connections we all share in this lifetime and beyond. They'll learn how they can use this knowledge to heal and grow, both physically and spiritually, by understanding themselves on a soul level and releasing energetic remnants of past-life trauma. *Bringing Your Soul to Light* includes a foreword by holistic healing pioneer and author C. Norman Shealy, M.D., Ph.D.

978-0-7387-1321-2
264 pp., 6 x 9 $16.95

SUN SIGNS & SOUL MATES
An Astrological Guide to Relationships
LINDA GEORGE

Understanding your relationships through astrology is a way to reach deeply and insightfully into the territory of your soul.

Today's overly materialistic and ego-centered world makes it difficult to recognize our inner selves, let alone connect on a spiritual level with another person. Thankfully, astrology reveals the true patterns in ourselves and in others.

Evolutionary astrologer Linda George looks at the nature of the soul and relationships through the lens of astrology, exploring the lighter and darker sides of the twelve Sun signs of the zodiac. She reveals the compatibility potential for each pairing and offers entertaining and insightful relationship clues to help you better relate to your partner. Learn about each Sun sign's strengths, challenges, and behavioral quirks. From deciding whether to date that flirtatious Gemini to identifying your soul's fundamental needs, *Sun Signs & Soul Mates* will help you understand yourself—and your partner—more completely.

978-0-7387-1558-2
240 pp., 6 x 9 $17.95

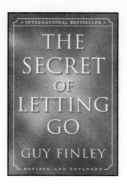

The Secret of Letting Go
Guy Finley

Llewellyn is proud to present the revised and expanded edition of our best-selling self-help book, *The Secret of Letting Go* by Guy Finley. Featuring an attractive new cover and fresh material, this Finley classic has been updated inside and out.

With more than 200,000 copies sold, Guy Finley's message of self-liberation has touched people around the world. Discover how to extinguish self-defeating thoughts and habits that undermine true happiness. Exploring relationships, depression, and stress, his inspiring words can help you let go of debilitating anxiety, unnecessary anger, paralyzing guilt, and painful heartache. True stories, revealing dialogues, and thought-provoking questions will guide you toward the endless source of inner strength and emotional freedom that resides within us all.

978-0-7387-1198-0
312 pp., 5³⁄₁₆ x 8 $14.95

JOURNEY OF SOULS
Case Studies of Life Between Lives
MICHAEL NEWTON, PH.D.

This remarkable book uncovers—for the first time—the mystery of life in the spirit world after death on earth. Dr. Michael Newton, a hypnotherapist in private practice, has developed his own hypnosis technique to reach his subjects' hidden memories of the hereafter. The narrative is woven as a progressive travel log around the accounts of twenty-nine people who were placed in a state of super-consciousness. While in deep hypnosis, these subjects describe what has happened to them between their former reincarnations on earth. They reveal graphic details about how it feels to die, who meets us right after death, what the spirit world is really like, where we go and what we do as souls, and why we choose to come back in certain bodies.

After reading *Journey of Souls*, you will acquire a better understanding of the immortality of the human soul. Plus, you will meet day-to-day personal challenges with a greater sense of purpose as you begin to understand the reasons behind events in your own life.

978-1-56718-485-3
288 pp., 6 x 9 $16.95

BEYOND REINCARNATION
Experience Your Past Lives & Lives Between Lives
JOE H. SLATE, PH.D.

Explore past lives, communicate with the departed, meet spirit guides. . . . According to Dr. Joe Slate, accessing the spirit realm is not only possible, it's beneficial for our present lives and future spiritual evolution. Past-life knowledge can offer direction and balance, explain fears and compulsions, build self-worth, and promote acceptance of others.

This introduction to reincarnation examines the mind/body/spirit connection and the existence of the ageless soul. Also presented here are Dr. Slate's simple, laboratory-tested strategies for exploring the nonphysical world. Readers can learn how to probe past lives and preexistence through self-hypnosis, astral travel to new spiritual dimensions, and communication with spirits through table tipping. The author's own fascinating experiences, along with personal accounts of his subjects who have tested his techniques, are also included.

978-0-7387-0714-3
216 pp., 6 x 9 $14.95

HOW TO UNCOVER YOUR PAST LIVES
TED ANDREWS

Knowledge of your past lives can be extremely rewarding. It can assist you in opening to new depths within your own psychological makeup. It can provide greater insight into present circumstances with loved ones, career and health. It is also a lot of fun.

Now Ted Andrews shares with you nine different techniques that you can use to access your past lives. Between techniques, Andrews discusses issues such as karma—and how it is expressed in your present life; the source of past life information, soul mates and twin souls, proving past lives, the mysteries of birth and death, animals and reincarnation, abortion and premature death, and the role of reincarnation in Christianity.

978-0-7387-0813-3
192 pp., 5³⁄₁₆ x 8 $8.95

Spanish edition:
Cómo descubrir sus vidas pasadas
978-1-56718-028-2   **$9.95**

To Write to the Author

If you wish to contact the author or would like more information about this book, please write to the author in care of Llewellyn Worldwide and we will forward your request. Both the author and publisher appreciate hearing from you and learning of your enjoyment of this book and how it has helped you. Llewellyn Worldwide cannot guarantee that every letter written to the author can be answered, but all will be forwarded. Please write to:

Ann Merivale

℅ Llewellyn Worldwide

2143 Wooddale Drive, Dept. 978-0-7387-1528-5

Woodbury, Minnesota 55125-2989, U.S.A.

Please enclose a self-addressed stamped envelope for reply, or $1.00 to cover costs. If outside U.S.A., enclose an international postal reply coupon.

Many of Llewellyn's authors have websites with additional information and resources. For more information, please visit our website at http://www.llewellyn.com